Portrait Photography

PORTRAIT PHOTOGRAPHY

How and Why

MARY ALLEN

FOCAL PRESS
London and New York

© 1973 FOCAL PRESS LIMITED

ISBN 0 240 50749 5

First Edition 1973
Second Impression 1977

Printed by Biddles Ltd, Guildford, Surrey
and bound by Wm. Brendon & Son Ltd,
Tiptree, Essex

CONTENTS

FOREWORD

MANY YOUNG photographers may have met with parental opposition when their chosen career has been photography. I was fortunate, for it was my father who suggested the idea to me, and who encouraged me to enter the profession. Replying to an advertisement in the *Times* for a premium pupil, I found myself, within a week, at work in a West End studio. Here I was initiated into the magic world of photography by Walter Stoneman, F.R.P.S.

Thus I embarked on what was to become a most interesting, frustrating, hard working, enjoyable and all engrossing career.

My first encounter with portraiture was a 15 × 12 in. photograph of a royal group taken at Goodwood. The rather large foreground area was covered with daisies. I spent the entire first week spotting out daisies in that one photograph!

At the Regent Street Polytechnic, where I attended the photographic classes in portraiture, the students were encouraged to formulate their own ideas and to work as individuals. No two students were expected to take similar portraits, although all received the same solid foundation of good composition, lighting and general technique.

This groundwork has remained with me through the years, and many of the same techniques can be seen in the work of most portrait photographers. It is the individual approach which makes one portraitist differ from another.

Who can say what a true portrait is? Each photographer will have his own ideas on the subject. There are no rules to apply, each one can only be true to himself. The challenge of portraiture is so great, and man is so complex, that I am forever exploring new techniques which will enable me to portray the personality before my camera to the best advantage.

Today, schools of photography show little evidence of any student interest in conventional portraiture. Students are tending to explore the scientific processes of the photographic medium, in an endeavour to find new ways of expressing their ideas and emotions. There comes a time, however, when the goal of technical perfection is no longer sufficient in itself—it must be used for a purpose. That is where this book comes in, for in it the techniques are to be perfected with the purpose of producing a "living" portrait.

The techniques of lighting, camera angle, exposure, and also processing have been discussed in relation to the widely differing characteristics found within the subjects before the camera. The elements of composition have been explained by means of original designs; so that the student is not confronted by a list of rules, but by exercises which, if carried out conscientiously, will teach him firstly to see, then to understand. Finally, he will be able to express his feelings about a subject with greater emphasis and clarity.

The applied techniques go beyond photography alone, touching on physiognomy and psychology. A study of the irregularities of the facial features, the character expressed in these as well as in some of the lines and wrinkles, teaches the student to recognise the various types at a glance. From this information he can judge the required camera and lighting set-ups, and the whole mood of the picture.

Psychology is used as a means of overcoming self-consciousness, and of unveiling the true personality. This "inner spirit" of the portrait is also obtained by a technique employing the long exposure coupled with low power light.

Colour photography is approached in a similar manner. Again, perfect technique is not sufficient as a goal in itself. It, too, must be used as a means to an end. In portraiture this is to express even more of the personality or mood than can be done in monochrome. The psychological effect of colour on the subject, the balance of colour as an expression of character, and the use of filters to obtain the required results are the main topics under discussion. The processing of colour materials is not included.

Although retouching on negatives is seldom required for portraits taken by the average amateur, it is an essential technique for the professional. The amount of retouching for each negative will vary from almost nothing to a considerable amount, and it is often knowing what to leave and what to remove that is all-important. The precise directions given for retouching and finishing of both negatives and prints, will enable the student to teach himself through practice.

My lectures to photographic societies in London and the provinces have made me aware of the recently renewed interest in portraiture among their members, and the ardent desire for more knowledge on the subject. This book will I hope, be of some interest to those who are already portraitists, as well as use to those who are just beginning, and also give some inspiration to those who have yet to become involved.

Any photographer who is contemplating portraiture as a career at the present time is fortunate, for, not only is there a revived interest in the subject among the amateurs, but a revival of portraiture in the professional field is now very much in evidence in both Europe and America. This fact was emphasized by the International Seminar on Portraiture, organized by Europhot, and held in Germany in 1969. This was attended by photographers of several nations and was a huge success.

Portraiture is reviving in a new form. The conception of the modern portrait, given to us by the photographers at the Seminar, is one that is posed naturally, has a characteristic expression, shows vitality, and, above all, reveals the "inner spirit". A photographer must have a knowledge of psychology to be able to communicate this essential quality through a portrait, as well as a complete understanding of all the photographic techniques necessary to produce the picture.

This conception of the modern portrait is the one which underlies every exercise and technique to be found within these pages.

This book is the outcome of my life's work in portraiture, in both the professional and amateur field. I have seen portraiture over the years to gradually decline in popularity, but never to die, and now it is coming back with renewed vigour and fresh vitality. The photographic techniques today are far in advance of yester-year, both in monochrome and colour, but the fundamental needs of portraiture are the same—a photographer who loves his subject enough to learn to understand human nature as well as the techniques of his art.

1 Equipment for Portraiture

PHOTOGRAPHERS are individualists. Like other creative people, they have their personal preferences and ideas of perfection. This is especially the case where it comes to choosing or recommending the tools of their trade. But it is not only because of personal feelings that the choice of photographic equipment can never really be a finite matter. Portrait photographers do not work under standard conditions and individual requirements vary according to the type of portrait, and the circumstances under which it is taken.

But the need to discuss some of the apparatus and accessories used for the studio experiments outlined in the following chapters reduces the question to manageable dimensions. So here it is possible to say not only which equipment is needed but why.

If you are a beginner in photography, and money is no object, you may, in your confusion, be tempted to buy the most expensive camera in the shop—with its accompanying case of shining accessories. The thought, uppermost in your mind at the time of purchase, may be that from henceforth the camera will make perfect pictures for you. It is natural for many beginners to think like this. They have yet to realize that it is not the camera, but the man behind the camera who has the vision and the ability to translate the image through the photographic media. The camera, then, as a tool in the hands of the photographer, is chosen to suit the particular work for which it is intended.

CAMERA

If you consider your main requirements first, you simplify your choice by selecting the camera in which the majority of these are incorporated.

1

For the type of portraiture discussed in this book you will find the following features are important:

1. A standard lens, and one of at least double the focal length of the standard lens.
2. Bellows extension or an extension tube.
3. Shutter with slow speeds.
4. Preferably upright and horizontal format.
5. Focusing screen.
6. Cable release, lens hood.

Having listed the items, let us consider the reasons why.

1. *Lenses*

With the standard lens you will experience difficulty in taking a close-up, head and shoulder portrait without showing distortion of some features. Taking the picture from a greater distance and enlarging the required portion of the negative is tolerable for occasional use, but if much portraiture is to be undertaken, or big enlargements are likely to be needed, a long focus lens is a necessity.

This not only reduces the risk of distortion, but allows for the subject matter to fill the negative frame, which is a distinct advantage in procuring good print quality. Also the decreased depth of field coupled with the increased subject to camera distance, gives a more pronounced feeling of roundness and vitality to the features.

2. *Bellows extension*

On a plate camera this feature is necessary if long focus lenses are to be used because the extra focal length requires a greater distance between the lens and the film plane. Some such cameras have double bellows extension, but failing this, extension tubes are supplied as a substitute. A long focus lens or one of telephoto construction is the usual choice for smaller cameras, and this should be a lens in the 90–135 mm range of focal lengths for 35 mm cameras, and 100–200 mm for 6 × 6 cm cameras.

3. *Shutter*

This should have a range of slow speeds such as $\frac{1}{10}$, $\frac{1}{4}$, $\frac{1}{2}$, 1 sec. This type of shutter is of much more use in portraiture than one which has only a few of the faster speeds, and then jumps to a time setting. The shutter can be a leaf (between lens) or a focal plane type. The advantage of the focal plane shutter is that it allows the independent changing of the lens.

4. *Format*

A rectangular format which can be used upright or horizontally is of more general use than a square. The size of film will depend on whether or not big enlargements are to be made from the negatives. A large negative format gives excellent results, but the camera is of necessity bulky, heavy and expensive, and the cost of each film needs to be considered. A reasonable film size with good proportions is the $3\frac{1}{2} \times 2\frac{1}{2}$ or the "Ideal" format *viz* $2\frac{1}{4} \times 2\frac{3}{4}$.

5. *Focusing screen*

You need to be able to focus accurately and quickly and on a particular point in the picture—this "point" is usually the near side eye. The ground glass screen with magnifier seems to be the best answer.

6. *Cable release and lens hood*

A cable release is a useful accessory as an aid to avoiding camera shake, and is quickly and easily operated. A lens hood is an essential to avoid flare in the lens from oblique light.

In considering all the foregoing features the selection of possible cameras is narrowed down considerably. You are likely to find your requirements incorporated in a single-lens reflex camera, but the size and price of the model remain very much an individual choice.

TRIPOD

Of almost equal importance to a suitable camera is a good, strong tripod. Many people think of a tripod simply as a means of steadying the camera to prevent a blurred image. This is only one of its functions.

A good tripod should, also, raise the camera to a height of at least 8 ft and lower it to ground level (or as low as possible); and as a third facility it should tilt the camera in all directions. With these points in mind choice does not offer much difficulty, but you may need more money than at first anticipated!

LIGHTS

Perhaps the next most important tools are the lights. Again, there is a great variety from which to choose, but your relatively simple requirements make it a fairly easy matter.

3

Basically, you need two spotlights and two floods, the floods being identical, and one or two smaller spots or floods, preferably also on telescopic stands. It is unnecessary to have more than these. Too many lights usually results in confusion. As subjects vary in character as well as in their physical features, you must have different qualities of light—soft and hard—and the scope to use them either reflected or directionally, diffused or undiffused. You must also take into consideration the measurements of the studio, as the available space will affect the size and power of the lights. Generally speaking, the smaller the studio, the smaller and less powerful the lights need be, but as some effects require strong lighting and others very little, it is advisable to compromise by having an average size in light but with interchangeable bulbs of a higher or lower wattage.

Your choice of lights, then, will include the spotlight for a hard, directional light, the flood for a less powerful, more spreading light, diffusers for both of them, and some suitable surfaces for reflecting light.

SPOTLIGHT

This is a lamp which, by means of a reflector and lens system, sends out a narrow light beam of high intensity which can be controlled in spread by a simple adjustment.

As the kind of studio envisaged is of relatively small dimensions the usual large spotlight, fitted with a 1000 W bulb is too cumbersome. But a smaller one of a similar design fitted with a 500 W bulb, would be very suitable. The stand, though heavy, is fitted with castors for ease of movement, and the central column being telescopic, extends to a height of 9 ft. The lamphouse is fitted with a focusing device to increase, or decrease, the width of the beam of light. Barn doors on each side can be extended to shield the camera lens from the brilliant glare and to shade off a part of the subject or studio.

Very small spotlights are useful for adding extra "effect" light to the clothes or hair. If these are supplied without a stand, they can be clamped to a suitable object quite easily. Black paper, or tin tubes or cones are easily made to fit over the light to control the width of the beam, or to shield the camera lens.

FLOOD

A flood is so called because the beam of light fans outward from the centre. This gradually disperses the power of the light making it much softer when it reaches the subject than when it left its source. This is different from the spot which sends its light out in straight lines.

The width of this spread of light, in its initial stage, depends on the width of the reflector. These range from very small, similar to a pudding basin, to very wide, and are either deep or shallow.

A good choice is a reflector of 10 or 12 in. in dia., with the bulb recessed well back, and the inside coated with a good reflective surface. This is a good average size, and the width of beam can easily be decreased by making a snout of stiff black paper and fixing it over the reflector; or the beam can be diffused further by means of a diffuser placed over the front. But the bulb must be well-recessed or any diffuser fixed over it will quickly burn.

Barn doors are not fitted to these lights by the manufacturers, but substitutes from black paper, or tin, can be made and fixed to each side of the reflector. The telescopic stand must be rigid, and show no sign of imbalance even at its greatest height. Many stands on the market extend to a height of only 6 ft, whereas 8 or 9 ft is the height more often required. Interchangeable bulbs of varying wattage, will give you plenty of control in lighting without too much equipment.

Two identical floodlights will make the lighting techniques discussed here more easily understood and practised.

In addition to the spotlights and floods you need reflectors and diffusers.

Reflectors. Any white reflective surface can be used to reflect light from the lamps on to the subject. Sheets of white polystyrene are light, easily fixed in position, and reflect adequately well. Stronger reflection can be obtained by using a mirror, or a piece of card covered with aluminium foil (dull side uppermost).

Diffusers. A floodlight can be purchased which incorporates a diffuser, but this either means having extra equipment, or using the diffused light for all subjects. If you make a diffuser out of a piece of translucent paper, butter muslin or similar material you can soften the light where necessary. Placing the diffuser between the subject and the light, has the effect of softening the light, whereas a piece of butter muslin placed immediately over the reflector will dull the light rather than soften it. A subtle difference, but one worth considering!

Dimmer. An electronic dimmer, placed within easy reach close to the camera, is of great value in controlling the intensity of the studio lights. A separate control for each light is necessary.

A useful instrument of this kind, made especially for the purpose, is the Varilux control unit, obtainable from Mr. Herbert C. Butcher of Wallington, Surrey. In this unit a separate control knob is provided for each light and the wattage capacity is quite high.

BACKGROUNDS

The background is so much a part of the individual photographer's preference that only a few suggestions can be made here.

Background and lighting are tied together. If the studio allows sufficient space, a white background can produce all shades of white, grey or black according to the amount of light it receives, which in turn depends on how far the model can be placed away from the background. Background paper is supplied in rolls 7 or 9 ft wide and in a range of colours. These can be pulled down to form a continuous ground behind and beneath for a full length portrait, if necessary, and the used portion torn off when soiled. Fixing an object in the beam of a spotlight, for the shadow to be formed on the background, can give an endless variety of exciting shapes to add interest to the picture. White polystyrene sheets, plastic materials, bamboo or reed screens, also make good backgrounds. Backgrounds can be as elaborate, or as simple, as the photographer aided by his lights, wishes to make them.

Simple, portable, backgrounds can be made by using a piece of hardboard 5 × 4 ft, either plain or painted in a suitable colour, or by stretching a piece of canvas across a light wood frame.

No special background at all may be needed if the studio walls can act as a substitute and care is taken over the inclusion of objects.

FURNITURE

As little furniture as possible should be in the studio while working. However it is a great advantage to have a selection at hand from which you can choose quickly the most suitable for a particular subject. Again, only a few suggestions can be made because individual ideas and requirements vary so widely.

You are photographing people—not advertising furniture and including a model to set it off and add sex appeal. You must choose the furniture according to the person's reaction to it. Have not you, yourself, noticed how different you feel when perched on a high stool, sitting on a chair or at a table, or curled up on a big cushion on the floor? You respond to each in a certain way. Others will also react—not necessarily in the same way—but they will respond more happily to one than the other. This reaction is the yardstick by which we choose the furniture.

Likely requirements might be stools of varying heights, a chair without arms, another with arms, a table, and several cushions, including one or two large ones for placing on the floor.

ACCESSORIES

It is an advantage if the studio decor allows for the occasional inclusion of the walls and curtains as a part of the background. This indicates plain, light-coloured walls—or light on one side of the room and dark on the other—and plain, rich coloured curtains, which hang well and extend to floor level. A few lovely pictures and some well arranged flowers add to the charm of the room and can be removed quite easily if necessary. The whole atmosphere of the room is happy, and is designed to attract and delight and the playing of soft music may help to allay nervousness.

The room itself and all the equipment are contrived to increase efficiency without appearing too clinical, to create an atmosphere of confidence, of serenity and of natural enjoyment.

All this is of little use unless you, as a photographer, are able to inspire these attributes. The atmosphere you create is your responsibility.

Confidence is obtained only by a thorough understanding and knowledge of the subject, and in the following chapters we will analyze together the individual studio techniques applicable to portraiture.

2 Looking at Light

If IT were not for the fact that white light, when passed through a prism, splits up into all the colours of the spectrum, there would have been no advance in photography at all and colour photography would be unknown. You will find many books and articles from which to study these and other astounding properties of light, but at the moment we are going to think about light in quite a different way. We are, in fact, going to train ourselves to *see* light, to observe everyday subjects under different lighting conditions, to note the effect that light has on colour and texture, and to understand something of the psychological effect that light has on us. At first we shall consider daylight out of doors, and then attempt to translate our findings into terms of artificial light in the studio. This should help us to a better understanding of light, so that we can use it as a descriptive medium in portraiture, and teach us to assess visually the contrasts between light and shade and the subtle changes in colour made by direct, as well as reflected, light.

OBSERVING LIGHT

Light enables us to see an object. Without light we are able to recognize things only by the feel of their shape and texture.

In the absence of light there is no colour. Normally we recognize things purely from a mental impression of them—if we know something to be brown, green or red, it stays that way in our minds, and we have to train ourselves to see the variations in colour produced by the changing direction and quality of the light. Similarly with texture—we know the surface of a particular object to be rough or smooth and we have to learn to see that the direction and intensity of light

8

have a visual effect on texture; a rough surface either being emphasized or being made to appear almost smooth.

If light never varied, either in colour, luminosity, or intensity, its use photographically, would be comparatively simple. It would also be very uninteresting and monotonous, and result in pictures that were merely a record of shapes.

Happily light does vary. Daylight can vary from one minute to the next, and we can make artificial light so versatile that it can become difficult to repeat a certain lighting effect unless careful records and measurements have been kept.

CLIMATIC CONDITIONS

We know that daylight varies in quality according to the time of day or the month of the year. But it also varies with changing climatic conditions. In this country we can compare the brilliant light produced by the overhead summer sun shining in a cloudless blue sky with the darkness resulting from overhanging storm clouds, or the soft brightness of an early morning heat haze with the cheerless hue of a November fog; or, again, the glistening white of fresh fallen snow in winter sunshine with the dreary grey of continual rain, or even the magic of dawn with the mystery of twilight.

Have you noticed that the description of the quality of light has included the texture and colour as well as the actinic value? The colour of light varies according to the colour of the sky from which it is reflected. An overall grey sky reflects grey light. A sky with an abundance of white cloud reflects white light, while the cloudless blue sky reflects blue light. The colour changes are most easily observed where part of the subject is in sunshine and part in shadow. When the sun is shining in a blue sky the sunlit area is tinged with yellow light—e.g. green leaves appearing yellow-green—while the shaded area is tinged with blue—the green leaves appearing blue-green. Or, the distant fields will appear yellow-green in the sunlight, but blue-green in any shaded areas. When the blue of the sky is obliterated by banks of white cloud, the reflected light is white—green leaves in the shaded areas will have a distinctly white appearance, and there is much less contrast between shadow and sunlit areas. Under a grey sky, without sunshine, all colours are dulled and contrasts are reduced to a minimum.

In the early morning sunshine the light tends towards yellow, being reflected by the golden hue of sunrise, and in the evening the light again changes towards the reds and yellows, caused partly by the dust-laden atmosphere, but mainly by the reflection of the glowing reds and yellows of the setting sun streaming across the sky.

The atmosphere is responsible for an apparent change in the texture as well as the colour of light. We talk of sunlight as being harsh and glaring, evening light as soft and mellow, light in snow conditions as crisp and clean or, perhaps, dull and heavy. We think of light through rain as being misty or clear and through fog as either thick white, or dirty yellow. Light is also termed exciting or depressing, warm or cold, and bright or dull.

It is because of this customary way of defining light in terms of mood and atmosphere, as well as the visual changes in texture and colour which occur with variations in its direction and intensity, that makes light such an important tool in the techniques of portraiture.

ACTINIC VALUE OF LIGHT

The intensity of light varies from hour to hour, from day to day and from month to month, according to the direction from which the sun's rays strike the earth. The power is greatest when the sun is directly overhead, i.e. at midday during the months of May, June and July. Decreases in intensity occur on either side, both in the hours of the day and the months of the year. The fewest hours of daylight in any one day occur in December; and the changes in the actinic value of the light occur more quickly then than in the long daylight hours of mid-summer.

The condition of the sky, which is reflecting the light, is a factor governing its intensity. When the sun is shining in a sky flecked with white clouds, the intensity of the light is greater than when reflected by an unclouded blue sky. This, as we have already seen, is because the white clouds scatter the light into the shadows. It is rather misleading for beginners in photography, because the sun in a cloudless blue sky appears so much more brilliant to the human eye and gives greater contrasts. The cloudy sky with no sunshine produces light of reduced actinic value, which, added to its lack of colour and texture, makes it a less favourable light for conventional photography, unless the subject is primarily one of mood.

PSYCHOLOGICAL EFFECT OF LIGHT

While we are still considering the nature of light in general terms, let us think what effect, if any, the variations of light have on our personal feelings. Sunlight is a joyous thing. In the bitter cold of winter, the sunshine can be exhilarating and can make us feel gay. When the first touch of warmth creeps into the sun's rays we are physically warmed and feel more kindly disposed towards life in general. Summer sunshine, associated in our minds with holidays and other pleasurable pursuits, makes us feel relaxed and happy, or, alternatively active and excited.

Wet weather, with its accompanying dull, monotonous grey light, can make us feel depressed and uninspired; misty light can fill us with awe or apprehension; thick fog can make us feel isolated, and perhaps, fearful. We could continue in this way at some length imagining our feelings under the varying conditions of light, but enough has been said to make us realize its importance.

We are used to changes in lighting conditions. Change is welcome, for we soon become tired of monotony. If it is dull and wet for too long we yearn for sunshine. If the sun shines for too long we look for the shade. Change has some excitement about it, monotony is always dull.

Can you imagine viewing an exhibition in which all the pictures were taken under identical lighting conditions, or seeing a series of portraits in which the lighting effects were all similar? Your response in each case, would lack any enthusiasm or interest. It can be said, then, that the light used for making a portrait can have an effect on the model, and the viewer, as well as the way the model's character is depicted, emphasizing the mood of the picture and formulating the features.

VISUAL LIGHT AND SHADE

We shall now begin to narrow our field of discussion from the nature of light in general, to its visible effect on a particular subject. You can choose any subject you like for this study, providing you can see it every day, and are able to observe the changes in it brought about by the various lighting conditions.

A TREE

The subject we have selected to examine now is a conical shaped cupressus—a coniferous tree completely covered in leaves from its pointed top to the ground. It is easily viewed from any angle as it stands isolated on a lawn.

Seeing the tree for the first time in sunlight we notice immediately the strong shadow it casts. This follows the shape of the tree, but varies in length according to the position of the sun. In the early morning sunshine the shadow is elongated,

11

but as the sun moves across the sky, the shadow of the tree becomes shorter until, when the sun is nearly directly overhead, it disappears from view, to re-appear on the opposite side of the tree where it gradually lengthens until the sunlight is no longer strong enough to produce any shadow. Although in bright sunshine, a shadow may appear dark, there is always visible detail within it—a point which will be referred to again when we attempt to translate the nature of light into terms of monochrome photography. The little pockets of shadow between the leaves are darkest when the sun is directly above the tree.

You will notice that there is, in addition to the cast shadow, a shaded area of the tree which is untouched by the sun's rays. The tree, or any other subject, when seen in slanting sunlight, will always have these two distinct types of shadow—the shaded area and the cast shadow. The only time, in sunlight, when these two shadows are not visible is when, from your viewing angle, the entire face of the tree is frontally lit by the sun. The shadows, of course, are behind the tree and therefore out of sight. If the sun at any angle becomes completely hidden by passing clouds, the cast shadows disappear and the whole tree is in shade.

Without sunshine some of the attractiveness of the tree is missing, but you will notice that the leaf detail is more in evidence. In fact it is the species of tree which you notice now rather than the shape. It can also be realized that both shade without sunshine, and sunshine without shade, make the tree appear flat and two-dimensional. To obtain a three-dimensional effect you must have part of the tree in sunshine, part in shadow, and, in addition, a well defined cast shadow. If the tree is to appear well modelled, the cast shadow must be of a suitable length for the height of the tree. In the late afternoon you can view the tree from an angle which will give sunlight over practically one third of the surface, leaving the remainder as a shaded area, apart from an outline of light on the far side. This back and side lighting is most attractive and gives a good rendering of the form, and character of the tree.

VISUAL COLOUR

Late afternoon sunlight also allows you to see quite clearly the change in the colour of the leaves under the different quality of light. In the sunlit area the green leaves have a distinct yellow tinge, while in the shaded area the tinge is blue. You can watch this interplay of colour throughout the day.

The light reflected from the pale gold of the early morning sky, mingling with the blue haze in the atmosphere, renders the leaves of the tree as a rich green.

12

As the sun rises in the sky the sunlit leaves become a yellow-green and those in the shaded area a blue-green. In the stronger sunlight, reflected by white clouds a golden yellow and a sprinkling of white intermingles with the yellow-green, while the blue-green of the shaded area is lighter in tone—appearing as a grey-green. The light reflected from a cloudless blue sky gives a distinct blue cast to the shaded areas, while in the sunlit area the yellow-green becomes green and silver-white. At midday the greens tend to become blue-green, while in the morning and evening they tend towards yellow-green. In sunlight the shaded area is always more blue than that which faces the sun. It is interesting to note that the colour is more saturated on a fine day when the sun is obscured by cloud, and so you find that the light which is giving greater detail in the leaves is similar to that which produces the strongest colour. Variety of colour tone and visual glitter and excitement are obtained only in sunlight.

A PIECE OF BARK

Now for a subject which can be observed in still greater detail—a piece of bark from an old silver birch tree. It is, in the main, gnarled and deeply grooved, and the colours range from browny-grey, through silver to moss green. But it is the surface texture which is of most interest. Looking at it in reflected daylight with the sun shining from a cloudless blue sky, though not reaching this part of the subject, the detail in the bark is very clear. If you concentrate, you can see every small crack and mark on it. It might be said that you are seeing it as a flat pattern, and this reflected light is the most suitable for such purpose. The piece of bark does not appear exciting in this light, in fact it looks rather old, tired and useless. Now turn it round allowing the sun's rays to play on it, and note what you see. Firstly the bark no longer looks decrepit—it has become re-vitalized. The grooves facing the sun have been "ironed out"—they are still visible but appear wider and more shallow. The over-all colours take on a white brightness, but the yellow-green of the moss, being in a more shaded position within a crevice, remains a saturated colour, and, incidentally, becomes a focus of interest. As you continue turning the bark, you will notice how the sun's rays alter the apparent depth of the grooves. We have already seen that they appear wide and shallow when filled with light. We now see that they also appear wide and shallow when filled with dark, i.e. when the sun's rays do not penetrate within the groove. The grooves appear the narrowest and deepest when the brilliant sunshine lights one side of the groove only, leaving the other as a contrasting dark tone.

13

This strong side or back lighting also makes the bark appear strong and hard and to have a very rough surface texture. Alternatively, when the whole surface of the bark is facing the sun, the grooves become scarcely visible, and the bark now appears younger, and softer, with a much smoother surface

The recognition of this apparent change in character and surface texture obtained with the varying conditions and angles of light is most useful when considering the skin texture in portraiture.

You have now learned that variations in the nature of light make a distinct difference to the mood, character, definition, contrast and colour of your pictures. To photograph a subject out of doors you have to wait for the most suitable light if you are to get the best possible results. The type of sky, the time of day, the month of the year, the weather, are all factors which have to be considered. These may have to be waited for (as many a photographer has experienced) possibly weeks or even months before conditions become ideal, and a pre-conceived picture can be taken. This is one advantage that the portraitist has over the landscape or architectural photographer. In the studio the lights are under control, and similar effects to those out of doors can be produced at will. If, at first, you consciously try to do this, even if it does seem to be stretching your imagination a little far, I think you will understand the control of studio lighting more easily. You should also resist the temptation to use too many lights, and evade the pitfall of "double lighting".

IN THE STUDIO—DAYLIGHT

Now suppose you go into the studio, with a model who is patient enough to sit for us during the experiments. It is a fine day with intermittent sunshine, and the light in the room appears to be quite bright. You check the light with an exposure meter and find a marked difference between the light near the window and that at the furthest point away from it. This fall off in illumination is due to the "inverse square law" which states that the power of light from a point source decreases, as a square of its distance from the subject. As a simple illustration, suppose your model is sitting 2 ft from the window and you make an exposure; she then moves back to 4 ft away from the window and you make another exposure. In theory the exposure time in the second case will not be twice our first exposure as one might suppose, but four times. But in fact a window is not a point source and window lighting is dependent upon so many other factors—the kind of light, the size of the window in relation to the subject, the colour of surrounding walls, etc. that this can only serve as a guide to

14

illustrate the point that light falls off more suddenly than you might expect. This fact must be continually taken into account when dealing with light in a confined space, especially with open artificial lights which follow the law quite strictly. It does not apply, however, to the spotlight whose controlled beam of light travels in a straight line instead of fanning outwards from its source.

With the movement of the model further away from the window in the light room it will be noticed that the light spreads more evenly over the features, giving a duller lighting, the quality of the light appearing much softer. It also, apparently, concentrates attention more on the character of the model than on the outward form, which latter was very much in evidence in the brighter light against the window.

The sun now appears from behind a cloud, and shines into the studio and on your model. The effect is warm, exciting and glamorous and you hastily make an exposure, only to be disappointed when you see the resulting print. The sunlight no longer looks warm and glamorous but cold and hard. The print is much too contrasty, because the emulsion has been unable to cope with the extreme contrast between the sunlight and shadow. Being indoors and therefore in a confined space, you have lost the vast area of reflected light from the sky, which has left the shaded areas virtually unlit. This "surrounding light" must therefore be produced artificially. It will need a powerful light to give a sufficient balance of tone with direct sunlight, and this can be achieved most easily by using flash, the most powerful of all the artificial light sources. A better plan is to use daylight without the actual sunlight for the main light, and make use of a white reflector to bounce the light back into the shaded area, and to simulate the reflected light from the sky. This gives a better balance of tone values, and shows visible detail in both highlights and shadows on the resulting print. The main point to remember is that as there is only one sun so there should be only one main light and whatever secondary light is used it should represent the reflected light from the sky. This means that it must never be used in opposition to the sun (or main light), but rather should suggest an over-all even light which is present whether the sun is shining or not.

As daylight is continually fluctuating in brightness, a careful check must be kept on exposure time.

By nature, as we have already seen, daylight can vary according to the season, the time of day and the weather. But, on the whole, in the studio it is a soft light without any glare. It is kind to skin texture and, being a natural light, it assists in overcoming self-consciousness in a model.

ARTIFICIAL LIGHT

Even with the limited number of lights at your disposal in the studio, you will find that you are able to reproduce by artificial means, almost every effect or mood that has been discussed with daylight out of doors.

VISUAL EFFECTS

Broadly speaking, you use the spotlight to replace the sun and the floodlights, with the additional help of reflective surfaces, to substitute for the sky. (At this stage we are solely considering the nature of the lights and their effect on mood and character. The actual positioning of each will be studied in detail in the following chapters).

Let us begin by visualizing a few effects using these artificial light sources.

BRILLIANT SUNSHINE AND BLUE SKY

For this effect you can use the spotlight for the sun and a diffused floodlight for the sky. The highlights will be crisp, clean and hard. The cast shadows and shaded areas will be dark in tone with sharply defined edges, giving strong contrast. The floodlight is diffused only to cut down the power and increase the spread of the light—it could be moved further back or fitted with a wider reflector—the essential thing is that the contrast between light and shade must be maintained but controlled.

HAZY SUNSHINE IN WHITE CLOUDY SKY

Less contrast is needed here and the shadow edges do not need to be clearly defined, but the result must still be gay and clean. The spotlight acting for the sun can be reduced slightly in its power, and an undiffused floodlight used for the sky. You must be sure to keep the right balance in light—the sun is always brighter than the sky, and if the sun is shining brightly there are always dark shadows, *but* detail is visible within them.

If the sun is hidden behind clouds wait until it re-appears before taking a picture, otherwise the resulting picture is dull and monotonous in its tone values. Similarly with a portrait, flat lighting is often dull and needs a touch of sunshine. Remember the evening light on the tree which was uninspiring until the sun came out from behind the cloud and lit each side from behind giving the tree a third dimension and adding tremendously to its beauty. To translate that effect in terms of artificial light, you need a spotlight each side behind the model, slightly reduced in power to prevent it from being too brilliant, and a flood for the frontal light, at a high enough position to give some modelling to the face.

SUNSHINE ON SNOW

An immense amount of reflected light is produced by the myriads of snow crystals under strong sunlight. White paper, or other reflective surfaces, must be placed everywhere around the model and floodlights brought in to bounce light off these. A spotlight can then be used for the sunshine (or two spots if they are placed behind the model). The cast shadows must be only very light in tone, but still visible as shadow. This effect is the true high key picture—too little reflected light around the model results in a grey tone which is more akin to dreary dirty wet snow when the exhilarating glamour has faded.

SUNLIGHT AND STORM CLOUDS

The dramatic effect which this description conjures up in our minds is easily produced by back lighting with an undiffused spotlight, and the careful use of reflected light for the remainder. In this case the reflected light can be positioned first and the depth of tone required obtained by adjusting its distance from the model—overlighting spoils the effect. This lighting is particularly effective with a subject seen in profile. All low key effects can be visualized as having dark clouds with a little sunshine, or maybe no sunshine at all.

MIST OR HAZE

For this rather soft and mysterious lighting effect you need plenty of reflected light, and if any direct light is felt to be necessary it must be diffused. As there is no sun, the spotlight is only used as an extra light on the background, or to be bounced off a reflective surface. The results of this lighting can be very dainty sketch effects, especially suitable for children.

PSYCHOLOGICAL EFFECT OF ARTIFICIAL LIGHTS

Spotlight. As we have seen the spotlight has all the attributes of strong sunlight. Its light is brilliant, exciting, sometimes dynamic, active, clean and crisp. It can be softened slightly by reduction in power or by a diffuser, but, normally, it is a hard light. It can either make a person feel attractive and gay, or more nervous and self-conscious, according to their temperament. The hardness of the light has both advantages and disadvantages. It can emphasize the character lines in the face, or it can obliterate them almost completely depending on the angle from which it is used. It can depict strength of character, and reveal the beauty and power which is latent within every human being. It can lift a nondescript type of face to one of distinction, and it can do much to remedy a sallow complexion. One of the disadvantages of the hard nature of the light is that it may give a hardness to the person's character which would be quite false. A grim, determined expression tempered with a warmth of feeling, shows positive traits, but the same expression, coupled with the cold, hard aloofness which the spotlight is capable of producing is too negative. Similarly, sophisticated glamour is flattering if it suits the personality, but the crisp contrast of light and shade can overshadow the attractive simplicity of some natures.

The spotlight can promote impact by force.

Floodlight. This light is much softer and less directional than the spot, which is why it was used to represent the sky in visual effects. The cast shadows have softer edges, as each shadow really has a dark centre and lightens outwards, owing to the cone-shaped beam of light. This cone of light can be controlled by the width of the reflector, as well as by diffusing screens, which means that the nature of the light can vary from fairly hard to very soft. The floodlight, then, becomes a light which can be made suitable for the majority of personalities, and for depicting many varied moods. The character lines in a face can all be shown, but the outer edge of each one has a softness which maintains the natural beauty.

Bounced light. When a flood, or any other light, is directed on to a reflective surface and the light "bounced" back to the subject, the quality of the light varies according to the material from which it is reflected. If white paper, or any white matt surface, is used, the reflected light is soft. If, on the other hand, a mirror or a shiny metal surface is used, the reflected light can be hard, and often too brilliant.

Soft reflected light is very suitable for children when a little sunlight can be added behind the child, and to middle-aged ladies who prefer the character lines in their face to be obliterated. The over-all soft light gives complete freedom of movement for the model. It is usually most effective for high key subjects, as the balance of tones in a full range can be upset by the over-all light, and somewhat flat, tone of the face.

18

When taking pictures out of doors, some of the most effective lighting arrangements are found when the sun is behind or to one side of the subject. For a similar reason, in the studio, the spotlight is nearly always placed behind the model (except in advertising photography or for special effects) and the floodlight in front. The spotlight then becomes largely an effect light, and the flood takes the important position of a modelling light.

Before putting into practice some of the lighting effects which have been visualized, you need to understand the effect that light has on the features, and the positions in which the individual lights must be placed to give both the correct modelling for the particular face, and accurate depth of tone for the shaded area and the cast shadows.

The next few chapters are in the form of exercises which will enable you to take your time and study each part in detail.

3 Light on the Features

IN ORDER to keep the whole problem of lighting as simple as possible it is necessary to experiment first with the effect of the height and distance of a light source on the various features of the face.

Using for this purpose a full face view of the head (square on to camera) ignoring all questions of arrangement of the body, each separate feature will be studied in turn, in order to understand how light affects the drawing of the face. In photography light is used as a drawing pencil. The shape of the face and the separate features is, therefore, dependent on the *position* of the light used.

The room should be dark, except for the one light to be used in the experiment, which can be of any type that is easily handled. A table lamp serves the purpose quite well.

Place the light squarely in front of the model, at a suitable distance for comfort and level with the model's face.

Study the effect of the light on the features, and try to imagine what the effect would be in a black and white photograph.

With the light level and square on to the model's face:

The whole effect is flat—two dimensional. The *eyes* are light in colour, appear to be on the surface, and lack depth and character. The *nose* is flat, shows no bone structure, lacks form. The *lips* are also flat, lack colour and form. The *chin* does not protrude and is hardly distinguishable from the neck. The *neck* is square and flat (Fig. 3.1).

EYES

While watching the eyes only, move the light slowly upwards. With this, the eyes appear to sink further and further into the head, at the same time gaining in colour tone and character. As the light moves higher there comes a time when

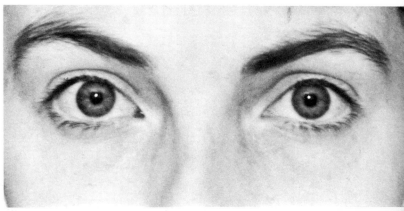

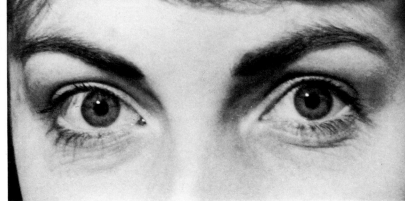

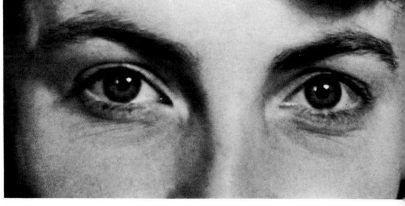

3.1 3.2
  3.3
  3.4

Fig. 3.1. Flat lighting from lamp
level and square
Fig. 3.2. Eyes: Light central,
level
Fig. 3.3. Eyes: Light central,
raised correctly
Fig. 3.4. Eyes: Light 25° to right
of central

21

the shadow of the eyelids crosses the eyes, when, obviously, the beauty of the eyes is lost. The correct position of the light for the eyes is that reached immediately *prior* to the shadow of the eyelid crossing the pupil (Fig. 3.3).

Now note the effect on the colour of the eyes when the light is close to the model or further away. The light being too close tends to destroy the character of the eye, but the further away the light the higher it has to go to reach the desired effect. Extend the light to its full height and position it correctly for the depth and colour of the eyes. Now move the light from the central position to approximately 25° to the right or left. Notice that the eyes now appear more rounded, and the whites of the eyes are graduated in tone, which gives the third-dimension effect (Fig. 3.4).

Proceed with the same experiment on the other features of the face.

THE NOSE

Start from the central level position when the nose appears flat and shapeless (Fig. 3.5). Lowering the light shortens the nose and puts the emphasis on the nostrils. As the light is raised the nose begins to gain form and length, the longer the shadow under the nose the longer the nose itself appears.

Continue to raise the light until the shadow from the nose begins to cross the lip line. This is obviously too far, as the drawing of the lips must remain clear. The most satisfactory position for the drawing of the nose is normally when the shadow from the nose is about half way between the nose and mouth (Fig. 3.6).

At this point note that if the model's expression is to be smiling, allowance must be made for the narrowing of the space between the nose and mouth, which will mean keeping the nose shadow slightly shorter than that required for a serious expression.

With the light placed centrally and at a height to produce a shadow half way between nose and mouth you can see that the bone formation of the nose and the length of the nose are well drawn.

To give a feeling of roundness or the third dimension, move the light about 25° to one side or the other. The position of the shadow from the nose should be such that it comes roughly half way between nose and mouth and follows round the nostril in a pleasing shape (Fig. 3.7). Lowering the light moves the shadow from the nose up the face giving an ugly triangular shape.

Raising the light gives a longer pointed shadow. In principle, the longer the shadow the longer the nose appears and, conversely, the shorter the shadow the shorter the nose appears.

22

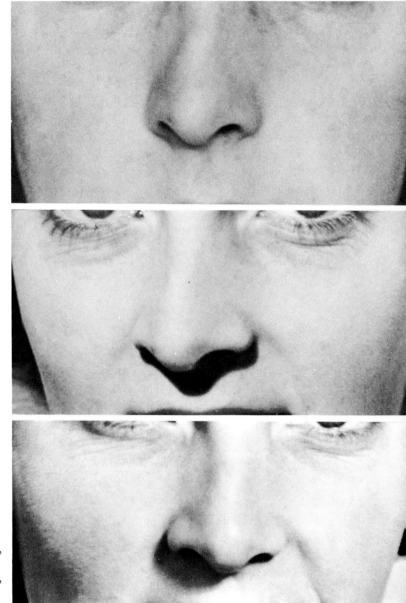

3.5
3.6
3.7

Fig. 3.5. Nose: Light central, level
Fig. 3.6. Nose: Light central, raised correctly
Fig. 3.7. Nose: Light 25° to right of central

For the average face the position of about half way between nose and mouth is the most suitable and the shape of the shadow is, obviously, most important. A very small adjustment to right or left will alter the shape; and overlarge or badly shaped nose shadows can be very ugly.

It is well to spend some time in experimenting with the effect of this light position on the face. Notice how a very slight movement of the model's head alters the nose shadow. This will prove to you how important the modelling light is, and why it is so often necessary to give a final adjustment to this light after time has been spent in arranging the other lights, and the model has been allowed a moment's relaxation.

Before advancing to a similar experiment with the lips, it is as well to note that, with the average face, when the light is positioned correctly for the nose it is also correct for the eyes. Of course, you can never make definite rules as all faces are different, and you usually have to compromise, but for the purpose of understanding the relative positions of the lights it is safe to base your studies on an average well-proportioned face.

LIPS

Return the light once more to the central level position. Observe the lips—they will be somewhat colourless and flat. Raising the light slowly you can watch the colour returning and the formation of the lips showing more clearly. The light is high enough when the shadow of the top lip is just beginning to show on the bottom lip, and, at the same time there will be a shadow underneath the lower lip. From this position the light gives the best drawing to the lips and gives good texture rendering, but for the third-dimension effect—and roundness in the lips —move the light to one side or the other to an angle of about 25° as before.

Now compare again the final positions for the eyes, nose and mouth and you will find the correct position for the one is virtually correct for all three.

This simplifies things a great deal. As the nose shadow is by far the easiest to see clearly, you can concentrate your attention on that, knowing that, given an average well proportioned face, if you get the nose shadow correct the other features will be similarly well drawn.

CHIN AND NECK

Yet again you must return the light to the level central position and study the chin and the neck. These two features may be bracketed together as the same lighting affects them both. It is a fallacy among many beginners in portraiture that there should be no shadows on the neck.

If a chin is to show form it must have a shadow underneath it. If a neck is to appear round it must have light and shade to produce roundness. In Fig. 3.8, where the light is level and central, the chin and neck are barely divided —the neck is merely a flat column. Moving the light downwards widens the neck still further and removes the dividing line between neck and chin entirely. The upward movement of the light gives an increasingly longer shadow.

Any lighting of the chin and neck will obviously include the jaw line, which does become a very important feature in portraiture when various types and ages of face are considered.

It is well, therefore, at this stage to notice the outline of the jaw—very clear-cut on each side of the face as the light moves higher in the central position. Moving the light too high obliterates the neck entirely by shadow and leaves the head isolated from the body. Bringing the light down again until the *nose shadow* comes half way between the nose and mouth you make the shadow on the neck a good shape—and the chin and jaw line are well contoured (Fig. 3.9).

Now move the light 25° to left or right. One jaw line will be in shadow whilst the other remains light in tone. The shadow spreading diagonally across the neck gives a rounder shape to the neck (Fig. 3.10). It is when the light at this off-centre position is too low that the ugly short shadow occurs between the jaw line and the neck that worries so many beginners.

To *sum up* the findings:

The modelling light used from the central position at a height to give the nose shadow half way between the nose and mouth emphasizes the contours of the face, gives strong outlines to the features and defines the bone structure. The frontal bones, the nasal bone, the cheek bones and the jaw bones are all well drawn. It is the clear cut drawing of the face which has made this particular lighting position so popular for glamour portraits (Fig. 3.11).

The off-centre position for the modelling light gives a greater feeling of roundness to the features. The outline of the face is not so clearly defined, which de-centralizes attention from the contours to the "withinness"—in other words the viewer can have contact with the character of the model rather than the shape of the model's face. Hence the off-centre light is often termed the "character" light (Fig. 3.12).

You will also notice that one side of the face is more in shadow than the other —one jaw line particularly being partly in shadow. This fact is a very useful thing

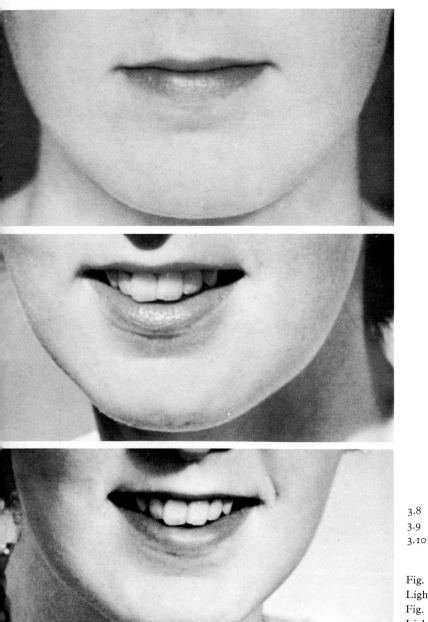

3.8
3.9
3.10

Fig. 3.8. Lips, chin and neck:
Light central, level
Fig. 3.9. Lips, chin and neck:
Light central raised correctly
Fig. 3.10. Lips, chin and neck:
Light 25° to right of central

3.11 3.12 3.13
     3.14

Fig. 3.11. Centrally placed correct angle modelling light gives well drawn bone structure

Fig. 3.12. Off-centre modelling light creates impression of roundness

Fig. 3.13. Three-quarter view sidelighting: small triangular highlight

Fig. 3.14. Division of highlights by the nose shadow—a pitfall to be avoided

27

to know when you are trying to subdue or emphasize various features with lighting.

45° MODELLING LIGHT

While studying the positioning of the drawing light, and its effect on the features it is as well to consider the 45° position which is so useful in pictorial portraiture, especially in portraits of men taken in a three-quarter face position. As it is seldom used for full face views it will do, for the present, to concentrate on the three-quarter face.

With the model's body still towards the camera, the head should turn to a position roughly 45° to the centre.

Now take the light towards the far side of the model's face until the face is divided in light and shade with the rear cheek light, the near cheek dark. Move the light slowly round towards the front, at the same time raising and lowering it until you produce a small triangular-shaped highlight on the near side cheek (Fig. 3.13).

The purpose of this highlight is only to prevent the near-side cheek from being flattened by shadow, in other words, to give the roundness and third-dimension effect you have been seeking in the off-centre position of the light.

The pitfalls to guard against here are (a) producing ugly-shaped highlights and (b) the division of the highlights on the cheek by the nose shadow. This latter fault is very common among beginners in portraiture, looks very ugly and destroys the simplicity and strength for which this lighting effect is so useful (Fig. 3.14).

This one light which you have been using to experiment with the drawing of the face and features is, as you will now realize, called the drawing or modelling light. It is the most important light in the portrait, and its function must be visible. Any other light used must aid the modelling light, not counteract it. Effect lights, to enhance the beauty of the picture, may be used from rear or side positions.

4 Basic Positions
of Modelling Light

The basic positions of the modelling light described in the following pages are:

Full face: 1. Central. 2. 25° to left or right of central. 3. 45° to left or right of central.

Three-quarter face: 1. Central. 2. 25° to left or right of central. 3. 45° to right of central only.

Profile: 1. Central. 2. 25° to right of central. 3. 45° to right of central. 4. 25° to the left of central, *level* for high key. 5. Dark rim outline for high key. 6. Rim for dark background.

In the following studies of these basic positions, the model is taken as turning in one direction only, from S. to E. If she were to turn in the opposite direction, all the instructions would need to be reversed. The camera remains in the same position throughout.

The "central" light is always central to the model, placed to give the central nose shadow half way between nose and mouth.

The light "25° to the right or left of central" is always placed to give a nose shadow which follows round the line of the nostril and finishes just under half way between nose and mouth.

The light "45° to the right or left of central" is always placed to give a small triangle of light on the shadow side of the face, not encroaching on the eye.

The following illustrations will determine the correct positions, and reference can be made to these at all times throughout the experiments described in the chapters on lighting.

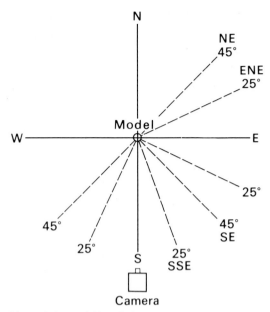

Fig. 4.1. Basic positions of the modelling light

FULL FACE CENTRAL MODELLING LIGHT

Model facing S.
Light used: 500 W flood in 12 in. reflector.
Height of lamp: 6 ft.
Distance of light from model: $4\frac{1}{2}$ ft.
Positioned to give triangular nose shadow, half way between nose and mouth (Fig. 4.2).
Camera position as near S. as possible, avoiding the lamp stand.

Note:

1. The depth of tone in the shadows decreases as the distance of the light increases. The shadow tone on the neck is not so dark as the shadow tone under the nose.

2. The face is lit evenly on both sides—the formation of the temple bones, the cheek bones and the nasal bone is well defined.

3. The chin is clear cut and the jaw line emphasized against the shadow on the neck.

30

4.2 4.3 4.4

Fig. 4.2. Full face, central modelling light, evenly lit and well defined bone structure
Fig. 4.3. Modelling light 25° to left of central
Fig. 4.4. Modelling light 25° to right of central

FULL FACE 25° MODELLING LIGHT

Model facing S.
Light used: 500 W flood in 12 in. reflector.
Height of lamp: 6 ft.
Distance of light from model: $4\frac{1}{2}$ ft.
Positioned to give well shaped shadow just covering the model's right nostril, and ending just under half way between nose and mouth.
Camera at S.

Note:

When the light is put in the 25° position to the *right* of central (for full face), the *left* side of the model's face appears wider than her right side. This is caused by the shadow tone falling over the side of the face (Fig. 4.4).

When the modelling light is put in the 25° position to the *left* of central (for

31

full face), the reverse is the case. In this position the right side of the model's face is in the full light, while the shadow tone divides the left cheek. This is useful to remember when trying to minimize irregularities in the face by means of light and shade (Fig. 4.3).

FULL FACE 45° MODELLING LIGHT

Model facing S.

Light used: 500 W flood in 12 in. reflector.

Height of lamp: 6 ft.

Distance of light from model: 4 ft.

Position: either 45° to the left of central, or 45° to the right of central. Careful adjustment is needed to produce a triangular shaped highlight on the shadow side of the face (Figs. 4.5 and 4.6).

Camera at S.

The clear cut definition of the nose structure by the dividing line of highlight and shadow. One eye is in light—the other in deep shadow. Interest is concentrated on one half of the face.

Fig. 4.5. Lamp 45° left of central position

Fig. 4.6. Lamp 45° right of central position

Fig. 4.7. Three-quarter face, central modelling light: well defined contours, small nose shadow

4.5 4.6 4.7

THREE-QUARTER FACE CENTRAL MODELLING LIGHT

Model facing S.E.

Light used: 500 W flood in 12 in. reflector.

   Height of lamp: 6 ft.

   Distance of light from model: $4\frac{1}{2}$ ft.

   Positioned to give triangular nose shadow, half way between nose and mouth (Fig. 4.7).

   Camera position S. The lamp has now moved further to the right of the camera—no longer in the path of the lens.

   The contours of the face are still well defined. The further cheek is outlined clearly in light against the dark background. The near side cheek has its outline drawn by the shadow tone.

THREE-QUARTER FACE 25° MODELLING LIGHT

Model facing S.E.

Light used: 500 W flood in 12 in. reflector.

Height of lamp: 6 ft.

Distance of light from model: $4\frac{1}{2}$ ft.

   Positioned: (a) about 25° off-centre of model's face to the left (Fig. 4.8). (b) about 25° off-centre of model's face to the right (Fig. 4.9).

   Camera at S.

   The near side of the face appears much wider than the far side (Fig. 4.8), there being no variation of light and shade, the area of light tone looks flat and uninteresting. The jaw is divided from the neck by a short, rather ugly shadow. The overall appearance is of a flat cheek and neck divided by a narrow black line. The nose shadow on the far side is not visible in its true shape. Compare this with Fig. 4.9.

   Here (Fig. 4.9), there is much greater interest. The outline of the face on the far side is well defined. The near side of the face shows good modelling, and the light and shade gives a much better feeling of roundness. It also shows far more character in the face than does Fig. 4.8. It is as well to take extra time studying this position, as it will be found suitable for the majority of types of faces.

THREE-QUARTER FACE 45° MODELLING LIGHT

Model facing S.E.

Light used: 500 W flood in 12 in. reflector or 500 W spot.

4.8 4.9 4.10

Fig. 4.8. Modelling light 25° *left* of central
Fig. 4.9. Modelling light 25° *right* of central
Fig. 4.10. Modelling light 45° *right* of central

Height of lamp: 6 ft.

Distance of light from model: 4 ft.

Camera at S.

Position: 45° to *right* of central. The height and distance of the lamp are adjusted until the only illumination visible on the near side cheek is a triangle of light (Fig. 4.10).

The position 45° to the left of *central* is not used—the triangle of light on the far cheek not being sufficiently visible to give any modelling.

Note:

The rear outline of the face and the nose formation are well drawn. The near side of face and neck are in shadow, apart from the triangle of light on the subject's cheek.

The effect of the third dimension is very strong, owing to the transition from light to dark tones.

PROFILE CENTRAL MODELLING LIGHT

Model facing E.

Light used: 500 W flood in 12 in. reflector.

Height of lamp: 6 ft.

Distance of light from model: 4½ ft.

Position to give triangular nose shadow, half way between nose and mouth (Fig. 4.11).

Camera at S.

The contours of the face are well outlined—the form of the nose, mouth and chin is defined more clearly in this head position and light combination than any other. The near side cheek and jaw and the neck are in shadow.

PROFILE 25° MODELLING LIGHT

Model facing E.

Light used: 500 W flood in 12 in. reflector or spotlight.

Height of lamp: 6 ft.

Distance of light from model: 4½ ft.

Positioned 25° to the *right* of central. Care must be taken that the nose shadow appears in its correct shape from the camera angle. The near side nostril should be in shadow, and the shadow continue in a rounded shape finishing well above the lip line, and *not* forming a pointed shape towards the camera (Fig. 4.12).

Camera at S.

The outline of the features are well shown, while there is good modelling in the near side cheek. This makes the face appear rounder than it does with the central light used in this profile position. The near side jaw line and neck are in shadow.

The lamp position 25° to the *left* of central has not been illustrated as its modelling effect is lost on the far side cheek.

The position 25° to the *left* of central can be used at a *level* elevation in a high key profile portrait. (See page 37).

PROFILE 45° MODELLING LIGHT

Model facing E.

Light used: 500 W spot.

Height of lamp: 6 ft.

Distance of light from model: 3 ft.

4.11 4.12 4.13

Fig. 4.11. Profile view: lit centrally from E
Fig. 4.12. Profile view modelled at 25° right of central
Fig. 4.13. Profile view with modelling at 45° right of central

Camera at S.

Position: 45° to right of central. Care must be taken in positioning the light to avoid flare in the camera lens. For this reason it is better to use a spotlight, with a more directional beam, for any modelling or effect light used behind the model (Fig. 4.13).

Note:

There is a rim of light outlining the profile. The rest of the face and neck are in shadow, apart from the triangle of light on the cheek.

PROFILE RIM LIGHT

Model facing E.
Light used: 500 W spot.
Height of lamp: 4 ft.
Distance of light from model: 3 ft.

36

Camera at S.

Positioned to give a rim of light running down the profile—forehead, nose, mouth and chin. If the light is raised the rim will be wider on the forehead and narrow down as it reaches the lower part of the face (Fig. 4.14).

Note:

This rim light, and any other *rear* lighting effect, emphasize the contours of the face and should be used only for faces with clear cut features.

The rim light can be used in conjunction with the 25°, to the right of central, in which case it acts as an effect light. In any case the rim light does not produce modelling in the face—it only draws the outline, as its name suggests.

PROFILE DARK RIM OUTLINE

Model facing E.
Light used: 150 W flood in 8 in. reflector.
Height of lamp: 3 ft (*level* with model's face).
Distance of light from model: 2 ft.
Camera at S.

Position of the light must be nearer to the model than is the camera. To produce the dark rim outline, the camera lens must see further round the face than the light. The light, which should have a narrow reflector, is placed slightly to the E. side of the camera to avoid obstructing the view of the lens (Fig. 4.15).

Note:

This type of lighting produces a flat two-dimensional face with no modelling at all. It is only suitable for use with a profile position against a really white plain background to give a type of sketch effect. Use two extra lights on the background to ensure that the background tone is lighter than the face. This lighting is also used (against a white background) for the high key treatment.

PROFILE 25° MODELLING LIGHT

Model facing E.
Light used: 150 W flood in 8 in. reflector with diffuser.
Height of lamp: 3 ft—level with model's face.
Distance of light from model: 4 ft.
Camera at S.

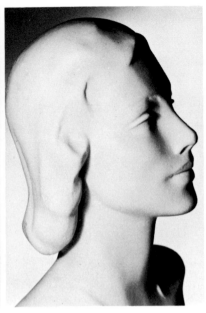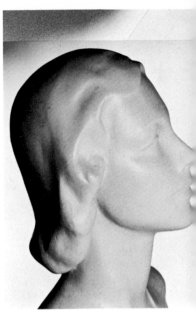

4.14 4.15 4.16

Fig. 4.14. Profile view: rim lighting
Fig. 4.15. Profile lit to give dark outline against white background
Fig. 4.16. Modelling light 25° left of central, nose shadow not visible

---

Position 25° to the *left* of central. The nose shadow will be on the far side cheek and will not be visible from the camera angle (Fig. 4.16).

Note:

The diffuser and lower powered light give added tone to the face and prevent the shadows from being too dark. Use a white background lit by two lights to ensure the background tone is lighter than the face.

This lighting can be used for high key photographs against a white background.

5 Rim Light as an Effect Light

THE RIM light is not a modelling light but is employed, as its name suggests, to rim or outline the head or features with light. It is, therefore, an effect light, and must be used in conjunction with a modelling light. Occasionally a silhouette may be required using the rim light on its own, especially for the profile position.

RIM LIGHT ONLY

Using the rim light only, its effect on the varying positions of the head are analysed below.

Full face position

With the model facing S. place a spotlight approximately N.E. To begin with, place it fairly high with the beam of light directed downwards. Notice the wider area of light on the forehead and the width tapering to nothing as it traverses the cheek. Moving the spotlight down to a level position gives a narrow area of light, but as the light travels downwards it outlines the neck and shoulder as well.

In Fig. 5.1 the spotlight behind the model's left shoulder is in the level position at N.E. while the one behind her right shoulder is at N.W. The latter is high and directed down in order to light the top of the head.

Three-quarter face position

Model facing S.E. position, one spotlight behind the model's right shoulder, approximately N.W. Direct the beam downwards until it outlines the hair and shoulder. On the other side the spotlight needs to be on the east side of N. and at a medium-high elevation. Care must be taken to ensure that the stand is not within range of the camera lens. The lens must at all times be shielded from the glare of the light (Fig. 5.2).

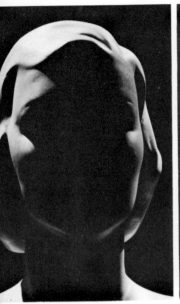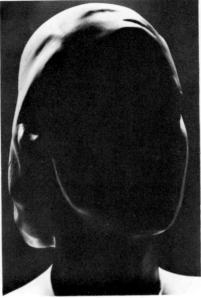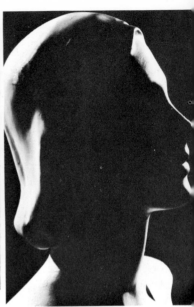

5.1 5.2 5.3

Fig. 5.1. Full face position; double rim lighting
Fig. 5.2. Three-quarter position; double rim lighting
Fig. 5.3. Profile position; double rim lighting

Profile position
Model facing E. Move the two spotlights further round until the outline is rimmed as with the other positions (Fig. 5.3).
Note: Great care must be taken when using the spotlights behind the model to shield the camera lens from the glare of the lights. A three-fold screen is useful for this purpose.

RIM AND MODELLING LIGHTS COMBINED

Full face position
The double rim lighting on a full face portrait is often used for a glamorous effect. It must be combined with a modelling light. The position for this modelling light can be either central as in Fig. 5.4, or 25° to the right (or left) of central as in Fig. 5.5.

It is incorrect to use the modelling light from the level position usually

5.4 5.5 5.6

Fig. 5.4. Double rim lighting; modelling light central
Fig. 5.5. Double rim lighting; modelling light 25° to right of central
Fig. 5.6. Double rim lighting; modelling light central level (secondary light position)

occupied by the secondary light. No modelling to the face is produced by this flat even light—the face and neck appear to be on the same plane, being divided only by a narrow black line under the jaw (Fig. 5.6).

Three-quarter face position (model facing S.E.)

The modelling light will again be central, 25° to the right of central, or 45° to the right of central positions (Figs. 5.7, 5.8, 5.9).

The rim light on the shadow side of the head should not encroach on the face, but light the hair only. On the right side of the face it can add a touch of sparkle to the modelling light, or help to emphasize the contours of the face.

In Fig. 5.9 a rim light has been used on the side of the modelling light but its effect is hardly visible. The spotlight has been used as the modelling light to form the clearly defined triangle of light on the near side cheek.

Profile

When the rim light is used on a profile position in conjunction with the modelling

41

Fig. 5.7. Double rim lighting; modelling light central
Fig. 5.8. Double rim lighting; modelling light 25° to right of central
Fig. 5.9. Single rim lighting; modelling light 45° to right of central

light it intensifies the contour of the face and neck. It is obvious that this lighting effect will only show to its best advantage against a dark background (Figs. 5.10, 5.11, 5.12).

Rim lighting (from rear)

A rim of light round the head can be obtained by placing a small light immediately behind the model. Care must be taken to see that the model completely obstructs the view of the lamp from the camera.

Fig. 5.13 shows the full face position with the head haloed by light from a lamp immediately behind the model's back.

Reducing contrast

Throughout these experiments the rim lights and the modelling lights have been used undiffused in order that the correct positions can be seen more easily. The result is far too contrasty for normal use, but we can control the contrast by

5.10 5.11 5.12
5.13

Fig. 5.10. Double rim lighting; modelling light central
Fig. 5.11. Double rim lighting; modelling light 25° to right of central
Fig. 5.12. Double rim lighting; modelling light 45° to right of central
Fig. 5.13. Rim lighting from a light behind the model

43

adding or subtracting light. We can add light to the shadow areas and subtract light from the highlight areas, thus producing the exact tonal range to suit our picture.

The main tools in this technique are lights, distance of lights and diffusers.

The light used for the purpose of lighting the shadows we shall call the "secondary light", as its function is always secondary to the modelling light. It is sometimes called the "fill-in" light, its purpose being to fill-in the shadows.

The correct use of the secondary light is really most important as the whole tone of the picture is controlled by the appropriate balance between the modelling light and the secondary and the effect lights. The direction on the chart from which the secondary light should come is easy enough to find, and it varies very little with the changing positions of the head. Deciding the distance from the model at which to place it needs considerably more study.

6 The Secondary Light

THE SIMPLEST way to determine the direction from which the secondary light should be used, is to turn off all other lights, and position the secondary light to give a flat even light over the face as seen from the camera angle. The light should not create any visible shadows. It should, where possible, assist in the modelling created by the first light, but should never oppose it.

This position will be found to be level with the model's face and on the line from S. (on the chart, page 30) when the model is facing S.—S.S.E. if the model is facing S.E.—and at S.E. when the model faces E.

Figs. 6.1, 6.2 and 6.3 illustrate this.

It is readily understood that the nearer the second light is to the model the lighter will be the shadow tone, and vice versa. You can, therefore, control the depth of the shadow tone by varying the distance of the secondary light from the model. This would be comparatively easy if you were using the secondary light on its own, but combining it with the modelling light necessitates a careful balance between the two. Other factors that also have to be considered are the variation in the power of lamps, the exposure and development of the film, and, perhaps, most important of all, the brightness range of the printing paper.

It is well known that a film is able to record a far greater range of tones than can be reproduced in the print—possibly a ratio of 130 : 1 as against 25 : 1. If you do not make allowance for the comparatively small contrast range of your printing paper you cannot hope to produce a picture representing the original you have in mind.

The brightness range of your picture must be controlled at the time of setting up the lights.

To do this you can make use of the "inverse square law" which states that

45

  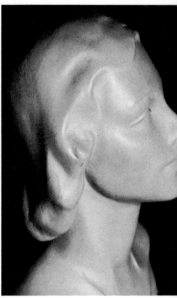

6.1 6.2 6.3

Fig. 6.1. Light at S; level with model's eyes
Fig. 6.2. Light at S.S.E.; level with model's eyes
Fig. 6.3. Light at S.E.; level with model's eyes

"the intensity of light on any one plane varies inversely with the square of the distance".

If a light is used at a distance of 3 ft from an object, and then moved back to a distance of 9 ft, the intensity of light falling on the object will not be one third as bright but one ninth as bright. Therefore the required exposure for a similar negative density would be nine times as much as that used when the lamp was at a distance of only 3 ft.

If two lights of equal power were used at the same time on one object, the one being at a distance of 3 ft from the object and the second at a distance of 9 ft from the object, the brightness ratio between the intensities of the two lights falling on the object would be 1 : 9.

Similarly, with one lamp at a distance of 3 ft from the object and a second lamp of equal power at a distance of 6 ft from the same object, the intensity of light on that object from the lamp at 6 ft would be one quarter that of the lamp

46

at 3 ft. The brightness ratio in that case would be 1 : 4.

Take one more example. If the modelling light is placed at a distance of 6 ft from a model and a secondary light at a distance of 9 ft, the second light is only half as far away again as the first light. The square of that distance is 2, therefore the brightness ratio is 1 : 2.

Now for a few experiments on the model's head, using the brightness ratios to control the depth of shadow tone produced by the combination of the modelling and the secondary light. If you were to cover the complete range of brightness ratios from 1 : 2 through to 1 : 10 with all the relevant varying factors you could fill a book with these experiments only. It is sufficient here just to select a few from which the results can be compared.

With the model in the full face position, place the modelling light in the three basic positions, but at two different distances from the model (a) 3 ft and (b) 6 ft. The secondary light should be used at S., level with the model's eyes, and at three varying distances to give brightness ratios of 1 : 2, 1 : 4 and 1 : 6.

The exposure is based on the modelling light only, and the reading taken off a white card and multiplied by 4. The rated speed of the film to be used for this case is 100 ASA.

FULL FACE: MODELLING LIGHT CENTRAL

Modelling light at 3 ft from model
   Model facing S. (Figs. 6.4, 6.5).
   Modelling light: central.
   Light source: 3 ft from model.
   Secondary light: S. level.
   Light source: 4½ ft from model.
   Brightness ratio: 1 : 2.
   Exposure: ½ sec. *f* 8.

Fig. 6.5 appears the brighter of the two because of the dark background. The reason for this is discussed on page 56.

   Model facing S. (Fig. 6.6).
   Modelling light: central.
   Light source: 3 ft from model.
   Secondary light: S. level.
   Light source: 6 ft from model.
   Brightness ratio: 1 : 4.

47

6.4 6.5 6.6

Fig. 6.4. Brightness ratio 1 : 2
Fig. 6.5. Brightness ratio 1 : 2
Fig. 6.6. Brightness ratio 1 : 4

Exposure: $\frac{1}{2}$ sec. *f* 8.

With the secondary light at twice the distance, the increased contrast can be judged quite easily by comparing the depth of tone in the nose shadow in the different examples.

> *Model* facing S. (Fig. 6.7).
> *Modelling light*: central.
> *Light source*: 3 ft from model.
> *Secondary light*: S. level.
> *Light source*: 7$\frac{1}{2}$ ft from model.
> *Brightness ratio*: 1 : 6.
> *Exposure*: $\frac{1}{2}$ sec. *f* 8.

A further deepening of the shadow tone and, consequently, an increase of contrast.

6.7 6.8 6.9

Fig. 6.7. Brightness ratio 1 : 6
Fig. 6.8. Brightness ratio 1 : 2
Fig. 6.9. Brightness ratio 1 : 4

Modelling light at 6 ft from model
  Model facing S. (Fig. 6.8).
  Modelling light: central.
  Light source: 6 ft from model.
  Secondary light: S. level.
  Light source: 9 ft from model.
  Brightness ratio: 1 : 2.
  Exposure: 1 sec. *f* 5·6.

  Model facing S. (Fig. 6.9).
  Modelling light: central.
  Light source: 6 ft from model.
  Secondary light: S. level.
  Light source: 12 ft from model.

6.10 6.11 6.12

Fig. 6.10. Brightness ratio 1 : 6
Fig. 6.11. Brightness ratio 1 : 2
Fig. 6.12. Brightness ratio 1 : 2

Brightness ratio: 1 : 4.
Exposure: 1 sec. *f* 5·6.

Model facing S. (Fig. 6.10).
Modelling light: central.
Light source: 6 ft from model.
Secondary light: S. level.
Light source: 15 ft from model.
Brightness ratio: 1 : 6.
Exposure: 1 sec. *f* 5·6.

With the light sources at twice the distance from the model in each case, exposure is increased by 4×, being the square of the distance due, of course, to the normal operation of the inverse square law.

There is an over-all increase in tone in the highlight areas.

50

FULL FACE: MODELLING LIGHT 25° RIGHT

Modelling light at 3 ft from model

  Model facing S. (Figs. 6.11, 6.12).
  Modelling light: 25° to right of central.
  Light source: 3 ft from model.
  Secondary light: S. level.
  Light source: 4½ ft from model.
  Brightness ratio: 1 : 2.
  Exposure: ½ sec. *f* 8.

The modelling light is now at 25° right of central. It is important to choose the correct brightness ratio for the off-side shadow. The 1:2 ratio renders it as a light grey, while any increase in the ratio makes the shadow progressively darker.

  Model facing S. (Fig. 6.13).
  Modelling light: 25° to right of central.
  Light source: 3 ft from model.
  Secondary light: S. level.
  Light source: 6 ft from model.
  Brightness ratio: 1 : 4.
  Exposure: ½ sec. *f* 8.

Here, the brightness ratio is 1:4 and the shadow appears much darker; below, a 1:6 brightness ratio gives even greater contrast.

  Model facing S. (Fig. 6.14).
  Modelling light: 25° to right of central.
  Light source: 3 ft from model.
  Secondary light: S. level.
  Light source: 7½ ft from model.
  Brightness ratio: 1 : 6.
  Exposure: ½ sec. *f* 8.

Modelling light at 6 ft from model

  Model facing S. (Fig. 6.15).
  Modelling light: 25° to right of central.
  Light source: 6 ft from model.

6.13 6.14 6.15

Fig. 6.13. Brightness ratio 1 : 4
Fig. 6.14. Brightness ratio 1 : 6
Fig. 6.15. Brightness ratio 1 : 2

Secondary light: S. level.
Light source: 9 ft from model.
Brightness ratio: 1 : 2.
Exposure: 1 sec. *f* 5·6.

Model facing S. (Fig. 6.16).
Modelling light: 25° to right of central.
Light source: 6 ft from model.
Secondary light: S. level.
Light source: 12 ft from model.
Brightness ratio: 1 : 4.
Exposure: 1 sec. *f* 5·6.

Model facing S. (Fig. 6.17).

52

6.16 6.17 6.18

Fig. 6.16. Brightness ratio 1 : 4
Fig. 6.17. Brightness ratio 1 : 6
Fig. 6.18. Brightness ratio 1 : 2

Modelling light: 25° to right of central.
Light source: 6 ft from model.
Secondary light: S. level.
Light source: 15 ft from model.
Brightness ratio: 1 : 6.
Exposure: 1 sec. *f* 5·6.

Increased lamp distances result in an increased area of light tone on the off-side of the face, decreased shadow area, and general softening of tone values.

FULL FACE: MODELLING LIGHT 45° RIGHT

Modelling light at 3 ft from model
  Model facing S. (Figs. 6.18, 6.19).

53

6.19 6.20 6.21

Fig. 6.19. Brightness ratio 1 : 2
Fig. 6.20. Brightness ratio 1 : 4
Fig. 6.21. Brightness ratio 1 : 6

Modelling light: 45° to right of central.
Light source: 3 ft from model.
Secondary light: S. level.
Light source: 4½ ft from model.
Brightness ratio: 1 : 2.
Exposure: ½ sec. *f* 8

With the modelling light at 45° right of central, the off-side of the face is in total
shadow apart from a small triangle of light—insufficient contrast for this lighting
in a full-face position.

Model facing S. (Fig. 6.20).
Modelling light: 45° to right of central.
Light source: 3 ft from model.
Secondary light: S. level.

Light source: 6 ft from model.
Brightness ratio: 1 : 4.
Exposure: $\frac{1}{2}$ sec. *f* 8.

Secondary light distance increased, giving greater contrast and a more definite shape to the light triangle on the off-side.

Model facing S. (Fig. 6.21).
Modelling light: 45° to right of central.
Light source: 3 ft from model.
Secondary light: S. level.
Light source: $7\frac{1}{2}$ ft from model.
Brightness ratio: 1 : 6.
Exposure: $\frac{1}{2}$ sec. *f* 8.

Edges of the light triangle clearer but the shadow area loses the contour of the face and the highlight is swamped by the shadow.

Modelling light at 6 ft from model
　Model facing S. (Fig. 6.22).
　Modelling light: 45° to right of central.
　Light source: 6 ft from model.
　Secondary light: S. level.
　Light source: 9 ft from model.
　Brightness ratio: 1 : 2.
　Exposure: 1 sec. *f* 5·6.

The modelling light is too distant to give a definite triangle in the shadow area and the whole lighting effect appears confused and unsatisfactory.

　Model facing S. (Fig. 6.23).
　Modelling light: 45° to right of central.
　Light source: 6 ft from model.
　Secondary light: S. level.
　Light source: 12 ft from model.
　Brightness ratio: 1 : 4.
　Exposure: 1 sec. *f* 5·6.

6.22 6.23 6.24

Fig. 6.22. Brightness ratio 1 : 2
Fig. 6.23. Brightness ratio 1 : 4
Fig. 6.24. Brightness ratio 1 : 6

An increased brightness ratio makes this better than other examples using the same set-up.

> *Model* facing S. (Fig. 6.24).
> *Modelling light*: 45° to right of central.
> *Light source*: 6 ft from model.
> *Secondary light*: S. level.
> *Light source*: 15 ft from model.
> *Brightness ratio*: 1 : 6.
> *Exposure*: 1 sec. *f* 5·6.

Increased distance of the secondary light loses all shadow detail.

It is interesting to compare the results of some of the brightness ratios 1 : 2 where the model has been taken against a white background as well as against a dark background. All other factors are the same. Against a white background the face appears darker than it does against the dark background. Take a cube of white sugar and put it on a piece of white paper and then place another cube on a piece of black paper. The sugar on the white paper will appear to be darker in tone than it does on the black paper. The contrasts between the light side and shadow side will appear softer against the white paper than against the black. This is partly an optical illusion, but also the white paper reflects light into the shadows which softens contrast.

The question of the background then, is very important and has a definite effect on the tones of the resulting picture. For high key portraits you always use a light background, and usually a dark one for a low key. This does not mean that every time you photograph a person with fair hair you need to make a high key portrait. Remember, white sugar looks darker when placed on white paper. Similarly fair hair can look even fairer against a dark background, or even a grey background, than it does against white, but the whole tone of the picture with a white background is more delicate and suits some types of children and very blonde young women better than darker renderings.

APPLICATIONS

Having now completed the exercises with the brightness ratio between the two lights used on the face you can now consider the results and how they can be applied in the studio.

First, compare the difference between the modelling light being at a distance of 3 ft from the model and 6 ft. At 3 ft the shadows down the side of the face are harder—that is, blacker in tone and with a more definite edge to the shadow. At 6 ft the light spreads further round the face and thus softens the shadows. At 6 ft, also, the skin tones are softer. It can be said, therefore, that the closer the modelling light is to the model, the harsher the skin tones and the greater the contrast.

The further away the modelling light is from the model on the other hand the softer the skin tones and the softer the modelling.

Contrast increases as the ratio increases. The 1 : 6 brightness ratio produces a print with a full range of tones and will be the chosen ratio for a strong portrait needing the maximum available tone scale. The 1 : 4 ratio produces a slightly softer result, and is suitable for general portraits, female portraiture and children. The 1 : 2 ratio is interesting as it can be handy for both ends of the scale—the light tones or the dark tones. It can therefore, be used for both high key and low key portraits.

EXPOSURE AND DEVELOPMENT

The exposure given in each case was the same. The reading was taken from the modelling light only, off a white card and multiplied by a factor of 4. When the modelling light was at a distance of 3 ft, the exposure was $\frac{1}{2}$ sec. at f 8. When the modelling light was moved back to 6 ft, the exposure given was 1 sec. at f 5·6. This was estimated by using the exposure meter again, as before, and proved the fact that at double the distance the exposure must be increased by 4 times (the square of the distance). For further details on exposure see Chapter 10.

The exposures were made in sequence on the same film and were given normal development time. This means that, by careful control of the brightness ratio, you can photograph all types of portraits, high, middle and low key on the same roll of film. This must be of great value to a 35 mm user.

7 Brightness Ratios Applied

By PUTTING the brightness ratio technique into practice, all types of portraits can be photographed on the same film for development at standard times in a standard developer.

Provided due consideration is given to the kind of subject to be photographed, and properly related to the desired result, the brightness ratio technique should always achieve your aim. Suppose, for example, the objective is a delicate high key result. Shadows on the face should be a soft grey rather than black, and the highlights should be delicate with separated tones. The selected brightness ratio should, therefore, be 1 : 2 as any other would make the shadow tones too dark. To preserve the delicate tones in the light areas on the face, the modelling light must be neither too bright, nor placed too close to the subject. For greater contrast between the light and dark areas on the face, producing an average print, use a brightness ratio of 1 : 4 and when the requirements are for even greater contrast choose the 1 : 6 ratio or any number thereafter, according to the depth of black tone required in the shadow areas.

HIGH KEY SUBJECT

So far in these experiments the same model has been used throughout. If the brightness ratio technique is applicable to all types of portrait we must give some consideration to the subject as a whole, and not solely to the face. A delicate high key print cannot be made from a subject which is not light in tone, so a live model, to be photographed as a high key subject, must have blonde hair with the accompanying fair complexion, and be dressed in light clothes and photographed against a light background.

The next set of illustrations show the model head in the full face position, and using a brightness ratio of 1 : 2. The model is dressed in white. The modelling light is placed at 4 ft, and the secondary at 6 ft—the exposure being based on the modelling light only. To prove the effectiveness of the technique the light on the background and the clothes will be measured and controlled to give the required result. White polystyrene is used for the background (or white paper is equally good). This must be lit in such a way that, in the resultant print, it will appear lighter in tone than the face. Any effect light striking the subject from behind will not show up against the white background. Effect lights can be freely used at each side of the model instead of from the back. The intensity of the lights can be controlled by means of butter muslin diffusers. Brightness ratios between the modelling light, the secondary light, the background light and the effect lights are checked by using an exposure meter and taking the readings off a white card. Each light is checked by itself, all other lights being turned off.

The modelling light, in this case a 150 W in an 8 in. reflector, is placed to give the required modelling, the light source being 4 ft from the model. The reading is taken off a white card. Then the modelling light is turned off, and a light placed for the background (in this case a 500 W flood in a 12 in. reflector) at a distance to give a reading off the white card of one quarter that of the modelling light. This means that the background is receiving 4 times as much light as the face.

When the effect lights are used, each one is controlled to give a light effect of twice the modelling light but half the background light. By this careful control of the power of the light, all the tones will be correctly produced in the finished print, because *exposure is for the modelling light only.*

The film used in these experiments is 100 ASA, rated at 25 ASA, and the reading taken off a white card. (See Chapter 10).

HIGH KEY: RATIO 1:2

Figs. 7.1, 7.2 *and* 7.3
   Model facing S.
   Modelling light at (7.1) central, (7.2) 25° to right of central, (7.3) 45° to right of central, light source 4 ft.
   Secondary light at S., level, light source 6 ft.
   Background: white polystyrene reflecting 4 times as much light as the modelling light.

7.1 7.2 7.3

Fig. 7.1. Modelling light placed centrally
Fig. 7.2. Modelling light placed 25° right of central position
Fig. 7.3. Modelling light placed 45° right of central position

---

Effect lights: directional or spotlights, dimmed, positioned at E. and W., to reflect twice as much light as the modelling light. In order to light the clothes only, and prevent any spread of light falling on the face, all the other lights should be turned off while the effect lights are positioned. Brightness ratio 1 : 2, exposure ½ sec. at *f* 8.

Note:

The position of the modelling light in Figs. 7.1 and 7.2 is suitable for high key, but in Fig. 7.3 the large area of shadow makes it a more suitable lighting for low key (Fig. 7.9).

Before leaving the high key effects with the brightness ratio of 1 : 2, we will set up the modelling light as suggested for the profile position mentioned earlier when the basic positions of the modelling light were discussed. These could be as follows:

61

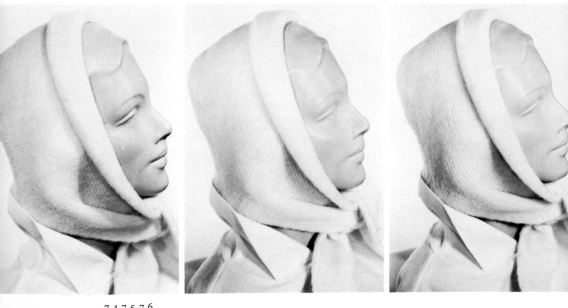

7.4 7.5 7.6

Fig. 7.4. Modelled at 25° left of central position
Fig. 7.5. Modelled at S.E. and level with model's head
Fig. 7.6. Modelled for a dark rim outline

Fig. 7.4

    Modelling light: 25° to the *left* of central—at 4 ft.
    Secondary light at S.E. level—at 6 ft.
    Effect lights, as in Figs. 7.1, 7.2 and 7.3, but near S.W. and S.E.

Fig. 7.5

    Modelling light at S.E. and level with the model's head. This is the position of the secondary light in Fig. 7.4, therefore no secondary light is needed.
    Effect lights, as in Fig. 7.4.

Fig. 7.6

    The modelling light is now in the position for the dark rim outline—positioned at S., but nearer to the model than the camera is, and in a level position. Again no secondary light is needed.

Figures 7.5 and 7.6 give soft tones, but the face lacks modelling owing to the level position of the light.

LOW KEY SUBJECT: RATIO 1:2

Before experimenting on the model we must give a little thought to the question of what we mean by the term low key. In the same way that a high key picture makes predominant use of the white and light grey tones on a grey scale, a low key picture has the majority of its tones in the lower part of the scale. It is made up of black, dark grey, middle grey and a small amount of white and light grey. This technique entailing the use of a 1 : 2 ratio, should not be confused with the popular version of low key which eliminates the mid-greys to give more dramatic contrast. For the latter a more appropriate ratio would be 1 : 10.

As we have already seen, the resulting picture is determined by the type of subject photographed. In a portrait, therefore, the model must be of a suitable type, and, for low key, must be dressed in dark clothes, but preferably not black. The colour black absorbs so much light and reflects so little, that with some materials it is difficult to produce a print with sufficient detail in the clothes yet maintain the right balance of tones in the face. Where the photographer has the opportunity of choosing the most suitable colour of the model's clothes he can make his task very much simpler. Colour is a question of great importance to the colour photographer, but is all too often neglected by those who work in monochrome.

Panchromatic films are sensitive to various colours in differing degrees. If you choose a colour which reproduces as a dark tone but not black, you will find it easier to obtain good tone rendering in the dark areas. All the *dark* hues of purple, green, blue, brown, orange, etc., will reproduce dark in tone, but will reflect a greater percentage of light than will black. The texture of the material itself will also make a difference. Material with a sheen to it, such as silk or satin, will give a better gradation of tone than wool or velvet. Black fur absorbs all reflected light, and only reflects such light as comes in direct contact with it. In other words, black fur needs a quantity of light from the correct angles if it is to be recorded in any detail.

Now to tackle a model in black—a black woollen sweater and a black fur hat. The background will be dark grey. The modelling light will be used at 4 ft and the secondary at 6 ft to give a brightness ratio of 1 : 2. Small spotlights will be used for the effect lights.

63

7.7 7.8 7.9

Fig. 7.7. Centrally placed modelling light
Fig. 7.8. Modelled at 25° right of central
Fig. 7.9. Modelled at 45° right of central

Figs. 7.7, 7.8 and 7.9

Model facing S.

Modelling light at (7.7) central, (7.8) 25° to the right of central, (7.9) 45° to the right of central, light source 4 ft from model, 150 W flood in 8 in. reflector.

Secondary light at S. level, light source 6 ft from model.

Background: dark grey paper lit by a small lamp.

Effect lights: spotlights used as rim lights at N.W. and N.E. Brightness ratio 1 : 2, exposure $\frac{1}{2}$ sec. *f* 8. Film speed 100 AS A rated at 25, and reading taken off white card for the modelling light only.

Note:

In Fig. 7.9 the edges to the triangular highlight are soft owing to the use of a floodlight for the modelling light—compare this with Fig. 7.12. The clothes are underlit. For the next set we will change the colour of the clothes from black to purple. The background as in Figs. 7.7, 7.8 and 7.9.

7.10 7.11 7.12

Fig. 7.10. Centrally placed modelling light
Fig. 7.11. Modelled at 25° right of central position
Fig. 7.12. Modelled 45° right of central position

Figs. 7.10, 7.11 *and* 7.12

Modelling light at (7.10) central, (7.11) 25° to the right of central, (7.12) 45° to the right of central. Light source 4 ft from model. Figures 7.10 and 7.11 are lit by a 150 W flood while Fig. 7.12 is lit by 500 W spot dimmed. The latter produces the clear cut triangle of light for comparison with Fig. 7.9.

Secondary light at S. level, light source 6 ft from model.

Effect lights: 150 W bulbs in small reflectors—one positioned N.W. at a fairly high elevation to light the top of the hat and rim the hair—the other approximately N.E. and almost level, to light the side of the hat and rim the hair, neck and shoulder. Using small effect lights means easy control, with no unwanted light spilling on to the face. Brightness ratio 1 : 2, exposure $\frac{1}{2}$ sec. at f 8. Film speed 100 ASA rated at 25, exposure calculated as before.

Note:

In Fig. 7.12 the small background light has been turned to face the camera

7.13 7.14 7.15

Fig. 7.13. Lighting ratio 1 : 4
Fig. 7.14. Lighting ratio 1 : 4
Fig. 7.15. Lighting ratio 1 : 4

but the model·obscures all light from reaching the lens. The light outline can be seen round the model's shoulders, and the background is now dark.

The control of the effect lights, and the careful balance of modelling and secondary light, results in a negative which is easily printable to any required depth of tone by printing for the highlight areas—the rest falls into place without difficulty. The 1 : 2 ratio is particularly useful for high key effects, but can be used successfully for all other subjects, including low key where the contrast range is to be kept low.

LONGER TONE SCALE SUBJECTS: RATIO 1 : 4

Perhaps the brightness ratio most often used for portraiture is the 1 : 4, as it is applicable to all subjects of average contrast. Provided the exposure is correct, the resulting negative will be capable of producing prints with clean highlights and good shadows. The first part of the foregoing sentence is important, as it

66

7.16 7.17 7.18

Fig. 7.16. Lighting ratio 1 : 6
Fig. 7.17. Lighting ratio 1 : 6
Fig. 7.18. Lighting ratio 1 : 6

is the density given by the exposure that gives the correct quality in the high-lights. The principle of the brightness ratio method is based on the assumption that the negative is exposed and printed for the highlight area. The remainder, if lit correctly, will automatically be produced in the right depth of tone.

For our experiments with the 1 : 4 ratio the model is dressed in a white cardigan with a red scarf round her shoulders, and a white beret on her head. (Notice that her hair has been painted black!)

The background is dark grey paper, the effect lights are two small lamps fitted with 150 W bulbs; the modelling light is the 500 W flood for the central and 25° to the right of central lighting, and the spotlight dimmed, for the 45° to the right of central (Figs. 7.13, 7.14, 7.15).

There is little need to elaborate on the set-up of the model and lights, as the arrangement is similar to that of Figs. 7.10, 7.11 and 7.12 with the exception of the distance from the model of the secondary light. This will now be 8 ft instead of 6 ft.

Brightness ratio 1 : 4, exposure $\frac{1}{2}$ sec. $f\,8$. Film speed 100 ASA rated at 25 and reading taken as before for the modelling light only.

Brightness ratio 1 : 6

For a more contrasty result, where extra strength is required in the shadow area, we have simply to move the secondary light back to 10 ft, provided the modelling light remains at 4 ft. This will give a ratio of 1 : 6. The exposure for the modelling light will be the same (Figs. 7.16, 7.17, 7.18).

If the brightness ratio is increased beyond 1 : 10, the effect will be similar to that of using one light only. The exposure will still be for the modelling light only.

To sum up

By the careful balance of all the lights, and the right selection of brightness ratio, there is complete control over the tonal range of the finished print. Consideration is necessary concerning the subject, and the required effect, rendering of colour in monochrome, tone of the background, careful placing of the effect lights, and the right balance between all the lights used.

By basing the system of lighting on the ratio method, controlling all the other lighting effects, and exposing for the modelling light only, negatives can be produced which allow plenty of latitude in making the print.

Another advantage is that dark, average or light subjects can all be photographed on the same roll of film, and processed in a standard developer for the normal time.

8 Effect of Camera Angle

FEW BEGINNERS in portraiture realize the difference that the height of the camera can make to the resultant "drawing" of a face and even the expression and mood of the picture. It is well, therefore, to study the question in some detail. If the model's head is photographed again, in the same series as before, a comparison shows the differences. The results will be useful for reference when discussing the many varied shapes of heads you are likely to encounter in the course of your work.

My normal choice for the height of the camera is a little above the model's eyes with the lens tipping downwards at a slight angle. Watching many beginners at work it would appear that often the tripod will not extend to a sufficient height to allow the camera to get a view from above the model's eyes. When the camera lens is on a level with the model's mouth the lower portion of the face will appear wide in comparison with the upper. This is the cause of so much of the distortion apparent in many beginner's portraits. It is intensified, of course, when the camera is moved fairly close to the model. (So far we are discussing the head and shoulder portrait, not the three-quarter length or full length, when, obviously a lower camera angle is necessary). Raising the camera to a position slightly above the model's eyes and tilting the lens downwards will present the face in better proportion. There are times when a low camera angle is needed, to emphasize the jaw line, and times when a much higher angle will give the better result. A level position is rarely the most suitable and yet it is so often the only one used.

To illustrate this Fig. 8.1 has been taken with the camera slightly above eye level, the lens tilting downwards. In Fig. 8.2 the camera was level with the model's eyes—not a very great difference in the actual height of the camera but enough to make a considerable difference in the presentation of the features.

Comparing Figs. 8.1 and 8.2 the following characteristics are apparent:

Fig. 8.1	Fig. 8.2
Model appears to look straight ahead.	Model appears to look up. A squarer shape to the top of the head.
A rounder shape to the top of the head—better proportion of hair visible.	Forehead slopes back more—less hair visible.
Nose well shaped, nostrils almost hidden.	Nose is shorter—tip tilted, with the underneath of the nostrils forming a wider based triangle of shadow.
The top lip is well drawn.	The top lip is somewhat thicker.
The chin is well modelled and pointed.	The chin is slightly rounder—the jaw line very slightly shorter.
The neck long enough in proportion to the face.	The neck appears longer.

The following experiments show the effect of exaggerated camera angles photographing the model's head from a level, low and a high camera position, with comparative results. Remember that it is most likely that you will normally need a camera position somewhere between these extremes rather than at them. The results will therefore be studied with this in mind—noting the tendencies rather than the extremes displayed.

In portraiture one has to compromise so much that it is as well to have as many techniques to choose from as possible and the height of the camera is among the most useful.

Before commencing your study make a note of the following:

Modelling light. Whenever the modelling light is said to be placed at the *central* position, it means that the light is square on to the model's face and at a height to produce the triangular nose shadow half way between nose and mouth.

When the modelling light is said to be at 25° it means that the light is placed about 20–25° to the right of central, at a height to produce a well shaped shadow following the curve of the nostril and finishing just under half way between nose and mouth.

When the modelling light is said to be at 45° it means that the light is placed about 45° to the right of central, positioned to give a small triangle of light on the near side cheek.

Use the chart for positions of the model.

70

  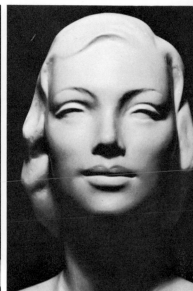

8.1 8.2 8.3

Fig. 8.1. Camera placed slightly above eye level
Fig. 8.2. Camera placed level with the eyes
Fig. 8.3. Camera placed level with the subject

MODEL FACING S.

Modelling light: central

Comparing the low and high camera positions (Figs. 8.4 and 8.5) with the "camera level" position (Fig. 8.3) you will find the following tendencies:

	Fig. 8.4	*Fig.* 8.5
Shape of the top of head	More square	More oval
Forehead	Slopes back	Protrudes more
Hair	Less shown	More shown
Eyes	Looking up	Looking down
Nose	Shorter—square tip	Longer—no nostrils showing
Lips	Both lips fuller	Top lip thinner
Chin	More rounded	More pointed
Jaw line	Shorter	Longer
Neck	Longer	Shorter

71

8.4 8.5 8.6

Fig. 8.4. Camera placed below the subject
Fig. 8.5. Camera placed higher than the subject
Fig. 8.6. Camera level with subject

With the modelling light in the central position none of the features are obscured by shadow with the exception of the underneath of the nostrils and the neck.

The outlines of the face are equally shaded on both sides. Therefore the shape of the face and the individual features are clearly drawn whatever the height of the camera. The tendency to flatness in the modelling that results from centrally placed lighting is avoided by reason of the height of the lamp.

In all other modelling light positions the relative shapes and sizes are governed more by the distribution of light and shade, the shadow areas subdue the contour lines and focus the attention on the highlight areas.

Modelling light: 25° right of centre
Comparing Figs. 8.7 and 8.8 with Fig. 8.6 we find there are the following tendencies:

8.7 8.8 8.9

Fig. 8.7. Camera below subject
Fig. 8.8. Camera above subject
Fig. 8.9. Camera level with the subject

	Fig. 8.7	*Fig.* 8.8
Outline of head and all features	Similar to Fig. 8.4.	Similar to Fig. 8.5.
Neck	Longer, wider, inclined to bulge forward	Shorter, much thinner, and receding
Focal point	The mouth	The eyes
Expression	More altert, forceful	Demure, withdrawn.

In all three illustrations the left side of the model's face appears wider than the right, due to the amount of shadow on the right cheek.

Modelling light: 45° right of centre
This is a dramatic lighting putting emphasis on to one side of the face. It is probably most successful in Fig. 8.9 where the neck is not so obtrusive as in

73

8.10 8.11 8.12

Fig. 8.10. Camera below the subject
Fig. 8.11. Camera above the subject
Fig. 8.12. Camera level with subject

Fig. 8.10. The predominance of light on the head and forehead of Fig. 8.11 coupled with short neck and overlarge shadow area distorts the head unpleasantly.

It is interesting to note that Figs. 8.10 and 8.11 depict the greatest extreme in the distortion of the shape of the face (of this model) that you will find in any of the combinations. Compare Fig. 8.10 with Fig. 8.11 and notice the difference in the whole construction.

The model is in the same position, the only difference lies in the camera angle and position of the modelling light.

MODEL FACING S.E.

Now turn the model to a three-quarter face position and proceed once more with the camera angle at the level, low and high positions. Starting with the modelling light in the central position, then at 25° and finally the 45° position.

Having already studied the different aspects of the features at the varying camera angles we will group this set together and then note any special differences.

74

8.13 8.14 8.15

Fig. 8.13. Camera below subject
Fig. 8.14. Camera above subject
Fig. 8.15. Camera level with subject

Modelling light central
Modelling light 25° right of centre
Modelling light 45° right of centre

The most noticeable differences in the three-quarter face position apart from those already studied are:

1. The backward slope of the forehead in the low camera angle position, especially in Fig. 8.16 where the backward sloping line of the shadow on the temple seems to emphasize it.

2. In Figs. 8.14, 8.17 and 8.20 there is no dividing line of the neck between the far cheek line and the shoulder. This gives the shoulders a hunched look.

3. The most dramatic aspect of the varying angles is Fig. 8.19, with the greatest width of highlight across the forehead, gradually narrowing to a rim light down the far side of the neck. This seems the most exciting of all the low camera positions so far.

75

8.16 8.17 8.18

Fig. 8.16. Camera below subject
Fig. 8.17. Camera above subject
Fig. 8.18. Camera level with subject

MODEL FACING E.

Modelling light central
Modelling light: 25° right of centre
Modelling light: 45° right of centre

The profile position would seem the most suitable for all camera angles provided the model has good features. The low angle gives even more emphasis to the lower portion of the face in the profile position than it does in the full face or three-quarter face.

The 25° or the 45° modelling lights give an added edge of light to the contours, and in Fig. 8.25 this rim light extends to the neck.

THE FINDINGS

The camera angle alone can alter the apparent shape of the head and the individual features.

The camera angle combined with varying positions of the modelling light can

8.19 8.20 8.21

Fig. 8.19. Camera below subject
Fig. 8.20. Camera above subject
Fig. 8.21. Camera level with subject

---

alter the direction in which the model is apparently looking, the expression and the character or mood of the picture.

A very slight difference in the height of the camera can make a noticeable difference in the resulting portrait, noticeable even on an average well proportioned face.

On an irregular face or irregular features or both, the height of the camera can make the difference between an acceptable portrait and an unacceptable one.

Though a general idea is given here of what happens with a change of camera angle, and why it happens, a successful portrait of a subject whose features are irregular must always ultimately depend on the photographer's own judgment. He must be able to *see* the irregularity in the first place, know what kind of corrective treatment is called for, and also understand how to carry it out with the camera.

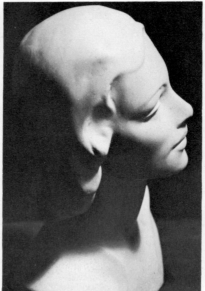

8.22 8.23 8.24

Fig. 8.22. Camera below subject
Fig. 8.23. Camera above subject
Fig. 8.24. Camera level with subject

As will be seen from the illustrations, the normal well shaped oval face can be photographed from almost any camera angle quite successfully. We will now experiment to find out what happens with some *irregular* shaped heads when photographed from a low or high camera angle.

8.25 8.26 8.27
8.28 8.29

Fig. 8.25. Camera below subject
Fig. 8.26. Camera above subject
Fig. 8.27. Camera level with subject
Fig. 8.28. Camera below subject
Fig. 8.29. Camera above subject

79

9 Camera Height and the Individual

In the foregoing chapters we have made various experiments on a model head. We have used the modelling, secondary and effect lights, on the full, three-quarter and profile positions, and have made comparisons in brightness ratios. Using the camera from a low, a level, and a high viewpoint we have realized the effect of camera angle on the drawing of the head and facial features. The experiments have all been made on the same 'still-life' figure, which has a well-shaped head and well proportioned features.

If every person who wanted a portrait made of themselves came under this category, the photographers task would be comparatively simple. But, fortunately, this is not so. I say fortunately, because under those conditions, portraiture would lose a great deal of its excitement and challenge.

The fact that all faces differ one from the other is well known. There are no two faces exactly alike either in construction or in character, each is unique and each requires a different treatment.

While you are studying the subject, it is safe to generalize. When the techniques are learnt and the time comes to put them into practise it will be found that they cannot in every instance be used in a straightforward manner. The human being is so complex, that when a technique is right for one feature it may be wrong for another and so on. So you often have to compromise.

Realizing that the vast majority of faces have irregular features, and that the height of the camera affects the drawing of them, it will be of considerable help if an easy method of determining the most suitable height to use can be discovered.

DIVISION INTO THIRDS

A well proportioned face can be divided up into thirds, these divisions being of more or less equal size.

In Fig. 9.1 lines have been drawn horizontally across the face (a) across the hair line, (b) across the top of the eyebrows, (c) across the base of the nose, and (d) across the base of the chin.

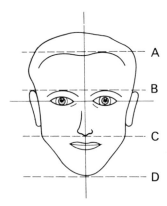

Fig. 9.1. The division of the human head into thirds

From this it will be seen that the division, AB, BC and CD are of equal size. Drawing these lines across the model's head used for the experiments with the camera, we find similar proportions. We therefore, know the varying effects that will be obtained with the various camera heights in relation to the face, by reference to the discussions on page 76.

IRREGULAR FEATURES

We will now divide a face with irregular features in the same manner.

From Fig. 9.2 it can easily be seen that AB and BC are larger than CD. Using the camera from too high a viewpoint increases these spaces and decreases CD. Too low a viewpoint could alter the shape of the face beyond recognition. A true presentation, therefore, would be from a camera angle level with, or slightly below, the model's eyes.

In Fig. 9.3 CD is much wider than BC or AB. Taken from too low a viewpoint CD would grow out of all proportion with the rest of the face and the result would be a distorted appearance to the face. The camera placed well above the

81

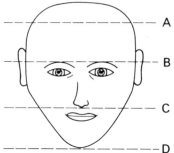

Fig. 9.2. Irregular features
divided at equivalent points

Fig. 9.3. Another irregular
head similarly divided

model's eye level would give a much more pleasing presentation of the face, and add emphasis to the eyes. The eyes, usually being the focal point of the picture, should always be carefully considered in the choice of viewpoint.

IRREGULAR SHAPED HEADS

Dividing these irregular shaped heads into thirds we shall occasionally find equal spacing, but more often irregular, the spacing being determined by the features.

Fig. 9.4. Long thin head,   round plump head,   triangular head,   square head

From the previous illustrations based on camera height with the normal type oval face, we can assess the best aspect and the most suitable lighting for these four irregular types.

LONG THIN FACE

Even when the division into thirds gives fairly equal proportions we should still not wish to use the camera from too high a viewpoint, as this would make the face appear even longer. The camera level with the model's eyes, or slightly below would give a more pleasing drawing. A long thin face usually has a long nose as one of its irregular features. When dividing the face into thirds the space BC would be greater than CD, which would normally call for a lower viewpoint. But a long nose from a full face position, and a level or low viewpoint looks ugly as the tip is widened and the nose foreshortened. This is not so apparent in the three-quarter face position. The profile position would show the full drawing of the nose if emphasis were required on this particular feature.

The central modelling light which emphasizes the contours would give predominance to the irregular shape, especially as one side of the face is usually longer than the other. The 25° modelling light would be suitable if the nose were not too long. When it is really long it is almost impossible to get a good shaped nose shadow without the shadow crossing the lip line. We are left, therefore, with the 45° modelling light, and provided that the ratio of modelling to secondary light is not more than 1 : 4, this should be the most suitable. If the shadow side of the face were allowed to become too dark, the thinness of the face would be apparent.

TO SUM UP

The most favourable drawing of the long thin face with a long nose would be:

Model facing S.E.
Modelling light: 45° to the right of central (at E.).
Secondary light: 25° to the left of central (S., S.E.) distance to give lighting ratio 1 : 4.
Camera: at S., level with model's eyes or slightly lower.

ROUND PLUMP FACE

On dividing the round plump face into thirds we are likely to find the space CD to be widest, as the irregular features we usually have to contend with here are the double chin and short neck. A high viewpoint would increase the forehead and minimize the size of jaw, but would probably entirely obliterate the neck. The head does not look well supported by the shoulders so we return again to a level position. If the model is of a cheerful disposition, we could get a dramatic effect by a low camera angle and strong lighting. This would give, at least, the illusion of a neck.

A three-quarter face position will be much the most suitable, full face making the face appear wide, and the contours being too rounded for a profile. The central modelling light would emphasize the outline too much, the 25° modelling light from the right would give good drawing, and while lighting the far cheek and jaw completely, the near side cheek bone would be lit while the jaw would be in shadow. This lighting would draw attention away from the rather heavy jaw to the upper part of the face and the eyes. Lighting 45° to the right could be used to advantage, keeping the shadow tones reasonably dark. This could be an exciting lighting effect. The model facing one direction with the head turned in the opposite direction and the camera low would give a good illusion of neck.

TO SUM UP

The round plump face with a short neck would be seen in its best aspect from a three-quarter face position with the head turned in the opposite direction to the body to give the illusion of a neck.

Two arrangements are suggested:

(A) *Model* facing S.W. head turned to S.E.
Modelling light: 25° to the right of S.E.
Secondary light: central (at S.E.) ratio 1 : 7.
Camera: at S. level with model's eyes.

(B) *Model* facing S.W. head turned towards S.E.
Modelling light: 45° to the right of S.E.
Secondary light: 25° to the left of S.E. distance to give ratio 1 : 7.
Camera: at S. *low*.

TRIANGULAR FACE

The triangular type face is not as common as the other four types, but belongs to a person with very interesting characteristics. The forehead is high and broad, the sides of the face irregular in length tapering to a long pointed chin. The division into thirds is likely to give reasonably equal spacing, though there would be a tendency for AB to be widest and BC to be wider than CD.

The camera, if level with the model's eyes, would give good drawing to this face, but in practise, one would usually require a slightly higher viewpoint to give emphasis to the aesthetic nature of the personality. (More will be said about character drawing later). A full face position would emphasize the irregular outlines of the face. Therefore a three-quarter face or profile would be suitable. The bone structure is usually well defined with clear cut features, all of which are well presented in profile.

The central modelling light would be unsuitable because of the irregular outline, but the 25°, 45° modelling light for a three-quarter position or the 25°, 45° from the rear, or the rim light could equally well be used for the profile.

TO SUM UP

Although irregular in the shape of head, the features are fairly regular. Therefore, provided you do not use the full face position or the central modelling light, you are free to make use of any of the other lighting positions for three-quarter face or profile. The camera should be on a level with the model's eyes or slightly higher. If the chin becomes too pointed from this viewpoint, the head should be tilted upwards very slightly.

SQUARE FACE

This is a strong, powerful face which can benefit from a print with low key, strong contrasts and rich dark tones to put over the characteristics.

Dividing into thirds will usually give CD as the widest space, suggesting the use of a higher camera angle. Your aim should be to prevent over-emphasis of the square jaw, not to alter its shape. A square jaw is an asset in a man—it shows determination, and a purposeful, strong nature. In a woman it is usually too heavy in appearance, therefore we can use the higher camera angle to flatter to a certain extent, bringing the shape of the face nearer to the oval. The oval face in a woman has always been the artist's ideal of beauty.

Again, a full face position is the least suitable. Three-quarter face is probably the best aspect, profile only being used if the nose is sufficiently well shaped.

The lighting plays a very big part in showing this face to best advantage. The modelling must be good—and the shadows strong.

Suggestions for lighting and positions:

(A) *Model* facing S.E.
   Modelling light: 25° to right of central or 45°.

85

Secondary light: central, ratio 1 : 7.

Camera: slightly higher than level (low for dramatic, powerful jaw effect).

(B) *Model* facing E.

Modelling light: central, 25° to right or 45° to right.

Secondary light: at S.E. ratio 1 : 7.

Camera: higher than model's eyes, or low for dramatic effect.

To sum up the effect of camera angle on the shape of the head and features:

A high viewpoint gives emphasis to the forehead and upper part of the face, including the eyes. The nose is apparently lengthened, the mouth and chin appear smaller, the neck shorter.

A low viewpoint can be used for dramatic effects emphasizing a powerful jaw in a man. In the case of a lady it is useful for a profile. If the model has a beautiful neck, the low viewpoint gives emphasis to the graceful line. A low viewpoint will draw attention to the mouth in preference to the eyes. The nose appears shorter, the eyes smaller and the forehead narrower.

Intentional distortion is a useful technique. But distortion which occurs through the camera being placed too low and too close to the model is always unsatisfactory.

As a general rule if you are working with a standard lens it is always much safer to photograph the model from a high viewpoint than a level one.

10 Exposure and Development

LET ME say to begin with, that there is no such thing as an "exact" exposure. There is, however, the most suitable or "correct" exposure for any given subject, which will produce a predetermined result when the negative is suitably developed. You cannot divorce exposure from development—they are inescapably united. The quality of any picture depends on the quality of the negative; which, in turn, depends on correct exposure and correct development (as defined above). We will first consider the exposure.

The type of negative most often aimed at by the portrait photographer is one which records detail in the shadow areas, but at the same time maintains separated tones in the highlights. If the exposure time has been too brief, the shadow areas will be devoid of detail, and only the brighter parts of the subject will be recorded. If the exposure time has been too long, the shadows may record plenty of detail, but all the gradations in the highlight areas will be lost. It is sometimes thought that underexposure will give greater contrast. This is a fallacy. Underexposure reduces contrast; the contrast is controlled by the lighting, the correct exposure and increased development time. It is well to note that prolonged development can never record detail in any area that has not received sufficient exposure. Therefore the golden rule is "never underexpose" —it is always safer, for average subjects, to err on the side of slight overexposure.

FACTORS GOVERNING EXPOSURE

The principal factors which govern exposure are:

1. The amount of light reflected by the subject.
2. The intensity, quality and angle of light.

3. The speed of the film.
4. The lens aperture.
5. The shutter speed.

Let us consider these factors and how they apply in portraiture.

1. *Light reflected by the subject*

In colour photography the depth and tone of colour in the subject are important considerations, but this is too often ignored when monochrome materials are in use.

This is a mistake, and note should always be made of the colour and texture of the model's hair and skin tones, as well as the clothes and other accessories.

A better understanding of the tone rendering of colour, and the reflective power of various materials, would not only be of value in assessing the required exposure, but would assist the photographer in controlling the contrast range of the picture.

To take one example. Let us imagine we have to photograph a model with light brown hair, wearing a fawn coloured wool jumper with a turquoise-blue skirt. The photograph is taken against a grey background, which looks quite attractive. The result in monochrome is very disappointing. It is severely lacking in contrast and looks dull and insipid. Had the model worn a fawn satin blouse in place of the wool jumper, and a darker background had been chosen, the result would have been much more satisfactory. Satin material reflects the light to a much greater degree than wool, and, therefore, more vitality and depth is given to the picture. The darker background would give added contrast.

The depth of colour tone as well as the textured surface of the material affect the exposure. The pastel shades of all colours will photograph as light in tone, but as the colours become more saturated, so they progressively deepen in tone. Dark shades of purple, brown, blue and green can too easily become black unless they receive sufficient light and exposure. Rough textured materials absorb more light than the smooth, and the dark coloured velvets reflect only a very small percentage of the light thrown on them.

In monochrome portraiture the rendering of colours in their exact tone value is rarely important. What does matter is the contrast in tone between the various coloured objects. In landscape or still-life photography filters can be used to produce the required colour tone and contrast, but in portraiture any filter, other than blue, would have a detrimental effect on the skin tones. A blue filter would tend to lighten blue eyes and darken the lips, but as most modern panchromatic emulsions cope with the skin tones of the face remarkably well, it is rarely advisable to add to the exposure time by using a blue filter. If you cannot use filters to control colour contrast, we must, where possible, advise the model on the most suitable garments to wear, both in colour and texture, and then contrast or harmonize the background with the subject.

2.   *Intensity, quality and angle of light*

The *intensity* of the light depends, not only on the power of the bulb, but on the distance of the light from the subject. As we have already seen, the intensity of the light diminishes or increases as a square of the distance. If the distance of the light from the subject is doubled, the exposure must be four times as long, not double the time as some might expect. The same increase in exposure time would be gained by opening the lens aperture by two stops. Again, if the light source is moved nearer to the model, the intensity of the light would be greater in proportion to the square of the distance—half the distance requiring only one quarter the exposure time, or a decrease in the lens aperture of two stops.

The *quality* of the light, or the nature and power of the light, is a straight-forward matter. A high powered lamp of 500 or 1000 W needs considerably less exposure than one of only 250 or 100 W used at the same distance. The spot-light, which condenses the power of the light into small areas, also requires less exposure than the flood, which spreads the light in a much wider beam, according to the width or "depth" of the reflector, allowing only a percentage of the light to fall directly on the model.

As for the *angle of the light*, a subject is most strongly illuminated when it faces the source of light. The illumination becomes progressively less strong as the light is moved further from the square-on position. To illustrate this we will refer once more to the chart on p. 30.

With a model facing S., and the camera at S., illumination will be greatest when the light source is at S.S.W., S., or S.S.E. or, in fact, anywhere within 45° angle either side of the camera. When the model faces S.E. and the modelling light is moved further round towards E., thus increasing the angle of light from the camera, the exposure will need an increase of one or two stops if moved as far as E.

In practice this is taken care of by decreasing the distance of the secondary light to maintain the equivalent brightness ratio.

3.   *Speed of the film*

This presents no problems. It is obvious that the fast film requires less exposure time, under similar conditions, than the slower type. A 400 ASA film will need only half the exposure of a 200 ASA and a quarter that of 100 ASA. But it is well to remember that speed is often achieved at the expense of quality, and that the finer quality is to be found in the slower emulsion. The latter may have slightly less latitude in exposure, but requires less development time and has a finer grain structure.

The choice of film speed, then, depends on the required exposure times. The maxim should always be to use a film of slow emulsion speed whenever conditions allow, only substituting a fast one when the need for the briefest possible exposure time becomes the deciding factor.

4. *Lens aperture*

Exposure calculation is made more simple by the lens manufacturers. The *f* numbers marked on the lens are arranged in a standard series—each *f* number passes double the amount of light of the preceding one as the aperture is widened.

Therefore, unless depth of field has to be taken into consideration, the variations in exposure times can be made by increasing or decreasing the aperture of the lens.

5. *Shutter speed*

The amount of light which reaches the film is controlled by the size of the lens aperture and the length of time that the shutter remains open. These are both adjustable and are used in conjunction with one another to suit the various requirements of a particular picture. For example, let us suppose that a calculated exposure gives $\frac{1}{2}$ sec. at *f* 8. The same result can be obtained by giving $\frac{1}{16}$ sec. at *f* 2·8 if speed is of greater importance than depth of field. If there is no risk of movement by the model, an exposure of 2 sec. at *f* 16 could be used equally well, and would give greater latitude in focusing, because of the increased depth of field.

CALCULATING EXPOSURE

By far the most accurate way of determining the nearest to correct exposure is by the use of an exposure meter. There are many makes on the market, but most of those generally used at the present time are either selenium cell or cadmium sulphide types which are marginally more sensitive at the lowest light levels.

An exposure meter does not automatically record the required exposure. A

10.1 10.2 10.3

Fig. 10.1. Average subject: 100 ASA rated at 25: underexposed
Fig. 10.2. Average subject : 100 ASA rated at 12 : correct
Fig. 10.3. Average subject : 100 ASA rated at 6 : overexposed

method of using the meter which will give consistently good results should be worked out by each photographer to suit his own needs. It is worth making several experiments with your own meter, always using film of the same speed and the same developing technique.

In this way you can standardize your working method and will be able to make full use of the meter under all conditions.

There are three main ways of using a meter. (I am only discussing those used for portraiture.) These are:

1. A direct reading of the reflected light off the subject.
2. Using the incident light attachment (or an incident light meter) and measuring the incident light.
3. Substituting an artificial highlight (you can also use an artificial mid-tone) of standard brightness for the subject and measuring the reflected light from it.

Let us consider each method in greater detail.

Direct reading

With the lights behind the model turned out, a reading is taken from the model's face, and the resulting figure doubled, or the lens aperture opened by one stop. Alternatively take a direct reading off the highlight area, followed by a reading off the shadow tones, and take the average between the two as the correct exposure.

Incident reading

Fit the incident light attachment to the meter as indicated in the maker's instructions. From the subject position, direct the meter towards the camera. This will give the correct exposure for an average subject without any further calculations. There is no need to switch off any background lights as these will not affect the reading.

Artificial highlight reading

The advantages of using an artificial highlight over a direct reading are firstly that the intensity of the highlight is standard; and secondly a reading can be taken under conditions where it might be difficult to use the direct method.

The artificial highlight used is a piece of white matt card about ten to twelve inches square. This is held in front of the subject and a reading taken from it. Care must be taken to avoid the shadow of the meter itself giving a false reading. This can usually be done by holding the meter about six inches away from the card and at a slight angle. If the subject is of average contrast, the reading obtained from the white card should be multiplied by 8; or the lens aperture increased by three stops.

SUBJECT TYPES

An exposure meter is calibrated for an *average* subject, having a fairly equal distribution of tones. It is therefore easily understood that calculations will have to be made for any subject which falls outside this category.

Dividing your subjects into three main groups, you have:

1. Average subjects.
2. Subjects predominantly light in tone.
3. Subjects predominantly dark in tone.

Average subjects

Any one of the three methods of taking a meter reading discussed above, can

10.4 10.5 10.6

Fig. 10.4. Light tone subject : 100 ASA rated at 25 : correct
Fig. 10.5. Light tone subject : 100 ASA rated at 12 : overexposed
Fig. 10.6. Light tone subject : 100 ASA rated at 6 : overexposed

be used. It is useful to understand each one of them, and, by experiment, you can prove for yourself that the same results will be obtained by all three methods.

Subjects predominantly light in tone

Because the meter is calibrated for an average subject, there must be a difference in the calculations if the subject is made up of mainly light tones, and has no dark shadows. The necessary calculations are as follows:

1. The direct reading $\times 2$ (or open lens aperture by one stop).
2. The incident light reading $\div 2$ (or close lens aperture by one stop).
3. The white card reading $\times 4$.

Subjects predominantly dark in tone

1. The direct reading $\div 2$ (or close lens aperture by one stop).
2. Invercone reading $\times 2$ (or open lens aperture by one stop).
3. The white card reading $\times 16$.

93

10.7 10.8 10.9

Fig. 10.7. Dark tone subject : 100 ASA rated at 25 : underexposed
Fig. 10.8. Dark tone subject : 100 ASA rated at 12 : underexposed
Fig. 10.9. Dark tone subject : 100 ASA rated at 6 : correct

It will be found that for a subject either predominantly light or predominantly dark in tone, the correct exposure can be taken as that mid-way between a direct and an incident light reading (with the attachment) without further calculations.

I have found that the simplest method of calculating an exposure is by using the white card and by dividing the film speed number by the required amount before taking the reading. No other calculations are then needed, and, by always using the same card, the results are standardized. Using this system a film speed of 100 ASA would be rated at 25 ASA, 12 ASA and 6 ASA for the light, average and dark subjects respectively (Figs. 10.1–10.9).

ASSESSING THE SUBJECT

Dividing your subject matter into these three groups requires some thinking about the picture you are hoping to produce. If you are photographing a model with medium fair hair and require only a large head, or head and shoulders, from a full face position having a brightness ratio of 1 : 4, the exposure would be calculated for a predominantly light tone, as the skin texture would be the important part of the picture. If the same model were to turn to a three-quarter face position with a 25° to the right of central modelling light, the exposure reading would be for the average subject; and if the 45° to the right of central modelling light were used the exposure would need to be increased again, so your reading would be for the predominantly dark subject.

When the position becomes three-quarter length instead of head and shoulders a compromise has to be made, and the full picture taken into consideration. The clothes may be either light in tone, a mixture of light and dark, or mainly dark. The exposure should then be chosen accordingly. If the clothes are dark and a factor of 16× on a white card reading is given, you must remember to move the modelling light further away from the face, or use a lower powered light to prevent the face becoming overexposed. But the clothes can, of course, be lit separately.

Do not be misled by the colour of the background. The background should be selected and lit to suit the subject, and then ignored as far as exposure is concerned. It is always the essential part of the picture which must receive the correct exposure, but everything else must be so balanced with lighting that the selected exposure is as near correct as possible for the whole. There may be times when you require the face only, or maybe even part of the face to be portrayed and the remainder of the figure to be devoid of tones. In that case do not light the clothes in any way. Concentrate on the skin tones and treat the subject as predominantly light in tone.

Do not expose for the shadows if no detail is required in them. If you do, the highlights will be burnt out and the whole effect lost. It is far better to expose for the highlights and lighten the shadows to the required depth by the auxiliary lights. The exception to this rule is in the case of a really low key portrait, when the shadow area is the main portion of the picture. The exposure is then calculated for the shadow area and the highlights are controlled by the lighting to make sure they register as required and do not become overexposed because of the exposure needed for the shadows.

For a silhouette effect against a light background, expose for the background only. The background may be of translucent material and the light placed behind it.

Should this have a figure silhouetted against it, the exposure must be calculated by the direct reading off the background and multiplied by 2.

DEVELOPING THE FILM

If you wish to prove for yourself the efficiency of the foregoing exercises in exposure, you will need to use a similar speed of film and developing technique.

The illustrations were made on an 100 ASA film and processed in the maker's normal fine grain developer, adhering to the specified dilution, time and temperature.

You are well advised to start in this way because you will then have a standard negative from which you can make the necessary deviations according to your requirements.

An alternative developer to give similar results is the Borax M.Q. developer, Ilford I.D.11 or Kodak D.76. This is a medium fine grain developer, very suitable for portraiture as it maintains the quality in the highlights and shadows. The contrast of the negative can be controlled by the length of the developing time.

Film speed and grain

I think it is still fair to say that high speed is gained only at the expense of quality despite what some manufacturers may say about certain products.

High speed emulsions have an inherently much coarser grain structure. Furthermore, grain size increases as development time is prolonged. But, unless falsification of tone values is deliberately required, high speed films need longer development time than slower, finer grain films. Portions of the negative which have received too much light during the exposure, start to appear almost immediately the film is immersed in the developer, and, therefore, have time to become really grainy in appearance before the allotted development time is up. Hence the need for minimum exposure.

The slower speed film, while having, perhaps, less latitude in exposing time, is capable of producing separated tones in the highlight and shadow areas to a greater extent than the high speed emulsions. The slight contrast, or more correctly, the clarity of tones produced, can be counterbalanced by lighting the original more softly if necessary. If the exposure is correct, and normal development given, the grain will be scarcely noticeable even at a considerable degree of enlargement.

Dilution

For a normal negative to be printed on a normal grade of paper it is advisable to keep to the maker's formula, including dilution. A more dilute developer

A pictorial portrait, full of impact, showing effective use of dark against light to enhance the charm of the young profile—*Richard Ustinich, U.S.A.*

This print won a first award in the Ilford competition. A low key portrait which shows originality in its conception, is pictorial as well as characteristic and conveys a depth of inner feeling—*Bill Carter, Britain*

A forceful character study with crisp definition. Off-centre lighting from left of central, gives the third dimension effect. The eyes compel attention—*Bill Carter, Britain*

Natalia Makarova, in rehearsal for her first television performance. The subject is so obviously unaware of the presence of the photographer that the picture is completely natural—*Richard Levin, Britain*

Silky. The somewhat slouching posture, the upturned collar and angled cap, the half hidden eyes and the alluring expression; the strong 45° lighting and simple background, combined with the great sensitivity of the author, all contribute to the making of this highly successful portrait—*Baron Wolman, U.S.A.*

Left
Peter Elphick, Architect. Frontal off-centre flood lighting and double rim spotlighting are used to maintain the triangular shape of the face, when the picture is taken from a low camera angle. The low viewpoint is employed to show the inherent strength of character—*Mary Allen, Britain*
Right
Strong 45° lighting, combined with critical definition, suits this type of subject, giving life and sparkle—*Hasse Karpheden, Sweden*

Left
Feel. Our imagination is called into play with this portrait. We realize that, although
we feel with our fingers, it is our inner thoughts and emotions which are aroused with
the sense of touch. This is cleverly conveyed by the toneless fingers which are doing
the touching, and the powerful tonal rendering of emotion in the face. The closed eye
emphasizes this impression—*Michael Mittelstädt, Germany*
Right
Song. Taken by available light, this portrait shows great sensitivity. The "significant
moment" has been caught. The closed eyes and flying hair imply movement and suggest
the singer's complete involvement with the song—*Michael Mittelstädt, Germany*

Mrs Gaye Pye. Technical excellence, together with the model's natural charm, produce this high key portrait. Earrings add a touch of glamour—*E. Johnson Taylor, Britain*

Draughtsman. The tone separation technique, suggesting the portrait as a design, symbolizes
one aspect of the subject's character – *Mary Allen, Britain*

Henry Geldzahler, Curator, New York. The photographer uses a mannerism to put over the character of a well-known personality. A forceful portrait in its simplicity of shapes and tones—*Va Wölfl, Kettwig, Germany*

A low camera angle and well-controlled back lighting contribute towards the success of this forceful portrait. The correct exposure for the highlights results in the wealth of detail in the essential areas—*Jozef Gross, Britain*

Puma. The clever distribution of tone values forms an effective design in black, grey and white. The relaxed expression of pleasant thought typifies the theme—*Michael Mittelstädt, Germany*

High. The author communicates his message by the technique of blurred image which conveys a feeling of movement and rhythm without recourse to the diagonal or circular line—*Michael Mittelstädt, Germany*

The hands, in their positioning and lighting, increase the character and depth of the picture, adding to the delightful interplay of light against dark—*Bill Carter, Britain*

A journalistic type of portrait, full of character. The vivid presentation tells its own story—*Wolfgang Kunz, Germany*

A glimpse of the hat and cuff form a vital contribution to this portrait of an intriguing personality—*Bill Carter*, *Britain*

J. H. Lock, Esq. A conventional portrait in the modern style, the low tones of which augment the thoughtful expression and depth of character—*E. Johnson Taylor, Britain*

Karen. A wonderful example of the fantastic effect that can be produced with the judicious use of accessories—*Baron Wolman, U.S.A.*

Master Robert Dickson. A charmingly natural child photograph to which the background adds distinction—*E. Johnson Taylor, Britain*

C. John Webb, solicitor. An interesting personality. His features suggest strong powers of observation, ability to concentrate and to reason logically. He is a good speaker and humorous conversationalist. The lighting and camera position have been organized to emphasize these characteristics—*Mary Allen, Britain*

Bob Kane. This portrait is another in the photographer's series "New York Personalities".
It is cleverly dramatized by the mastery of black tone over all others. A strategic placing
of white against black is the climax of the character portrayal—*Va Wölfl, Kettwig,*
Germany

Shelley Hewitson. The character is shown in the frank, open eyes, and the silent determination in the closed lips. The dark tones suggest the hidden mysteries within the mind of such a child—*Mary Allen, Britain*

Sommer-Sprossen. A portrait which tells a story in simplified tones of black and white. The turn of the figure, the isolation in the picture space and the rejection of half-tones, can form the basis for many different themes. The picture is an outline. It is for us to fill in the story content in our own way—*Michael Mittelstädt, Germany*

An imaginative, striking portrait, skilfully produced. The diagonal lines and bright contrasty lighting on the figure, give a dynamic aliveness to the picture. The soft background in reduced scale supplies the illusion of depth and power—*Per Wiklund, Sweden*

The impact of this portrait lies in the magnetic quality of the eyes. The strong texture rendering of the skin tones is produced by the double rim lighting—*Hasse Karpheden, Sweden*

 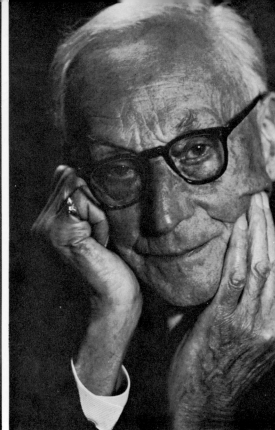

Left
Face. This is one of a number of pictures depicting emotion made by this photographer. It gives a vivid impression of a singer during performance—*Michael Mittelstädt, Germany*
Right
Andy Warhol. A portrait showing unusual dramatization of the subject resulting in great impact—*Stephen Shore, U.S.A.*

No luck. The bold arrangement of lines and shapes suggests action, while the empty jar and hopeless expression indicate frustrated hopes—*Bill Carter, Britain*

Central lighting coupled with the 1:10 ratio emphasizes the form. The figure, curving backwards, demands sufficient picture space and the alive expression and freedom of movement has to be recognized and captured within seconds—*Richard Ustinich, U.S.A.*

This picture of two heads is imaginatively conceived and skilfully produced. It has sensitivity in its tonal arrangement and beauty in line and form—*Richard Ustinich, U.S.A.*

Andy Warhol. The impenetrable dark eyes hinder penetration to his thoughts. The firm, yet sensitive, mouth, together with other facial features, proclaim a man of artistic talent; this is further exemplified by the general presentation of this very fine character portrait— *Va Wölfl, Kettwig, Germany*

An ethereal, symbolic photograph with the effect of mist and haze creatively reproduced. The techniques using grain and distortion have been masterfully handled. The
resulting picture is poetically intriguing—*Per Wiklund, Sweden*

results in a softer negative, but again at the sacrifice of true tone value. The stronger the concentration of the developer the more quickly will it develop, and the more contrasty will be the result.

Temperature

The standard temperature of the developer should be 68°F (20°C). Temperature affects its activity. Any decrease in temperature must be compensated for by extra time, and any increase by less time. Increase in temperature may increase the size of the grain, and also perhaps introduce the additional hazard of fogging. It is advisable, then, to keep to the standard recommended temperature of 68°F for all the solutions.

Agitation

Keep to the maker's instructions for developing time and agitation. The two are interdependent. Continuous agitation makes the film develop more rapidly, while intermittent agitation will slow down the process. Agitation should be gentle but definite—quick jerky movements will only probably increase the grain size by making the developer more energetic.

WORKING WITH STANDARD DEVELOPERS

1. Correctly exposed film

The process of development of a correctly exposed film is a gradual build-up in density of the varying tones. The first to appear are the highlight areas, then the mid-tones and lastly the shadows. Development must be continued until all the tones have their correct value and the required negative density is reached. If the result is too contrasty it indicates that the highlights have been overlit in the first instance. Curtailing development time will give a softer negative but true rendering of tone value will not be achieved.

2. Underexposed film

The highlights will appear first although more slowly than those of correct exposure. Mid-tones make their appearance more slowly still and the shadows refuse to develop at all. No amount of developing will produce detail in areas which have received no exposure.

A slightly underexposed negative can produce an acceptable print on a rather contrasty grade of paper.

If the film is known to be underexposed, it should be developed in one of

129

the developers which actually boosts the speed of the film, often by approximately one stop.

3. *Overexposed film*

If the film has received too much exposure the highlights appear almost immediately, followed in quick succession by the half tones and shadows. The negative will be dense and difficult to print through. If developing time is curtailed the negative will be flat. A film known to be overexposed should be developed in one of the developers which normally require an increase in exposure time.

Slight overexposure and a shortening of the developing time in the normal developer is one way of coping with subjects of extreme contrast. Nevertheless this should be the exception, rather than the rule.

Another exception to this developing technique is when electronic flash has been used for lighting the subject. A film which has received such a high intensity of light for such a short exposure time can develop more slowly, and might, therefore, require an increase in development time, possibly up to 50 per cent.

To sum up

A correctly exposed film of a subject with well balanced lighting, should be developed in a normal fine grain developer, under the maker's specified conditions. Such negatives will produce prints on a normal grade of paper to match the tone values in the original subject.

11 Interpretation and Design

WHENEVER WE set out to make a portrait we have a number of aims in view. Unless the project is a purely pictorial portrait, we are attempting to convey a likeness of a particular person and to express our emotional response to some character trait, or some physical feature, which has stirred our imagination.

The source of our inspiration is a human being; animated by thoughts and feelings, a moving, breathing, alive personality. We have to describe our feelings about them, not by well chosen words, but (more often than not) by a monochrome photograph—a two-dimensional drawing within a rectangle—without colour and without movement.

Having studied the techniques of lighting, camera angle, exposure and development of the film, all of which contribute to the success of our endeavour, we must now consider ways of composing the picture. Composition deals with arranging of the subject within the frame, the interplay of lights and shade, the vitality of line, and the required balance of all the elements into one harmonious whole.

The word itself—composition—has become increasingly unpopular over the past few years, perhaps because its importance as a technique has been over-stressed. No picture, portrait or otherwise, can be built up solely on composition or any other technique.

Some time ago I noted a quotation, "Technical perfection means little unless it is guided by artistic conception and inspired by imagination". I do not remember the author of these words, but you will surely recognize the truth encompassed by them. An artist must be free to make his own creations, not copies of another's, but he must also have the ability to express his ideas in his chosen medium in such a way that the message can be received.

131

We all use descriptive words in our endeavour to communicate with others, but how many of us could paint in words such an expressive picture of a sunrise as Shakespeare did when he wrote about "The glorious morning, gilding pale streams with heavenly alchemy". Shakespeare was inspired by the subject, he knew the techniques, and was a master of his tools.

SIMPLICITY

One of the essential elements in composition is simplicity—the inclusion of only that which is necessary to convey the intended idea. It has been said that, when Michelangelo was asked to define art, he said: "Give me a block of marble, and I will hew off everything unimportant". Unwanted elements can be "hewn off" at a number of stages in the making of a photograph. To mention but a few, there is the use of lenses of different focal lengths; the choice of viewpoint; darkroom techniques; enlarging only a portion of the negative; printing controls. Also, the judicious trimming of the final print.

The essential truth to be learned is that nothing should be included in the picture that does not contribute in some way to the subject or theme.

We have suggested that an artist must be free to make his own creations; but there are two kinds of freedom. There is the freedom of self-expression when through ignorance no techniques are consciously applied, or the freedom of self-expression which emanates from a knowledge of technique so well understood that the sense of design and the relationship of shapes and lines become an inherent part of the artist's way of seeing.

The former freedom built on ignorance may well be successful when the author is a born artist, or on the rare occasion when chance, or luck, takes a hand, but the beginner in photography knows only too well how much time and material can be wasted, and how many pictures can be lost through lack of knowledge. The art of seeing, and the comprehension of the techniques of graphic design, can probably best be learned through the study of some of the other arts as well as of photography.

CULTIVATE THE IMAGINATION

Some people are much more imaginative than others, but by consciously exercising your imagination, you will find yourself becoming progressively more able to visualize thoughts. Each one must choose his own form of art, or particular artist, on whose work to base his studies. A choice can be made from dancing, music, poetry, sculpture, painting, drama, ballet, ice-skating etc. as well as from photography. There is a wide scope for your selection. Try to analyse for yourself why you have made the particular choice, what does it make you feel, and why. How has the arrangement of sounds, colours, shapes, or movements contributed to the success of the whole? If you like a phrase, or a movement, is it repeated? How often? Or is it used as a climax? What different feelings do you get when music is played loudly? Softly? Fast? Slow? If you are a lover of ballet or ice-skating, spend some part of your time, while in the audience, to analyse the movements—the lines of the body, the graceful curves, the exciting diagonals, the strong uprights and the peaceful horizontals. Notice the background music, how it harmonizes with the particular theme, how it crescendos as the tension mounts, and fades to almost nothing taking with it the excitement of the moment and leaving an atmosphere of peace.

Take a painting that appeals to you and try again to analyse your feelings about it. What effect do the colours themselves have on you? Do they make you feel gay, fearful, depressed, peaceful? Are the colours conveying the reality of the subject matter, the texture, the solidarity or translucence of the material, the mood of the picture? Ignore, for a moment, the reality of the subject matter and study the shapes—the shapes of the objects, the shapes of the background spaces. Are the shapes themselves pleasing to the eye? How are the shapes related to one another? Does the arrangement give a feeling of harmony, or discord, strength, or weakness? What about the direction of the leading lines in the picture. Are they mainly upright, horizontal or diagonal? What effect do these have on your feelings? Do the upright lines give a feeling of height, stability, strength or aspiration? Do the horizontal lines convey a sense of calm, repose, unending space? And what about the diagonal lines? Do they convey to you the feeling of movement, of falling over, of vitality? Now consider the picture as a whole. How have these elements contributed to the mood or reality of the subject matter? Have you received the message the artist was trying to convey?

Now you can apply the same techniques to a monochrome photograph. You can study the relationship of the spaces, one with the other and consider the effect, you can analyse the direction of the lines and the part they play in conveying the mood of the picture. But, instead of feeling the effect of colour on your emotions, you must substitute the varying shades of grey, from dead white to pure black.

Maybe it requires a little more imagination on your part to do this, because you are better acquainted with colour and its effects on your feelings in everyday

133

life. But, if you persevere in the exercise, you will very quickly find you are able to see in terms of monochrome tone values instead of colour.

Return now to the photograph you have chosen to analyse. Once more ignore the subject matter and concentrate only on the tone values. How do the various tones affect you? Begin with the darker greys. Do they appear to you to be rather heavy? Perhaps depressing or sombre? Are the deep blacks more exciting? Is there a greater feeling of strength and solidarity about them? Or, a richness which may not be evident in any other tone? What about the lighter greys? Are they not quieter? perhaps rather nondescript, mysterious, spacious? And the pure whites. Do you not find them bright, and clean but cold and unemotional in any large area?

It is difficult to visualize a large area of single tone without an illustration. We will side-track for a little while, and use sheets of paper instead of a photograph. Take three pieces of paper—one white, one grey and one black, to represent the monochrome tones. Let your imagination arouse in you some emotional response to each tone, such as the white giving a feeling of emptiness, the grey one of dull monotony, while the black becomes impenetrable and suffocating. In each case, but more especially with the white, you are most likely to feel a strong desire to put some mark on it, to introduce some other tone, in order to create interest—a focal point. It is this placing of one tone upon another, in varying shapes and sizes and the addition or subtraction of the intensity of tone, which creates the design or composition of a pictorial photograph.

BUILDING YOUR OWN COMPOSITION

The following exercise may take a little time but it is a sure way of teaching yourself the techniques of composition. Not only is it a fascinating experiment but it will give you endless ideas of design and arrangement with varying shapes, and suggest to your imagination ways of using the tone values to convey such things as distance, proportions, scale, mood, impact, vitality, etc.

You will need a small quantity of black, grey and white paper. From each shade cut several circles of varying diameters, also a number of triangles, squares and oblongs of assorted sizes. A few long strips are needed to represent straight lines, and some curved strips shaped like an elongated figure S are also useful, and any other shapes made up of straight or curved lines which appeal to your artistic sense. Any number can be cut, and you will probably keep on adding to the collection as new ideas come into your mind.

134

You also need three pieces of card, one of each colour; black, grey and white to serve as the picture base.

The exercise is to so arrange the various shapes and lines on the cards to form pleasing compositions, i.e. pleasing to you. Then try to analyse why they satisfy you, what interpretation your imagination can construct from the way in which you have used the various colour tones and shapes.

Begin with a few very simple arrangements, as the basic elements on which to build.

1. Take a piece of white paper for the base, and place a small black paper circle over the central point. What are your reactions to this arrangement as a composition for a single object in space? (Fig. 11.1).

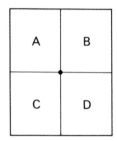

Fig. 11.1. A basic geometrical arrangement

It is a geometrical arrangement. The spaces A, B, C, D are equal in size and shape. The composition has impact, but lacks variety and the object appears static.

2. Fold the base paper into equal divisions of three, both horizontally and vertically. Place the small black paper circle on any one of the points where the folds intersect. Do you consider there is more vitality about this arrangement? (Fig. 11.2).

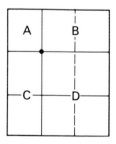

Fig. 11.2. Subject at the intersection

135

The spaces A, B, C, D are now of differing shapes and sizes, which adds variety to the composition without the loss of impact. The object is no longer static, the available space along the diagonal AD implies a movement in that direction.

You will find that in a great number of paintings and photographs, the main focus of interest is on, or near, one of these points.

3.   Take one oblong shape of paper in each of the shades, black, grey and white. Arrange them on the base as shown in Fig. 11.3. The horizontal format gives a feeling of restfulness and continuing space in the sideways direction.

The black paper at the base suggests the foreground, the grey becomes the middle distance and the white completes the illusion of space in depth.

The widths of these shapes can be varied to give the suggestion of differing viewpoints. Experiment with these strips and note the different effects. Try leaving out the grey and the resulting feeling is stronger, harder and has greater

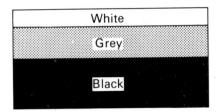

Fig. 11.3. The horizontal format

impact than when all three tones are used. Now leave out the black and use only grey and white, and at once a more restful, quieter mood is felt. Use narrower strips, and intersperse the white with the black, and the result becomes more exciting, but could become discordant unless modified.

Leave out the white, and use only black and grey in the arrangement and a more sombre, heavy mood is suggested.

4.   Continue with oblong shapes of black, grey and white paper, but this time arrange them on the base in the vertical format, as in Fig. 11.4. The vertical format gives a feeling of strength, solidity and height. The black looks quite solid and immovable.

The grey and white, which created the feeling of distance in the horizontal format, now extends to nothingness, sideways, which is unsatisfying.

The black tone, as well as being impenetrable, is heavy and appears to over-weight the left side. The balance can be restored by adding a small strip of black to the right side or by cutting a piece off the black and inserting it between the grey and white.

136

Fig. 11.4. The vertical format

5. Cut the oblong shapes into varying sizes, and, by using the black and grey on a white base, form them into as many pleasing designs as you can, overlapping where necessary. Figure 11.5 is a suggestion for one such design.

Here the spatial relationships are important, such as: width to height, width to width and height to height.

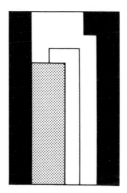

Fig. 11.5. Design in the vertical format

6. Again using the black, grey and white oblong shapes arrange them on the base as shown in Fig. 11.6 and Fig. 11.6a.

The spatial relationships are used to show perspective: Fig. 11.6 illustrates a higher viewpoint than Fig. 11.6a. The shapes get progressively smaller in size and lighter in tone as they overlap.

7. Take a triangular shape this time, in each of the three tones, black, grey and white. Cut the grey one slightly smaller than the black, and the white one smaller than the grey. Arrange them on the base as shown in Fig. 11.7.

137

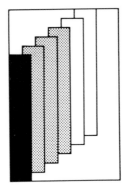

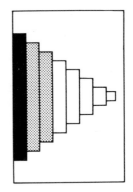

Fig. 11.6. Implied viewpoint   Fig. 11.6a. Implied perspective

This is another example of spatial, combined with tonal, relationships—the illusion of space between the objects and of distance from near to far. The triangular shape differs from the oblong or square, in that it introduces the diagonal line. This arrangement is shaped like an arrow, and is, therefore, a clear indication of movement. In a single triangle, the two opposing diagonal lines meet at

Fig. 11.7. Illusion of space and distance

the apex which arrests the movement. This point is often used as the prime focus of interest in a design, or in a portrait. This will be discussed further later on.

It is the implied diagonal line connecting the tops and the bases of the oblong shapes in Figs. 11.6 and 11.6a, which is, to a great extent, responsible for the feeling of movement towards the distance. Both the oblong and the square shapes are enclosed and are apparently static or limited in their movement—the oblong can move vertically or horizontally—but they must both be composed

138

with the diagonal line for any other direction. The triangle does not appear to be so inhibited. Its three points can revolve, like a star, and its implied movement is in all directions. The triangular shape can give stability to a composition if the base of the triangle is level with the base of the picture.

8.   The last shape is the circle. Take five circles—two black, one grey and two white, together with three other circles of half the diameter. The smaller

Fig. 11.8. A complete design

circles will be one of each tone, black, grey and white. Arrange these on the base as shown in Fig. 11.8.

Perhaps some explanation of this design is necessary. Why have I chosen to show a complete design in preference to a simple illustration of spatial relation-ships with three circles, of black, grey and white tone?

We could use three such circles separately spaced as in Fig. 11.8a—the

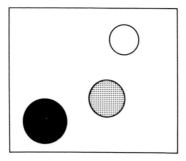

Fig. 11.8a. Distance and movement

139

circles getting progressively smaller in size and lighter in tone as they move across the base.

This does produce an illusion of distance and a sense of floating up and away, but such an arrangement is limited in its use as a design. A circle on its own has no direction, it is enclosed within itself, and the overlapping of just three circles in varying tones has little or no meaning. Therefore we must increase the number of circles, vary the size as well as the tone, and arrange them in such a way as to imply movement.

Note that an uneven number of each sized circle is chosen, and that nowhere does the circumference of one circle just touch another. The interplay of black, grey and white tones, together with the varied size of semi-circular shapes, produce a sense of rhythm.

The low position of the small grey circle on the large black one directs the eye to the small white circle. This in turn leads up to the small black circle, which, owing to its place in a large area of white, becomes the focal point. Herein lies the implied movement in a circular direction.

DIRECTION OF LINE

Let us now look at the direction of each line and see what interpretation can be put on this in a composition.

9. First, examine the upright line. Take some narrow strips of paper in varying lengths and widths, of each tonal value, black, grey and white. Arrange them on the base as in Fig. 11.9.

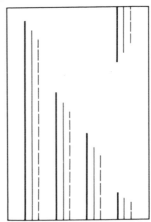

Fig. 11.9. Movement and strength in lines

140

The dark line represents black tone, the lighter line, grey tone, the dotted line, white tone. What can be deduced from this illustration?

(a) The upright line moves from a stationary dot in a vertical or downwards direction, thereby conveying height or depth.

(b) The upright line needs no support—and can therefore be used as a symbol of strength. It can stand alone in a composition.

(c) The black tone has the greatest impact and appears to be more solid.

(d) Tall upright and short upright lines used together can give a sense of scale.

10. Now to examine the horizontal line; using similar strips of paper, arrange them on the base as shown in Fig. 11.10.

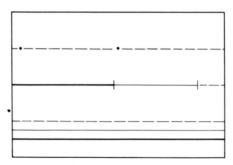

Fig. 11.10. Dynamics of the horizontal line

From the illustration Fig. 11.10 it can be seen that:

(a) The line moves horizontally from a stationary dot, leading the eye in the direction in which it is apparently moving.

(b) The motion of the line can be checked at any given point by intersecting it with an upright line.

(c) The blacker the line the greater the momentum.

(d) A short horizontal line appears stationary.

(e) As the line lies horizontally it is a symbol of rest and quiet.

11. Now look at the diagonal line.

First place some strips of black paper on the base as in Fig. 11.11.

Study the arrangement and you will realize that your attention is drawn firstly to the line from C which leads your eye into the picture, then to the line from A which also leads in towards the centre. The lines from B and D, however, appear to be lines which lead the eye from the centre outwards. The reason for

141

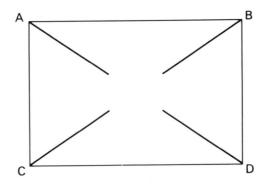

Fig. 11.11. Dynamics of the diagonal

this can only be that we are more used to reading from left to right, and we instinctively follow the lead in from the left.

By placing the grey and white strips alongside the black, we get the feeling that the black is pushing the other two either in a downward or an upward direction according to whether the grey and white are above or below the black, (Fig. 11.11a).

Fig. 11.11b shows the diagonal line radiating from a central pivot, and Fig. 11.11c illustrates how quickly the direction is altered when the line is intersected by an opposing diagonal.

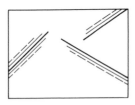

Fig. 11.11a. Dynamics
of parallel lines

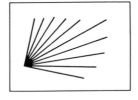

Fig. 11.11b. Dynamics
of radiation lines

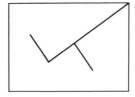

Fig. 11.11c. Dynamics
of intersecting lines

From these arrangements we have learned the following characteristics of the diagonal line.

(a) The diagonal line is the longest line possible in a picture.

(b) It is a versatile line, being used to express movement and radiation. One of its functions is to lead the eye into the picture, and from one point of interest to another. It is, therefore, often called "the leading line".

(c) An opposing diagonal immediately arrests the movement and turns it in another direction.

142

(d) The movement can be fast or slow according to the angle at which it rises from an imaginary horizontal line, or falls from an imaginary upright.

(e) To give stability to a picture the falling diagonal requires an upright line to support it.

12. The circular line is not to be confused with the circle already described. The circle is enclosed. The circular line proceeds from a stationary dot in a circular movement but forms an ever widening circle (Fig. 11.12). It can twist and turn to form other circles (Fig. 11.12a). The flowing turn from one circle

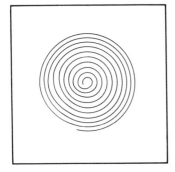
Fig. 11.12. Dynamics of the circle

Fig. 11.12a. Dynamics of the flowing line

to another becomes the S curve, which is commonly talked about in the subject of composition.

We can assume then, that:

(a) The circular line is a flowing line.

(b) It has movement, with a sense of continuation.

(c) Its speed depends on the steepness or otherwise of the curve—it can be slow and rhythmic or fast and whirling.

(d) It has a beauty and grace inherent in itself, and can be satisfying as a composition on its own.

FEELING FOR DESIGN

If you have really practised these exercises you will already be developing a feeling for design and arrangement. The elements of composition should become so much a part of a photographer's way of seeing that the use of them in picture making is more subconscious than deliberate.

If you have understood the reasons for the arrangements of the different shapes, the tone values and the nature and use of line you will now be able to translate any idea, mood or subject into monochrome, using composition as your descriptive medium. You can for example now think of any adjective and describe it solely by tone values, shapes and lines. You can return to the study of music, sculpture, ballet or poetry, such as were discussed earlier, and interpret your emotional reactions in terms of photography. You should be able to analyse paintings and photographs and understand how the artist has used composition to communicate his ideas and emotions. You may also be capable of producing an abstract photograph built solely on your own feelings for design and imagination.

GRAPHIC DESIGN IN PORTRAITURE

Having studied the meaning of the various shapes and lines used in a picture, and how to express moods and emotions by tone values, their use in portraiture must now be considered.

Tracing over a portrait
It is of great benefit, to all who are studying composition, to discover how successful portraitists have themselves dealt with the subject. It is not always easy, at first glance, to isolate the lines, shapes and basic tone values from what looks initially like very complex tonal structure. The best way of doing this is to cover a photograph with a piece of tracing paper, and pencil over the lines and shapes which are visible through the paper. Transfer this tracing to a sheet of paper which you have cut to the same size as the original format. Then shade in the basic tones of black and grey, leaving the white as the blank paper. The direction of the lines will then be clearly indicated and you will be able to note the size relationship of figure to background, the background shapes, and the predominant tone values.

PORTRAIT HEAD USED AS A DESIGN

Fig. 11.13 is a study of one side of the face only with the eye as the centre of interest, and the tone values simplified. The background of black and white is so arranged that the shadow side of the face is seen against the white. The whole forms a simple design. Fig. 11.13a is a traced copy of the outlines, and the shadings represent the three tones, black, grey and white.

We can summarize the analysis of this picture as follows:

144

 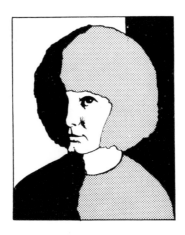

11.13 11.13a

Fig. 11.13. Simple tonal arrangement
Fig. 11.13a. Showing the tones: black, grey and white

1. The eye becomes the focal point because it is a very small area of black in a large area of white. The area of white tone, on its own, is dull and flat, but, with the introduction of the dark tone, the eye zeros at once on to the dark. The introduction of a small white on a large area of black would have the same effect.

2. The size relationships between the head, the body and the background are such that the head predominates, but is well balanced by the body, and the background.

3. The tones are well balanced, and there is a good interplay of light and dark across the picture.

4. The strong black upright shape on the right, together with the horizontal oblong shape of the body, give a solidity to the composition.

5. The upright line of the shadow down the face and the horizontal line of the eye convey a static, quiet dignity.

145

6.   All spacings are unequal: the distance from the top, back and front of the head to the border all differ; least on top, slightly more at the back, more still in front. This adds variety.

7.   The body is attached to the border on both sides, giving security.

8.   There are no points in the picture—there is a slight space between the jaw and the shoulder lines. Points are best avoided in an otherwise straight and curved line composition.

9.   The dark shoulder line against the white background attracts attention, and its diagonal direction towards the eye, which is the focal point, makes it a strong leading line from the bottom left of the picture (Fig. 11.11).

10.   The body turning away from the camera, with the pull of the eye towards the lens, gives slight variety to the background shapes. In a normal head and shoulders portrait, the head itself would be turned towards the camera. If it were so turned in this instance, the width of the light cheek would be decreased, thereby losing much of the impact of the eye.

Diagonal composition

To obtain a greater feeling of vitality, use can be made of the diagonal line in head and shoulder composition.

1.   In Fig. 11.14 the body is turned in one direction, while the head is turned to the opposite side. The subject is leaning forward with her left shoulder lower than her right. This gives a diagonal line to the shoulders. An imaginary line through the centre of the face forms an opposing diagonal, both to the shoulder line and to the line of the eyes.

2.   The spacing between the head and the border is varied, there being least above the head, slightly more behind, and very much more in front. There must be space in the direction of the eyes.

3.   The eyes have impact—partly owing to the fact that each one is on one of the diagonal lines of the picture, which is a strong position, and partly because the dark colour of the pupil is adjacent to the whitest area in the picture, and these two contrasting tones are isolated in a large area of mid-light tone. The impact is lessened by the direction of the glance being turned away from the viewer. This conveys a feeling of aloofness which is characteristic of the model, whereas a glance towards the camera or the lens denotes greater intimacy.

INTIMACY IN A PORTRAIT

As human beings we are not accustomed to looking at one another's faces at very close range. It is too embarrassing for both parties. Nor do we look straight

11.14 11.14a 11.15

Fig. 11.14. Diagonals in head and shoulder composition
Fig. 11.14a. Traced copy of lines and masses
Fig. 11.15. Opposing diagonals of face and shoulder

---

into each other's eyes for any length of time. It is too much like encroaching on a person's freedom of thought, into their inner sanctuary. A straight look is a sign of truth and trustfulness.

The eyes are the windows of the soul, and a mutual deep and searching glance into the eyes can only be maintained when the two persons concerned are prepared to reveal their inner emotions.

Fig. 11.15 is a portrait consisting of the head only, the eyes being the focal point. The eyes are directed towards the viewer and are in a very strong position in the picture space similar to those illustrated in Fig. 11.14. An opposing diagonal line runs down the centre of the face. This is supported by the opposing diagonal line of the shoulder, and the dark, solid, shape of the background.

The dark hair frames the face above and on each side, sufficient of it being shown to maintain a reasonable balance between the light and dark areas, and to keep the eyes in the strong position above the half-way line.

147

12 Character
and the Facial Features

IN PORTRAITURE you embark on a far greater challenge than when tackling a still life subject, for example. You are dealing with people—each one with a unique personality and each presenting individual problems. Your next step, then, is to try and learn something about the actual subject before the camera.

Before dealing with individuals it is as well to look more closely at the physical features of the face in general and find out as much as possible about the personality trends which usually accompany a particular type of feature.

A note of warning must be given here. It is not easy to classify any person's features from a list of shapes and sizes. Most people's features are a mixture of two or three types, resulting in a person with breadth of character. But on occasions it will be found that one particular facet of character is very strong and is easily recognizable in the appropriate feature.

The study of the physical features can begin by taking another look at the shape of the head in which the features are set. If you will refer back to the diagrams on page 77 you will see the lines across (a) the hair, (b) the eyebrows, (c) the base of the nose, (d) the chin, dividing the face up into three sections. If these sections are of equal size, as with the majority of people, it denotes, in theory at least, a well balanced personality, with no one particular character trait being predominant.

The *upper* portion, the forehead area, being the widest would be associated with an intellectual, "brainy" type of person. The emphasis being on the *middle* area would indicate a broad-minded, philosophical, friendly personality, interested more in spiritual than physical matters. If accompanied by a long nose,

148

which is often the case, the nature would be more forceful and active. The predominance of the *lower* third denotes a strong, determined character, with physical strength but lacking depth of feeling.

Now for the individual features:

FOREHEAD

A forehead can be high or low, narrow or broad, receding, projecting or almost vertical. It is easier to assess from the profile view in conjunction with the full face, rather than from full face only.

High forehead: an intellectual, analytical mind.
Low forehead: shows less capacity for thought, little imagination.
Narrow forehead: a somewhat narrow minded person.
Broad forehead: a constructive mind, imaginative, resourceful, a good leader.
The slope of the forehead can be seen from the profile position.
The normal forehead is slightly receding and denotes average intelligence.
Vertical: suggests an inclination towards idealism and art.
Projecting: in a projecting forehead the fullness may be found in different areas:

1. Above the eyebrows: ability in tasks requiring precision.
2. In the centre: a good memory.
3. At the top: logical reasoning powers.

A forehead which projects without any marked depressions or fullness, and is usually low and narrow implies limited mental activity.
Receding: if full and wide: a practical turn of mind with executive ability. Receding severely with no height or fullness infers limited intelligence.

EYES

Colour

Blue: affectionate but not excessively emotional. Energetic, businesslike.
Grey: a colder nature, self-controlled but inclined to be hard in judgement.
Hazel: warm, affectionate, gentle nature.
Brown: emotional, less self-control, strong likes and dislikes. Artistic and moody.
Black: passionate and emotional, quick to anger.
The size, slant, set and brightness of the eyes should be studied.

149

Large: usually wide open and often showing a rim of white below the iris—upper eyelid curved.

An emotional, sympathetic person—often artistic and observant. If very wide open the character would be more shallow and emotions stronger. Protruding large eyes would indicate a nervous disposition and lack of deep thought. If deep-set, a person with hypnotic power or interested in occultism could be indicated.

Small: usually deep-set under the brows—observant, calculating, analytical, and great power of concentration. If set too close together a more secretive nature can be expected.

Eyes slanting upwards from the nose—an alert mind, inclined to be selfish. Quick on the uptake.

Eyes slanting downwards from the nose show an agreeable nature, talkative, with a desire to please.

Bright eyes—an alert, intelligent mind, usually optimistic and happy.

Dull eyes—usually a sign of ill health, or a slow mind.

EYEBROWS

Eyebrows can be dark or fair, coarse or fine, straight or curved, thick or thin. They are not necessarily similar on both sides of the face, more especially regarding the slant. Dark brows are considered attractive, and the smooth curve is aimed at by the majority of models who use the art of make-up though, admittedly, they are subject to changes in fashion. Where a natural eyebrow is visible one can deduct the following personality traits.

Thick bushy eyebrows will denote strength, vitality, strong likes and dislikes, power of concentration; irritability if the eyebrows meet over the nose or are coarse and ruffled.

Thin fair eyebrows indicate a calm, sensitive disposition. Eyebrows slanting upwards from the nose denote a changeable nature and, if thick, a rather unsociable disposition. Arched and well above the eyes, depict a dreamy, somewhat impractical and credulous personality. A downward curve from the nose gives a practical mind with analytical ability.

NOSE

Generally speaking the nose shows the force of character and energy. The best nose is one which is well proportioned, measures the one-third of the face and protrudes slightly at the tip. This shows a person who has a well balanced personality, is ambitious, intellectual and generous.

Other types are: *Roman,* a fairly large nose with a bump high up on the ridge —showing power to command, courage, and physical strength. The wider this nose the more the character is emphasized. (Large nose similar to the Roman but with a wide ridge all the way down has more vivacity and love of excitement; a narrow ridge gives a sharper appearance, is peace loving, refined and quick to make decisions).

Grecian. This nose is straight and well proportioned. It goes with an even tempered, artistic and courteous personality.

A straight or slightly concave nose, with a wide ridge all the way down, depicts strong powers of thought, serious, and logical.

A straight or slightly concave nose which is narrow at the ridge, broadening towards the tip, indicates ability for sound reasoning when the mind is applied but easily swayed by intuition.

The convex nose when viewed in profile, shows less natural force and energy. It is usually short with an upturned tip. Impulsive, cheerful, sociable, sometimes hiding shyness under an abrupt manner. A sharp tip is more alert than a blunt one.

MOUTH AND LIPS

A small mouth, small that is, in comparison with the rest of the features, implies a self-centred nature, and, if pursed up, severity and thriftiness.

The fairly wide mouth with medium-sized lips, belongs to a good-natured, sociable, but firm and decisive person. If the lower lip is full, the nature is more generous, open-minded and sympathetic.

The corners of the mouth turning up mean an optimistic, happy, sociable personality, but a downward turn means a more serious outlook, sometimes pessimistic.

The straight mouth gives a good balance between the two.

Protruding lips denote an impulsive, moody nature somewhat quarrelsome; emotional but kind.

Lips which are normally apart, showing the teeth, go with a lack of self-confidence.

If the line of closure between the lips is made up of curves instead of a straight line the person can be expected to have ability in acting, or singing and is inclined to be emotional.

151

CHIN

The good *average* chin is on a straight line with the lips when seen in profile, or may be very slightly receding. The *protruding* chin shows a determined, somewhat stubborn nature, with strong powers of endurance. The *receding* chin shows a lack of firmness and self-reliance. The *square* chin—physical strength, reliable, independent, courageous, usually an outdoor type. The *round* chin—easy-going nature, fond of physical comforts, sociable. The *oval* chin—reliable, artistic, capable. The *pointed* chin, carefree, unmethodical, cheerful. *Dimpled* —artistic, self-willed.

EARS

The top of the ear is usually on a line with the eyebrows. If it is noticeably higher, it would indicate an excitable nature.

Large ears, well shaped, denote a physically strong person, with go-ahead ideas. Large lobes to the ears means a friendly disposition.

Medium sized ears, thin and finely shaped, show a friendly person with artistic or musical talent. Small ears belong with a more cautious nature; projecting ears, a courageous person; ears lying close to the head, more cautious and ears pointed at the top, changeable or witty.

FEATURE STUDY

Realizing how difficult it is to study a living face in detail, we will make our task easier by using photographs. To make a fair assessment, the photograph must be made like a map—on a flat plane. The face must be lit with flat, even lighting such as you would use for making a copy of a flat original. The model must be square-on to the camera, and both a full face and a profile view should be taken.

We have already discovered when we were studying the differing shapes of faces that one side of the face always differs from the other. No person's face is completely symmetrical, and within reason the greater the difference the greater the character or the more mature the personality. We can then expect the features to be a mixture also.

To make this easier to understand we will divide each face (from different age groups) in half and put the two left sides of the face together and the two right sides together.

First we must shoot the photograph, as described, with the model square-on the camera with the lights level and at equal distance. Care must be taken to see that the face really is square-on to the camera, that the same amount of ear can be seen each side, that the head is straight and not tilted in any way. Following that, a profile view should be taken with the lights and camera still level. From these negatives we will make 8 × 6 in. enlargements. Two identical prints must be made from the full face negative. The negative is then reversed in the enlarger carrier, and one further print made. Only one print need be made from the profile.

One print from the normal negative and the print from the reverse side must now be cut up the centre. This cutting must be accurate. The easiest procedure is to mark the centre point between the eyes, between the nostrils at their base, the centre of the lips and the centre of the chin. Rule a straight line through these points with a pencil, and then cut along the line. The two left sides of the face and the two right sides can then be mounted together on a card.

Immediately the differences in the shape of the face, and the individual features and also the characteristic expressions become apparent.

We have studied the physical features and learned some of the character traits we may expect to find therefrom, but, so far, no mention has been made of the expressions. From these composite photographs we can realize that we have still one step further to go in our analysis of the face—the reading of the lines and wrinkles which help to form the expression.

Some faces, especially those of photographic models, or any user of the art of make-up, will show little sign of lines or wrinkles. Although these faces may appear beautiful they will have to rely on their physical features for portraying their character. Lines and wrinkles are an asset—they give added strength and character to a face provided that the strong characteristics can be shown and the weak, undesirable ones modified.

In a later chapter on retouching, reference will be made again to these character lines, as it can so easily happen that lines which have been etched in a face over many years and speak of courage, concentrative powers, sympathy, wisdom or wit—all positive traits, can be removed at a touch of the retoucher's pencil. Some of the negative traits, on the other hand, which could well be eliminated, might remain.

This, then, is an important part of the study of faces, so let us consider these character lines before progressing any further with the composite photographs.

FACIAL LINES

Lines *across* the forehead caused by contracting and relaxing the muscles when in thought indicate a logical mind, able to concentrate on problems.

These must not be confused with the slightly wider lines which traverse the forehead of a younger person through continued perplexity or worry.

Vertical lines between the eyebrows: there may be one, two, or three such lines, caused by contracting the brows in concentration. The characteristics usually to be found are: precision, a love of justice and notable sense of duty. These attributes are the stronger where the lines are more marked.

Horizontal line across the bridge of the nose denotes a person able to command, a natural ability to lead.

Horizontal wrinkles from the outward corner of the eye are the laughter lines, and show a happy personality.

A horizontal wrinkle under the eye, more than the full length of the eye, indicates the passionate or emotional.

A curved wrinkle under the eye may show a good speaker.

Oblique wrinkles from the inner corner of the eye can betray a selfish, greedy, rather spiteful nature.

A downward line from the base of the nose to the mouth—the normal position for this line is one which starts at the curve of the nostril and ends a little way out from the corner of the mouth.

If the line is short it shows less power of concentration, if long—continuing below the corner of the mouth—it shows greater determination.

Vertical line in the centre of the lower lip indicates a jocular type.

A vertical line in the cheek running down towards the chin goes with a good talker or public speaker. If this line is short and shallow, it indicates merely a pleasant conversationalist.

A vertical cleft in the bottom of the chin shows a methodical person, fond of approval. A circular cleft (dimple) in the chin means artistic talent. A circular dimple near the mouth indicates a good-natured, sociable, probably artistic personality. A long dimple in the cheek is similar, but shows a more serious disposition.

SUBJECT 1

We are now ready to make the first analysis.

Turning to the previous page we can observe the following:

1. *Shape of the head*: A mixture of square and triangular.

154

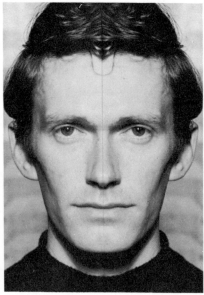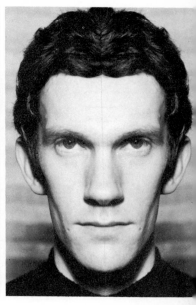

12.1 12.2 12.3

Figs. 12.1, 12.2, 12.3. Full face, two lefts, and two rights

---

2. *Division into thirds*: Average.

3. *Forehead*: Square and moderately high. A good forehead showing honesty and good judgement. Constructive ability. Strong perceptive powers.

4. *Eyebrows*: Thick, lying low over the eyes, bushy. A mind for details intense nature, uncommon abilities—(more obvious on the right), moody.

5. *Eyes*: Hazel in colour—kind, affectionate nature. The top eyelid covers the upper portion of the iris. There is an upward slant from the nose, more especially on his right side—depth of thought and concentrative power; a quick discerning mind; a degree of self-interest, more obvious on the right.

6. *Nose*: Seen in profile, the nose is straight from top to tip—a talent for the fine arts, music, poetry, painting, etc.
Left side: The ridge is narrow between the eyes widening slightly towards the tip—swayed by impressions and intuitions.
Right side: The ridge is wide down the full length of the nose—power of thought and logical reasoning.

155

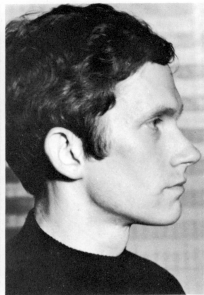

12.4 12.5 12.6

SUBJECT I
Figs. 12.4, 12.5. Two profiles of the subject
Fig. 12.6. The right side of a more photogenic outline

7. *Mouth and lips*: Wide mouth, medium full lips, and a slight upward turn at the corners. The line of closure is made up of several curves—well controlled feelings and emotions, a sociable and friendly disposition and probably artistic tendencies.

8. *Chin*: On his left the chin is square in shape, on his right more oval. Physical strength is shown on his left, and the artistic tendencies on his right.

9. *Ears*: Small, well-shaped, protruding slightly—cautious, some originality.

The horizontal wrinkles in his forehead, already becoming clearly marked, show a desire and ability for work with difficult problems.

Conclusion

Apart from an exercise to teach us to understand and recognize the character traits likely to be found, in some degree, in the person we are discussing, how will this help us in taking the portrait?

The more photogenic outline, as seen from the profile position, is on his right. The shape of the head, the more rounded tip to the nose and the oval chin, are more attractive than the same features on his left side, and the expression is more relaxed. Hence we can use the right side of his face for emphasizing charm of his physical features, and to portray the sensitivity of his nature and his artistic abilities.

If we wished to portray the sterner characteristics, the physical strength, and determination, we should concentrate on his left side and emphasize the square jaw.

From our study we have also found out something about his personality. He is capable of deep thought, is sociable, fond of the outdoors and of the fine arts. At least we have a subject for discussion—art in some form, or the countryside. Also music, which can be played in the background, will help to overcome any feeling of self-consciousness, because he will react emotionally to the sound, which will therefore have a calming influence.

SUBJECT 2

1. *Shape of the head*: Mixture of oval and square.
2. *Division into thirds*: More or less equal—forehead wider on her left.
3. *Face*: Left side of her face longer and thinner than her right.
4. *Forehead*: *Left*—high and narrow, *Right*—low and wide. Intellectual, timid, trustworthy—a good mixture!
5. *Eyebrows*: Thick, curved over full length of the eye. Powers of observation and concentration; a mind for detail.
6. *Eyes*: Brown in colour; affectionate nature. Large eyes, slight upward slant from the nose, especially her right eye—observant, an alert mind, the subtleties of which are sometimes difficult to understand.
7. *Nose*: Fairly short, slightly concave in outline, more rounded tip on the left. The left side is also wider across the bridge—cheerful, sunny-nature, rather impulsive and an abrupt manner which is sometimes a cover for shyness.
8. *Mouth*: Full lips on fairly wide mouth; lips slightly apart when relaxed, showing the teeth—warm, affectionate nature, generous, energetic, though lacking in self-confidence and inclined to be irritable.
9. *Chin*: Slightly projecting—resolute, decisive opinions. Laughter lines beginning to show at the side of the left eye.

157

 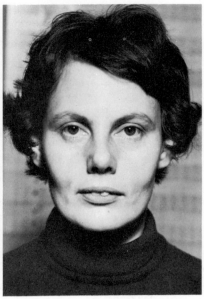 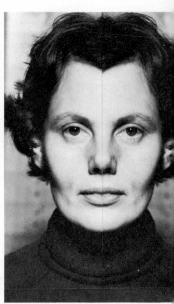

12.7 12.8 12.9

SUBJECT 1
Fig. 12.7. The left side for the sterner characteristics
SUBJECT 2
Figs. 12.8, 12.9. Full face view of the subject, and two rights

Two vertical lines in the forehead above the bridge of the nose are faintly visible, formed by the endeavour to analyse a situation.

Conclusion

In taking the portrait we will select the right side of the face for a profile position, because the outline is more attractive. It is obvious that the camera must be higher in order to emphasize the upper half of the face, to lengthen the nose and focus attention on the eye. The clear cut jaw line needs to be subdued by the lighting effect. This powerful jaw shows strength and determination in character, and can be emphasized in a man's portrait. For a woman we need a softer effect, and we will in no way destroy the character if we use light and shade to subdue rather than emphasize the bone formation. For a full face or three-quarter face position we will use the left side of her face nearest to the camera. This will give the good outline of the right side against the background and allow full concentration of the character revealed in the left side of the face.

158

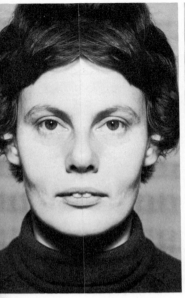  

12.10 12.11 12.12

SUBJECT 2
Figs. 12.10, 12.11, 12.12. Two lefts, and profiles of the subject

Look again at the two lefts and two rights. The warm, affectionate and generous attributes are distinctly visible in the expression in the eyes and the face generally on the left, while the right side shows a withdrawn, critical, straightforward but unsympathetic nature. You can communicate with the person revealed on her left, but the one on the right will be difficult to penetrate.

SUBJECT 3

1. *Shape of the head*: A mixture of oval and triangular—oval on the left, and triangular on the right.

2. *Division into thirds*: Lower third narrower than the other two, especially on her left.

3. *Face*: The left side of her face is longer and wider than her right. This is uncommon—the longer side is usually the thinner.

4. *Forehead*: As far as we can see the forehead on the right is full and high

12.13 12.14 12.15

SUBJECT 2

Fig. 12.13. The right side for an attractive outline
Fig. 12.14. The left side and low camera angle
Fig. 12.15. The left side and higher camera angle

—the left appears lower and a little less wide. Intellectual and a good memory on the right. Less ambitious on the left.

5. *Eyebrows*: Thick and arched. The ends curve upwards to a more marked degree on the left than on the right—fine powers of observation and concentration on the right; more unsociable, self-centred disposition on the left.

6. *Eyes*: Dark brown in colour—emotional, artistic, demonstrative, sympathetic, shows moods easily. The eyes are large and rounded; a rim of white shows between the iris and the lower eyelid. Outer ends of eyes slant upwards from the nose giving a dreamy yet penetrating appearance. These features indicate a creative talent and the ability to remain silent or speak at the right time also to meditate and reflect—withdraws within herself. Quick on the uptake, can size up situations and make use of opportunities. Not an easy person to understand.

7. *Nose*: Shows an inward curve from top to tip, is narrow across the bridge,

12.16 12.17 12.18

SUBJECT 3
Figs. 12.16, 12.17, 12.18. Full face, two lefts, two rights

widening towards the tip—changeable nature with a great zest for life, but enjoying ease.

Capable of clear thinking but being easily swayed by intuitions.

8. *Mouth and lips*: Medium top lip, full lower lip on a wide mouth; top lip shorter than lower on the right; line of closure made up of curves—a kindly, generous nature with strong affections. Animated, sociable. Aptitude for dramatic expression in singing, dancing, acting, etc.

9. *Chin*: Oval, average with firm contours—artistic, appreciation of colour, reliable, determined.

10. *Ears*: The top of her right ear is noticeably higher than her eyebrow level, showing her impetuous, excitable nature. Both ears are well-shaped, fine in texture and lie back close against the head—a sign of a sensitive person, able to appreciate music.

11. *Neck*: Wider on her right, more photogenic on her left.

161

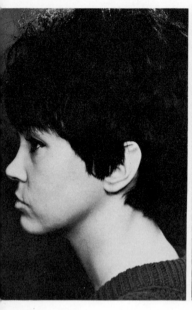 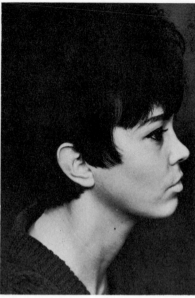

12.19 12.20

Figs. 12.19, 12.20. Profiles

12.21

Fig. 12.21. The right side emphasized against a dark background

162

Conclusion

The contours of her face are more attractive on her right side. The cheek and jaw bones are more clearly defined, the triangular shape of her face is distinctive. On the other hand there is a certain angularity about the features, and the expression is somewhat penetrating. There is a more "puckish" expression in the eyes on her left, and the oval face with more rounded contours, shows the more charming sociable side of her nature.

Here is a face and personality combined which is a joy to photograph. The positions and styles of arrangement and lighting are almost unlimited and you can use the softer or the more clear cut outlines to suit the mood of the picture. But, if you want a happy, smiling expression you have to capture it quickly— the moods change swiftly and her intense nature is shown in the moods.

The whole charm of the personality is behind the smile in the mouth and eyes, and this must be caught, or you will be left with a mask.

Likewise in the serious, triangular shaped side of her face, the intensity of the character can be shown with vitality and drama, or the introspective, withdrawn characteristics with an accompanying sullenness of mood.

The clear cut outline of the right side of her face can show well against a dark background. The oval chin and jaw line, and the softer contours of the cheek bone, together with the good line of the neck are seen to advantage in the turn of the head. The hair style, being drawn away from the eyes, to reveal the height and breadth of the forehead, adds distinction to a thoughtful, yet interested mood.

SUBJECT 4

1. *Shape of the head*: A mixture of long and square.
2. *Division into thirds*: Average.
3. *Face*: The left side of her face is wider and fuller than the right, and there appears to be more character revealed in her right side.
4. *Forehead*: Wider across the top, narrowing towards the temples. Measures one-third the length of the face, and having several horizontal wrinkles in the upper part, and two vertical (not so clearly marked) above the nose. An intellectual forehead, capable of working out problems but the position of the wrinkles denotes a tendency to worry and be over-anxious. An ability to concentrate.
5. *Eyebrows*: Wide and thick following the curve of the eyelid. A strong character with decided likes and dislikes. A practical person, with patience and perseverance over details.
6. *Eyes*: Colour—dark brown, affectionate and emotional. Deep set, narrow

163

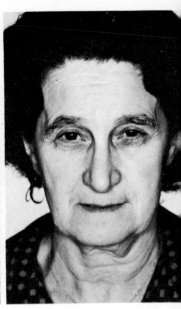

12.22 12.23 12.24

SUBJECT 3
Fig. 12.22. Outlining the longer left side of the face
Fig. 12.23. Different hair style reveals the height and breadth of forehead
SUBJECT 4
Fig. 23.24. Full face

___

eyes, pointed at both ends. The lids are drawn more closely together on her left, but this may be the effect of the light. The eyes show a person able to make her own judgements and keep her thoughts to herself when necessary. Her right eye is the more outward looking, and therefore the more indicative of a sociable nature.

7. *Nose*: A long straight nose, with a lump immediately before the tip. A wide ridge, which is wide all the way down on her left, but broadens towards the tip on her right. A well proportioned nose seen in profile. This denotes a generous person, with executive ability. She is deep thinking, quick but sound in her judgements, though sometimes swayed by intuition. She thinks more than she speaks.

8. *Mouth*: Medium thin lips on a fairly wide mouth, with the corners of the mouth turning up. Self-control is again borne out in the shape of her mouth, and the upward turn shows her happy, sociable disposition.

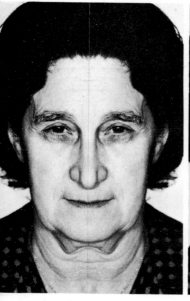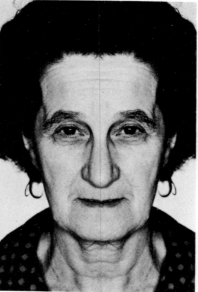

12.25 12.26 12.27

SUBJECT 4
Figs. 12.25, 12.26, 12.27. Two lefts, two rights, and profile

---

9. *Chin*: The chin, slightly projecting, is rounder in shape on her left, more square on her right. The easy-going nature depicted on her left, whereas the right shows more of the firm and decisive qualities.

10. *Neck*: Shorter and wider on her left, which makes the right side the more photogenic.

Character lines: Mention has already been made of the nervous tension in the forehead. Laughter lines are evident at the corners of the eyes on both sides of the face. The lines from the nose go with an averagely sociable person.

Conclusion

Her right side would appear to have both the better outline and the most positive character. A three-quarter face position, with the right side of her face nearest to the camera. Camera position slightly above eye-level, to concentrate attention on the eyes. The neck must be kept in shadow, or, if a characteristic

165

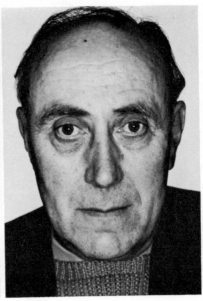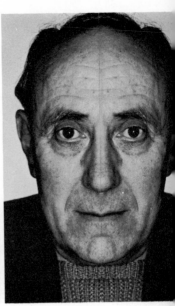

12.28 12.29 12.30

SUBJECT 4
Fig. 12.28. Shows the character in the right side of the face
SUBJECT 5
Fig. 12.29. Full face
Fig. 12.30. Two lefts

pose can be found with the hand up to the face, this can be used to hide the neck lines almost completely from the camera lens. A dark background and some back lighting will help to convey the serious decisive side to her nature as well as the more vivacious and sociable.

SUBJECT 5

1. *Shape of the head*: Mixture of long and oval.
2. *Division into thirds*: Average.
3. *Face*: The left side of his face is slightly shorter and thinner than his right, and shows the most character.
4. *Forehead*: High, wider on his right than his left, with a fullness in the top centre. This denotes an intellectual person with an ability to describe events or things in detail. An interpreter.
5. *Eyebrows*: Thick and dark, lying low over the eyes. Strength of character and the ability to analyse.

166

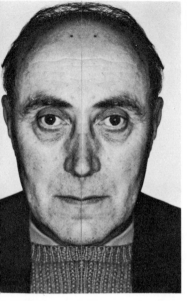

12.31 12.32 12.33

SUBJECT 5
Figs. 12.31, 12.32. Two rights, and profile
Fig. 12.33. The left side of the face showing the more positive characteristics

---

6. *Eyes*: Brown in colour—sympathetic, warm-hearted. Large round eyes—kindly, straightforward nature, interested in the arts. The lids show sign of mental strain or worry.

7. *Nose*: Seen in profile the nose has a bump in the outline just above the centre. On his left, the nose widens towards the tip, on his right it is thin down its entire length. Capable, ambitious, enthusiastic, courageous, energetic, are the adjectives attributable to his left side while the right side shows an acute mind but less broad in outlook.

8. *Mouth and lips*: Medium full lips on a wide mouth, upward trend to the corners, dip in the centre of the top lip. There is also a long space between the nose and the top lip. Firm self-control and a happy sociable disposition. He shows plenty of perseverance, is understanding and tactful.

9. *Chin*: A well-balanced chin, showing both artistic and scientific abilities.

10. *Ears*: Thin ears, well-shaped, lying back to the head. These show sound

167

sensitivity, and therefore the owner is possibly musical. The ear on his right slopes in towards his face showing that, with all his courage, he has his pessimistic moments!

11. *Neck*: Short and thicker on his left than his right.

12. *Lines and wrinkles*: The lines on his forehead show a mixture of logical thought and nervous strain. On his left the line denoting a good speaker is clearly visible.

Conclusion

This is a strong personality, with an analytical mind, and an ability to interpret, or to describe events in detail and is a good speaker. He is sociable, generous, kindly and artistic. The left side of his face shows these characteristics to the best advantage.

From a three-quarter face position, the left side of his face being nearest to the camera, a fairly low camera angle will emphasize the power and determination in his character, and, by lengthening the neck, will separate his head from his shoulders. A strong back lighting will illustrate his vitality and enthusiasm, and, if the eyes are directed towards the camera, it will better convey his desire to communicate. To overcome any apparent self-consciousness while being photographed, it would be good tactics to have soft music playing and encourage him to talk on some recent occurrence.

13 Psychological Approach to Portraiture

IN THE foregoing chapters we have been studying the techniques of lighting, of camera angle, of exposure and of composition. We have analysed a few of the different types of faces, and noted some of the characteristics depicted by the individual shape of the head, the features, and the predominant lines and wrinkles. There has been no great difficulty in understanding or in practising these exercises, because the lighting could be demonstrated on an inanimate head, and the character lines were discussed with the aid of photographs and diagrams, quite adequate means for describing the purely *physical* aspects of the subject.

We now come to the point where we must substitute a live person for the model head and think of them as something other than a diagram, and look beyond the interpretation of facial geography. We have a completely new dimension to deal with—human personality.

Personality is, perhaps, the most difficult part of portraiture to understand, but we will make a start by comparing two pictures taken under similar lighting conditions, one of the familiar model head and the other of a living person (Figs. 13.1 and 13.2).

INANIMATE HEAD AND A LIVE PERSON

We can see at a glance that an inanimate head can appear to have good modelling in the face, and some vitality in the features by the careful positioning of all the lights. In this model the eyes are represented by eye-lids only but if the eyes were present, they would be seen as a surface shape, and have no quality or

169

depth of feeling. The mouth is well modelled, but cannot express any emotion. It is the outward form only which is portrayed.

If a live person were to be photographed in a similar way, that is with no expression in the eyes, and in a completely static arrangement, the result could be a good record of the facial features, but could not be classed as a true character portrait.

CHARACTER THROUGH THE FEATURES

The two facial features which express the emotions, and through which we can get a glimpse of the individual personality, are the eyes and the mouth. As we have seen from previous illustrations there are many different types of eyes— e.g. deep-set eyes with the somewhat penetrating glance—sparkling, laughing eyes that seem to dance with the reflected lights—wide, affectionate eyes with emotional appeal. The eyes can speak a language all their own—the emotions of love, hate, joy, sorrow, interest, endeavour, boredom, can all be expressed in them. Emotions which have been felt deeply enough remain buried in the sub-conscious mind, a reflection of which can be seen in the expression in the eyes.

Mouths, too, can be varied in shape. They can be large or small, have full relaxed lips, or the thinner variety more often tensed with concentration. But whichever shape the mouth may be, it has no inner depth of character to be revealed, such as can be seen through the eyes. Although the mouth can move to order, it will not show emotion unless it has moved voluntarily to co-ordinate with the eyes.

All emotion is felt in a person's inner being, the reflection of which is expressed through the eyes. If the mouth is smiling while the eyes remain serious, the model is self-conscious and unnatural. If the eyes are dancing with merriment with the mouth remaining firmly closed, the model is trying to stifle his or her inward feelings and is again unnatural.

In Fig. 13.2 we can see the lack of co-ordination between eyes and mouth. The eyes are wide open showing vitality and interest, but are only acting the happy mood which the mouth has tried to convey. This is understandable when we realize that the photograph was taken among a series of exercises, but it serves its purpose to show what happens in a portrait when the model is not really feeling the emotion. This is where co-operation between model and photographer plays an important part, and we shall return to the subject at a later stage in this chapter.

170

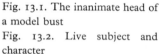

13.1 13.2

Fig. 13.1. The inanimate head of a model bust
Fig. 13.2. Live subject and character

CHARACTER THROUGH PERSONALITY

The model head, used for the demonstrations, is an inanimate object, and no amount of different lighting techniques or camera angles can make it anything else. It can neither feel nor reflect any emotions. Having no personality it can reveal no character traits. At best it can only reflect an image which has been created in the mind of the photographer, aided by various accessories.

The live person, on the other hand, is a very complex individual, and in order to make a true character portrait of him, or her, we must try to understand something about their psychological make up.

If you look back to Chapter 12 where the individual character revealed through the lines and wrinkles, etc., was discussed, you will realize that little mention has been made of the negative traits in any one character—yet there must be some. There must also be some lines in the face to denote their presence. This has been done intentionally. It is easier to learn to recognize only the positive traits and to be able to emphasize these, than it is to learn the complete sum, and then have to decide which to eliminate. (The question of elimination will crop up in a later chapter where retouching is discussed, but thinking about it at the studio stage is a hindrance rather than a help).

Unlike the inanimate head, which has been mass produced, every single

171

person who comes before our camera is unique, there is no one else exactly similar in the whole wide world. A wonderful thought! Yet within each person is a mixture of positive and negative character traits, which, in varying degrees, add up to one complete whole.

Each positive has its negative—such as courage—fear; generosity—selfishness; love—hate; kindness—cruelty; justice—unfairness; energy—laziness; pride—carelessness; happiness—sorrow, etc. The list is endless and so is the degree to which any one element is found in any one person's make-up. Experiences through life develop the personality, altering the balance between the positive and negative traits.

A just portrait should reveal as many positive characteristics as possible, and you must start looking for evidence of these as soon as you meet the model, and decide on the techniques which will show them to the best advantage.

CHARACTER THROUGH MANNERISMS

The inanimate head has no body or limbs, no hands, and no ability to move in any way.

The live person is more or less continually on the move. In fact he is probably known and remembered as much by his actions and mannerisms as he is by his facial features.

Even though you do not intend to photograph the full length figure, it is wise to notice every movement of the body and especially of the hands. This is an additional clue in reading character, and will help in posing the model naturally. It is good fun as well as being instructive, to sit in a café by the window and watch the passers-by. Watch how a person walks. Is it a jaunty walk with the head held high, or a slow casual amble with hands in pockets? Perhaps it is the nervous quick step or the impatient rush of someone always in a hurry. Some couples walk arm in arm, some (especially young lovers) hand in hand, some talk as they walk along, some remain silent. While still in the café look around at those sitting at the tables. Some have their elbows on the table allowing their faces to rest on their hands. Many perhaps have their elbows on the table but few will be adopting a similar position for the hands. Some have their faces resting on the whole palm of the hand, some on the back of the hand, in some cases only the finger tips touch the face. Some people have two hands to their face, some have the two elbows on the table and the two hands clasped together, or the fingers of one hand touching the palm of the other. There are some people

172

who do not sit forward at the table at all, but are inclined to lean back in the chair resting their hands in their laps. Watch the people who are smoking, how they hold the cigarette.

Make a mental note of the positions you think would be photogenic because it is not only a natural pose that is needed but one that will look pleasing in a photograph. An overlarge hand, distorted by its proximity to the camera lens, can detract from the character instead of add to it.

Returning to the studio you can now study all these movements on your live model. Note the way the person stands or sits. Is he or she, perhaps, more natural standing up? If so you can take a head and shoulder portrait with the model standing—provided the camera tripod will extend to a sufficient height. Does your man model stand with his arms folded, or with one hand in a pocket? Does the model stand with one elbow resting on the other hand, and the finger tips touching the face?—a favourable position, and photogenic too. Does the model gesticulate with the hands while talking? When sitting down, does the model sit well back into the chair, or on the edge and lean forward? Are both feet resting on the floor or does one leg cross the other? If a table is placed in front of the model what use is made of it? You will know what to look for after your time spent in the café!

While studying the hands and their most photogenic positions, it is as well to realize that the hands themselves—their shape and type—reveal a certain amount of character. Look around you, and what do you see?

PRACTICAL HAND

This is a thick-set, strong hand with rather thick fingers and a short broad thumb. The thumb is often double jointed and can be bent backwards. I have called it the practical hand because it belongs to one whose work involves the use of his hands. In course of time the hand has become firm, sometimes hard, but strong and dependable. The hand can grip well, and the owner gives a really firm handshake. This type of hand is seldom used for gesticulating during conversation, not being sufficiently pliable, but the inclusion of the hands in a portrait can add strength to the interpretation of character.

ARTISTIC HAND

The artistic hand is much more pliable. The hand itself can be of any size, but is usually long and thin. The fingers are long and tapering and bend easily at the top joints. All the fingers bend backwards, slightly, from the base, which gives the hand freedom of movement. This hand is often used in gesticulating, and, being very pliable, presents few problems to the photographer. The owner of such a hand is usually of a nervous disposition, highly emotional, is practical in the arts or crafts, but has little knowledge of mechanics.

SHORT SQUARE HAND

The short, square-looking hand, with the short fingers usually belongs to a person who loves to organize everything and everybody. This person is efficient, neat and orderly, and is intolerant of any who fall below these standards. The short hand is not quite so easy to arrange in photography, sometimes because of the shortness of the fingers, but often because the owner is self-conscious about the hands, terming them "dumpy" and unattractive.

SMALL HAND

Perhaps the easiest hand of all to photograph is the one which appears small in proportion to the rest of the person, and has beautifully shaped fingers, and a small, well-shaped thumb. The owner of this small hand may be an idealist, more imaginative than practical, but possibly nervous and self-conscious in the presence of other people. This nervousness is only superficial, and unlike the highly-strung person, he has an inward calm, and his features rarely lose the look of composure. This person will usually co-operate well with the photographer.

As you continue your study of hands you will find other types which seem to fit specific personalities. You will also find that a number of hands are a mixture of two or more types, which is really what you would expect, as character is a complex matter.

PSYCHOLOGICAL EFFECT OF CLOTHES

For several of the foregoing experiments the model head was adorned with a variety of hats and scarves or dressed in a blouse or sweater. Although the model is incapable of feeling any difference, she certainly looks different. She can be made to look attractive, sophisticated, young, old, intelligent, athletic, etc. just by being dressed in suitable clothes. She sometimes looks almost human! (Figs. 13.3–13.8).

Her appearance is different when seen in dark or light coloured clothes, in

174

13.3 13.4 13.5
13.6 13.7 13.8
Figs. 13.3, 13.4, 13.5, 13.6, 13.7, 13.8. Even the facial appearance of a model bust can be altered with clothes

close-fitting or wide-brimmed hats, and with black or blonde hair. Through these accessories, a character is being imposed on the model at the whim of the photographer.

A similar thing can happen with a live person. A model can be dressed in any clothes to depict a certain type of character, which, is, of course, what happens in the theatre. But normally the clothes worn befit the person. People are made to look more attractive, more sophisticated, younger, older, more intelligent or more athletic, etc., according to the type of clothes they wear, in the same way that the model head does. The difference between the two is that the model head does not *feel* any different, but the live person does. Clothes have a great bearing on feelings of self-consciousness, of inferiority or of superiority. Clothes can make one *feel* younger or older, stiff or free, old-fashioned or modern, attractive or just plain, formal or informal. Even the neck-line to the dress or sweater can make a difference. Ask any woman what she feels about it and in every case she will have a preference.

One may say she prefers the high neck line as it gives her poise and self-confidence. Another might feel more attractive in a round one, with, perhaps, a collar or scarf. Others still, favour a V neck as it makes for a slimmer outline. The type of garment, too, makes a difference, whether it be formal or informal. One person will be self-conscious and very difficult to photograph when wearing, say, a dress, but, having changed into slacks and a sweater, immediately becomes natural and readily co-operative with the photographer.

Although by no means all models feel self-conscious, even with a completely natural person it is advisable where possible to portray him or her wearing a variety of clothes. It is not only the question of whether or not a certain garment suits the wearer best, or that it is more photogenic, but that it reveals another side to the character. If a man changes from his city suit to an open neck shirt or polo neck sweater, he is sure to show, automatically, different aspects of himself.

Although a photographer can guide a model as to the suitability of a certain style of dress—the colour and the texture of the material, and whether it is patterned or plain, the essential point is what effect the particular garment has on the model. It is the right one if the model feels happy and self-confident wearing it—it is the wrong one if it has the opposite effect. However photogenic the garment itself might be, you are not interested, at the moment, in fashion pictures, but in a character portrait in which the person inside the clothes matters more than the clothes themselves.

Before passing on to something more interesting than clothes, we must give

176

a thought to hats. From the illustrations of the model's head it can be seen that a hat does add a distinctive quality to a suggested characteristic. A hat can lend elegance, dignity and charm to its wearer. It also has an effect on the personality, especially of a woman. It has been said that if a woman feels depressed she should go out and buy herself a hat—it can boost the ego.

Hats, then should not be neglected as an accessory for the portrayal of character. Also, a hat, as well as making a plain person look distinctive, can turn a somewhat ordinary picture into one that is quite exciting and has greater impact than normal.

Now let us turn our attention from the clothes which are on the outside of the person, to the self which is on the inside.

There are a great number of adjectives pertaining to the word "self", but the one that is most often used in connection with photography is "conscious".

SELF-CONSCIOUSNESS

It is the fear of feeling self-conscious in front of a camera that prevents a number of people from ever being photographed. The appearance of any suggestion of self-consciousness in a picture can ruin its vitality and appeal. The word "self-conscious" really means to be aware of oneself. One can be fully aware of oneself, one can act, make a speech, sing or "impersonate" in front of a mirror, being fully aware of every movement, and yet be perfectly natural *providing one is by oneself*. The moment we are observed in our actions we become nervous through fear—the fear of being ridiculed, the fear of destructive criticism, the fear of insecurity, the fear that one's self-command is lost. This is what self-consciousness has come to mean, the awareness of oneself coupled with the fear of being observed by others. In the studio there can be a twofold self-consciousness, the model on the one hand and the photographer on the other; because the photographer can be almost as self-conscious as the model.

There is no harm in both the photographer and the model being aware of themselves, aware of what they are doing and saying, provided there is the harmony between them which makes each one feel as natural as if they were alone and unobserved. This harmony is the essential ingredient for success—the "something" which exists between model and photographer; moreover, this is a link which, once formed, must not be broken throughout the whole session.

It is the creating and the maintaining of this "something" that needs such careful handling in the studio.

The more sensitive a model is the more he or she will suffer from nervous self-consciousness and it is this very sensitivity which, rightly used, is at the very heart of our pictures.

Lack of sensitivity in the photographer can have the opposite effect to what he intends. The model's personality, instead of being drawn out, can be withdrawn until little more than a mask remains and the features may appear completely unnatural.

PSYCHOLOGY APPLIED IN THE STUDIO

Let us imagine you are about to photograph a female subject you have never seen before. You have to make all your initial observations without the model being aware of any scrutiny whatsoever. To enable you to do this you will have a short time prior to the studio session just sitting down talking with your subject to become acquainted. A cup of tea or coffee with a cigarette will help both of you to relax. The conversation can be turned gradually towards subjects which are of interest to the model—holidays, hobbies, achievements, children, etc. You must appear to be relaxed, but all the time be really on the alert—taking part in the conversation, but simultaneously making mental notes of the model's mannerisms and as many character traits as possible. If you have put enough time into the studying of people's behaviour and deciding on photogenic positions, then it should not be long before you have visualized a few positions, at least enough to make a start in the studio.

If the studio looks attractive the model may even remark on it. Always try to make the studio a cheerful, comfortable room, not like the dentist's surgery which so many people seem to expect! Put flowers on the table, several pictures round the walls, and have a record or tape playing a selection of musical pieces very quietly.

Ask the model to select the type of chair or stool she prefers to use for the first picture. As she tries several of them note the effect produced as this will be found handy later on. As you already have an arrangement in mind you can suggest the position and arrange the lights quickly and confidently. As the pose is a natural one, the model will probably adopt it easily, but if she is unable to do so the idea can be demonstrated. She can then try again. If it should still be unsuccessful, either pretend to make an exposure, or drop the idea until later. Anything which has taken too long to arrange will look stilted and artificial.

Never be tempted to touch the model, by moving the hand or fingers to suit your requirements. If you do not know your model sufficiently she may be someone who objects strongly to being touched, and, if so, your link would be

178

broken right at the beginning of the session. So, it is better to play safe. Also the model must never get the idea that she is awkward and cannot do exactly what is needed. Rather you must encourage her to think that she is an excellent model and is being very co-operative. This will give her confidence in herself. Flattery is cheap and should never be indulged in, but sincere encouragement, and praise where applicable, will always boost the ego, and prevent nervousness.

Consider the model's comfort at all times. The studio must be warm in winter and cool in summer. The lights must be switched off occasionally to prevent everyone from becoming overheated. The glare of the light must be kept off the model's eyes, either by diffusing the lamp or by reducing its power. Do not keep the model in a fixed position for too long or she will become stiff and self-conscious. For this reason it is always good to give her a moment's relaxation before making the exposure, unless, of course, it is a spontaneous position or expression which you must lose no time in capturing—such as a genuine smile with the twinkle in the eyes. It is almost impossible to immediately repeat a happy smile—saying "cheese" may produce a beautiful "grin" but, at best, will be purely superficial.

During a short break the model can change her clothes. You re-arrange the studio, alter the background, make any necessary alterations to the lighting equipment, and be ready to welcome her back for another series. A refreshing drink before she starts again will not be amiss. You can now compliment her on the colour, style, etc. of her dress, and indicate that her new appearance has given you fresh inspiration. You should, by this time, show real enthusiasm about everything you are doing, and enthusiasm is catching! Once the model reaches this stage in co-operation, there is no self-consciousness left, and model and photographer can work on in complete harmony.

Perhaps you will say that all this sounds too simple, and that we have been discussing an ideal subject. Also that there must be a number of people who would react very differently from the same treatment.

I agree with this to a point. There are many differences in people, and we cannot treat any two in exactly the same way and get a similar response. Our demonstration model was nervous at the beginning of the session, but this very soon wore off and she enjoyed being photographed. This is the essential goal, the ingredient for successful co-operation. You meet many people who are self-confident, happy and relaxed at the very beginning of a session, but others may take a long time to reach that stage. We tend to think of self-consciousness as being something which makes a person nervous—somewhat shy and timid. But this is not always the case. It can do the opposite, and make the sufferer arrogant, boastful, domineering and brusque. Self-consciousness can make a quiet person talkative, a serious-minded person jocular, a kind hearted person appear hard and thoughtless, an intelligent person appear morose and dull, and even a public speaker can be made to lose normal composure.

In all these more difficult cases, the preliminary treatment is the same as before, i.e. a time for relaxation, refreshment and conversation, is allowed before the sitting commences. This custom is dispensed with only when circumstances demand that the sitter has little available time, all of which must be spent in the studio.

In spite of all our efforts to relax the tension, we may sometimes have to commence work in the studio before the barrier of self-consciousness has been broken down. If this should happen we may be thankful that we have had the forethought to ask our subject to bring with him something in which he is interested. This could be something pertaining to his career or hobbies, such as a guitar or other musical instrument. An artist for example could bring some of his paintings—these would be both a subject for conversation and for inclusion in the picture. An animal lover could bring a dog or even a cat!

The wearing of a uniform or dress relating to the model's normal occupation will assist in giving greater self-confidence, particularly if any rank or qualifications are denoted.

With the aid of various accessories, but chiefly with the confidence, understanding and enthusiasm of the photographer, tension will be relaxed and creative co-operation begin to take over.

There is a danger that the self-conscious negative atmosphere emanating from the model will influence the photographer too. This can easily happen when the photographer does not feel sufficiently confident to deal with the situation.

Here lies the difference between portraiture and any other branch of photography. Portraiture is a two-way interchange between two complex personalities, it is one of the great arts that deals with the unseen as well as the seen. There is an intimacy between two souls, a sometimes silent communication, which is sacred between the two concerned. Portraiture can be likened to the medical profession in this respect, that the photographer is often entrusted with intimacies which he cannot reveal to any other person, but which may sometimes be revealed through the portrait and find an echo in the heart of a viewer. Portraiture is a very personal subject. A portrait can often be liked or disliked according to the effect the subject has on the critic, especially if that subject is unknown. On the other hand, if the subject is well-known, the feelings of like or dislike of the personality, can be the deciding factor.

The same two-way communication operates in the studio. A careful balance must be maintained all the time—in fact we naturally return time and again to the word co-operation. Any successful portrait is the outcome of complete co-operation between model and photographer.

The more books a photographer can read on psychology, and kindred subjects, the better will he understand the complexities of human nature. In other branches of photography, such as architecture and landscape, this understanding of the subject is covered by the word "love". To love your subject you must understand it, and, vice-versa the thorough understanding of it leads to love.

The portrait photographer must have more than just a liking for people—he must learn to love them. The rather narrow definition seems to be placed on the word love when applied to people, but if I turn the word "love" up in my dictionary I find such descriptions as "an affection of the mind caused by that which delights; pre-eminent kindness; reverential regard". These definitions can surely apply to the subject of our photography—we aim to produce a portrait which delights. We strive in all our dealings with the model to show pre-eminent kindness, and we certainly must have a reverential regard for the creation of the wonderfully complex yet whole personality of our subject.

14 Low Power Lighting Techniques

IN EARLIER chapters, when we were studying the basic positions of the light to obtain certain modelling of the features, we were using lamps of 500 W. There are occasions, however, when these lamps will be found too powerful for the conditions under which we are operating, and also times when, for special effects, much less light is needed.

In this chapter then, we will discard all lamps of high power, and use only those of 100, 150, or at the most 200 W. One distinct advantage is that these lamps are easily obtainable. They are ordinary household bulbs. It is advisable, if possible, to use these lamps with the proper reflectors and telescopic stands, but makeshift lights such as ordinary office desk lamps can be utilized provided they can be held or fixed at the correct angle, and that a cone-shaped paper reflector is made to replace the shade.

WORKING CONDITIONS

Let us first consider the conditions under which we are operating, when the low power lamp has a definite advantage over that of the high power.

1. *Working in a confined space*

A common fault among amateurs practising portraiture at home is the use of too bright a light in a small room. The lamps have to be placed fairly close to the model, with the disastrous result that skin tones are "burnt-out". A simple remedy is to exchange the lamps for others of lower power. This does not necessarily mean an increase of exposure time over that required for the higher powered lamps at a reasonable distance. Applying the inverse square law the effective power of the light diminishes as the square of the distance, so that a lower powered lamp placed closer to the model will have similar actinic value to the higher powered one at a greater distance. Hence the general rule should be that the smaller the room space, the lower should be the power of the light used.

2. *Lamp stand of insufficient height*

In order to obtain lower contrast in modelling the features the light has to be moved away from the model, and, simultaneously, raised to a greater height. Frequently, the light cannot be raised sufficiently owing to either (1) the limitations of the stand or (2) lack of height in the room. The changeover to a lamp of lower power will enable the light stand to be moved closer to the model, yet preserve the modelling without excessive contrast between highlight and shadow areas.

3. *Models suffering from weak eyesight*

In the course of our study with various types of people, we are sure to come across someone with poor eyesight, who is incapable of facing a bright light without the eyes watering and becoming sore and inflamed. A diffuser placed over the reflector helps to minimize the glare, but it is very much better to change the bulb for one of lower power. If necessary the diffuser can be used as well. It is possible, of course, to use the higher powered lamps and bounce the light off white reflectors. In this way no direct light will shine on the model, but the lighting technique becomes very restricted, and often results in lack of modelling in the features.

4. *Portraying the older woman*

The lighting of an older face engraved with a network of lines and wrinkles, presents certain problems. The high powered lamps with frontal lighting will iron out the wrinkles but, at the same time will flatten the modelling. If used to one side, the lines and wrinkles become emphasized and the skin appears coarse. There are times when this technique may be advantageous, especially in a male portrait, but it is unsuitable if we want to portray the face with full modelling, maintaining all the character lines, but softened, so that although no essential line is omitted, the lines themselves are unobtrusive. Placing a diffuser over the bright lights will soften all the lines, but in so doing the light is spread from

183

the highlights into the shadows, at the expense of some of the vitality in the final print. The surest way to maintain the full quality of the light in the highlight areas, while avoiding the deep black shadows, is to switch over to lamps of lower power. They give a clearer, cleaner and brighter result than that obtained by diffusing a more brilliant light. If the model's temperament will allow a moderately long exposure, the low power lighting will give even greater detail in both the highlight and shadow areas.

5. *Lighting the hair in a confined space*

It often happens that the light used for the hair is too powerful when positioned close to the model, resulting in highlight areas being too dense on the negative to allow good enough tonal quality in the print. The highlight tones, instead of remaining separated, are forced to merge with overexposure. A lower powered lamp would overcome this difficulty.

6. *The effect of light on some temperaments*

We soon find when we start taking portraits of different types of people, that not all of them react to light in the same way. There are some, of course, including the trained model, who react successfully under any lighting conditions. There are some who appear to become even more alive and free under the influence of strong artificial light than under normal lighting conditions, but others react quite differently—people who are more reserved and not used to being in the limelight, will often become self-conscious and awkward as soon as the powerful lights are switched on. For this latter group, low powered lighting will often lead to success.

LOW LIGHT TECHNIQUE

Naturally, if low powered lighting is used at the same distance as photofloods the exposure times will have to be drastically increased. But we have already seen in practice this is not always necessary. If the portrait is taken in a small room with light walls the exposure may still be very brief. But, supposing our aim is to give a very much longer exposure in order to get *greater depth of character* then lights of low power become essential.

Long exposures are an important part of this particular technique, and worthy of consideration. The theory of this long exposure technique is based on the fact that we are photographing a live human being and not a still-life subject.

This human being is very complex in character, a limited amount of which is shown on the surface. A photographer can capture an instantaneous expression, however brief its duration, by using electronic flash; but, with the brevity of the exposure of approximately only 1/800 sec., the expression can easily appear frozen, and the skin texture rendered as a hard surface. The outward features are clearly presented, but the inner personality of the model remains hidden.

The human brain is continually at work, the heart is pumping the blood to all parts of the body all the time—life is going on—thoughts are going on. It seems reasonable to suppose that the longer the exposure time the more of the personality will be captured, and the more lifelike will be the resulting picture. It is a well known fact, in other branches of photography, that a really long exposure in dim light will reveal details in the shadow areas which are scarcely visible to the human eye. You must have heard the story of the photographer with the half-plate stand camera, and the slow speed film, who set up the camera in a dimly lit church, focused the picture on the ground glass, set the lens aperture at approximately $f\,64$, inserted the film, opened the shutter and left the church locking the door behind him. After a good lunch and a stroll around the town he returned to the church, closed the shutter and replaced the sheath in the plate holder. The resulting picture showed perfect detail in every part, in fact more than could possibly be determined with the naked eye. This may be a slight exaggeration but the principle remains, and if it works for architecture it will work for portraiture, as the two subjects are very much akin.

The main difference between the two as far as the photographer is concerned is the question of movement. However long the camera shutter remains open in the case of architecture, there will not be any movement on the part of the subject. But this cannot be said of portraiture. There is a definite limit to the time during which a person can remain sufficiently still and keep natural and relaxed. For any exposure time over one second there will always be a scarcely perceptible movement due to the natural pulsating of the heart and the rise and fall of the chest in the act of breathing. This very slight movement during an exposure time of say eight seconds is an asset: it results in a realistic effect of soft skin as opposed to the hardness of solid stone.

The character lines in the face have softened edges which make them appear more natural, but the most remarkable thing is the depth of character revealed in the eyes. There is a quality about the eyes which gives one the impression that real thought is going on behind them. This living quality, in which we really see the eyes as "the windows of the soul" cannot be so readily obtained by any other means.

14.1 14.2 14.3

Fig. 14.1. Normal lighting and exposure
Fig. 14.2. Low power light and long exposure
Fig. 14.3. Exposure 4 sec. $f8$ 12 in. Cooke Portrait Lens ¼ plt. medium speed film

You cannot visualize this? Maybe you would like to see a comparison, so we will photograph the same model, using the brief exposure first, followed by the long exposure, without altering the pose, or the lighting effect. Naturally the power of the lamps, and the distance at which they are placed, will have to be changed to allow for a correctly exposed negative with a time of 8 sec. It is as well to stress here that "long exposure" does not mean overexposure. The lights must be controlled to make 6 or 8 sec. the "correct" exposure for the subject (Figs. 14.1 and 14.2).

The 500 W bulbs used for 14.1, are replaced by 100 W for 14.2, and moved to the required distance to allow for an exposure time of 8 sec. Both pictures are on the same roll of film, and therefore development time for each is identical.

We will select for our model someone who is of a fairly serious disposition, and who will therefore be able to sit still naturally. The long exposure technique is one which can only be used with certain type of people—it would be of no

186

use with children, or with any highly-strung individual whose varied expressions flit across the features so rapidly that only the briefest exposure will capture the characteristic personality.

In both cases the model is to be relaxed, comfortable, and seated in a completely natural position. It is unfair to expect anyone to sit still for any length of time if any muscles are being tensed, or if the pose is not one which they are in the habit of adopting. The model will be asked to blink the eyes quite naturally during the long exposure. This will ensure that the expression in the eyes does not become fixed and staring. If the model were to blink during an instantaneous exposure the resulting picture would show the eyes closed, but several blinks during an exposure of 8 sec. are still too brief to register, and are definitely an aid to obtaining a more natural appearance.

To make a fair comparison we will ask the model, in both cases, to co-operate with us by concentrating their thoughts on a particular subject during the exposure. This is because the human brain is incapable of thinking about two things at the same time, and, if the thoughts are elsewhere than on the camera, there is less chance of a self-conscious expression.

COMPARING FIGURES

Fig. 14.2. There is a greater feeling of serenity about this picture due to the softening of all edges, both of the contours of the face and features, and of shadows. The highlights are well separated in their tones and merge quietly into the shadow tones instead of jumping from light to dark, which is inclined to happen in Fig. 14.1. The eyes have greater depth, better colour rendering, and appear to have more thought behind them. There is an inward aliveness which is not visible in Fig. 14.1. This is an emotion which is so often missing in an otherwise technically perfect portrait, mainly because the eyes themselves are underexposed—especially if they are brown in colour. As it is mainly through the depth of expression in the eyes that we can contact the personality in the picture, it is important that in a serious study especially, we use any technique possible to prevent the eyes from becoming blank and expressionless.

Another noticeable difference is the amount of detail visible in the dark areas.

SOFT FOCUS

We have already seen that a long exposure results in a more realistic effect of soft skin texture, due to almost imperceptible movement. This soft focus effect

187

14.4 14.5 14.6

Fig. 14.4. A very long exposure need not show subject movement

Fig. 14.5. Low power lighting and a long exposure. Exposure 8 sec. ƒ16

Fig. 14.6. Serenity is observed with long exposures

itself can be used as another technique for portraying character. It shows a sensitivity which is lacking when everything is in sharp focus. It displays the tender emotions, and gentle, affectionate characteristics, and gives an added flexibility to the features.

This is well illustrated in Fig. 14.3.

The soft focus effect in this portrait of a rather shy girl has given it a quality and charm which would have been lacking had it been produced with critical definition. Clear cut edges to the shadows would have displayed the more sophisticated characteristics rather than the tender emotions. Here the soft contours of the lips give the mouth an appearance of reality—of the ability to move, to speak, to smile. The eyes have a quiet depth which can hold our interest, and through which we can contact the sensitivity of the girl's inward self.

The soft focus effect is emphasized by the very slight movement of the model during the exposure. However, it is important to realize that a long exposure does not necessitate movement to any noticeable extent. A model can sit still for a much longer exposure than the 4 sec. given to Kathryn. There is no sign of movement in Fig. 14.4 although the exposure in this case is 8 sec. This portrait, taken in a library with little available space, is lit by two 100 W household bulbs.

These are placed some distance from the model owing to the proximity of the books enforcing the use of a wide lens aperture.

It is interesting to note the depth of thought behind the eyes, the soft, pliable, rendering of the skin tones, the amount of tone in the forehead, the detail in the clothes and the subdued tonal reproduction of the books.

TONE IN THE FOREHEAD

A man's bald head, or a forehead with receding hair, is often overlit, thereby losing some of the character in the person. Low power lighting and long exposure is a sure way of overcoming this difficulty. This can be seen in Fig. 14.5. The character lines in the forehead are clearly seen, the eyes have thought behind them, the mouth is relaxed but firm, and there is good skin rendering in the hands. The lighting is by two 100 W household bulbs. The exposure time is 8 sec., and, again, there is no sign of any movement. The model, seated at a table to give support to the body, has adopted his own natural position. This is important. No one can sit still and look natural unless he is in a natural pose. Deep inward serenity and kindly thought are two characteristics which add charm to this picture of a well loved personality.

THE MODEL'S THOUGHTS

We have agreed that longer exposure time, coupled with low power light, softens all contrasts, harmonizes all tones and gives greater depth of character to the eyes. You may wonder why the character in the eyes is not lost in a self-conscious expression, resulting from the model staring fixedly at the camera for as long as 8 sec.

The apparent naturalness is due partly to the normal blink of the eye-lids, which we have already seen is permissible, but mainly to diverting the model's thoughts to any subject other than the camera. As I said, the human brain cannot concentrate on two things at the same time, so, if the model is thinking of something which is of real personal interest he need not be aware of the

189

photographer, or the camera, or even of the time of exposure itself. This is where the co-operation between model and photographer becomes so essential. It requires an effort of mind and will to turn one's thoughts elsewhere than on the camera when one is sitting looking straight into the lens. But it can be done, and it is one of the secrets of success of the long exposure technique.

In my opinion there are times when the wisdom and serenity within a personality cannot be captured by any means other than with a long exposure. Such is the case with the Rev. Sydney Sharpe (Fig. 14.6), a kindly, humorous personality, with a keen logical mind.

The portraits are taken at home, by daylight, using one 500 W flood as an effect light. The normal lighting techniques deal adequately with most of his characteristic expressions and emotions, but are unsuitable to capture that inward peace which pervades his whole being and which makes him the trusted and loved man he is. The long exposure with concentration on something other than the camera is the technique required. This subject's mind, full of many varied experiences, easily allows him to concentrate on one particular encounter for as long as may be required—but the lighting creates a problem. The confined space, white walls, daylight and the 500 W flood make lengthy exposures very difficult. By diffusing the light and stopping the lens down to f 16, an exposure of 8 sec. is possible.

Before leaving the subject of long exposures for portraying the quieter emotions we will compare two pictures of the same model—one in a gay mood, the other thoughtful.

The happy mood (Fig. 14.7) is expressed by the diagonal arrangement of the body with the eyes on the opposing diagonal, by the lighting effect and by the expression. The high powered spotlights and floods allow an instantaneous exposure which captures the smile and twinkle in the eyes.

In Fig. 14.8 the power of all the lights is considerably reduced, giving a much softer rendering of all shadows, and allowing for a longer exposure time to record more of the hidden characteristics of the model.

If, during the same sitting, we need to vary the power of all the lights in use, we shall find it impracticable to keep changing the various bulbs. A new piece of equipment has recently come on the market which is invaluable for controlling the power of light. But a rheostat or variable resistance placed in the circuit such as a Varilux electronic control unit can stand beside the camera. Any light which is plugged into it can have its power varied at will by merely turning a knob. The light can be used at full power if necessary, dimmed very slightly or dimmed considerably with continual adjustments possible through all the stages

190

14.7 14.8 14.9

Fig. 14.7. Happy mood conveyed with composition of opposing diagonals and strong lighting
Fig. 14.8. Lower powered light bulbs and 6 sec. exposure for a more serious mood
Fig. 14.9. Exposure: × 16 off white card

in between. This ensures the correct balance of light, quickly and easily, without moving the lights.

If the spotlight, which is being used for the effect light on the hair, is attached to the Varilux, the light can be dimmed sufficiently to show brilliance with detail for every shade of hair—blonde, brunette, auburn or black—without having to diffuse the light or alter its position.

With a rheostat control unit it is possible to change from one technique of lighting to another within seconds. This allows the photographer a greater freedom of choice in the technique he considers best suited to the character traits he is trying to portray.

PHOTOGRAPHING COLOURED PEOPLE

The ability to reduce the power of the light to any visual effect is of great benefit when photographing coloured people, especially those with very dark brown or

191

Fig. 14.10. Exposure: ×32 off white card

Fig. 14.11. Lengthened exposure times with coloured subject improves quality in highlights and shadows. Exposure: ×64 off white card

black skins. The attractive soft, velvety appearance of the black skin is completely lost with the harsh contrasts of high powered lights. The moment that any light is thrown on a black face extreme tonal contrast is created. We have already seen that low power light reduces contrast, so, where possible, the low power light and long exposure technique will give the most pleasing results.

The arrangement of the lights, as well as their power is different from that used when photographing white-skinned people. With the latter, the primary light is of stronger power than the secondary. For black skins the primary light is reduced in power while the secondary remains brighter. Excessive contrast is reduced but modelling retained (Figs. 14.9, 14.10, 14.11).

Comparing the above illustrations it will be seen that the quality of both highlights and shadows is improved, the separation of tones is increased, and the apparent vitality of the subject is more obvious as the exposure time is lengthened. Without the ability to decrease the power of the individual light used for the primary, we should find the highlights burnt out with overexposure. By maintaining the full power of light for the shadow area while decreasing the power for the highlights, we are able to expose fully for the shadows. Thus we can increase the effect of modelling and reveal the true skin texture without altering the position of the lights.

15 Mental Impressions
as Artist's Sketches

ALTHOUGH inward emotions are visible in the expression on the face and in the eyes, people are sensitive to criticism and would become embarrassed by the searching glance of a photographer.

TRAINING OURSELVES TO SEE

How, then, can we study the face in front of the camera without the knowledge of the person concerned?

This is something we have to train ourselves to do. It takes time, and a lot of thought, but gradually our powers of perception become stronger until we find ourselves able to see a person's face with greater clarity of understanding, and also to recognize various mannerisms and attitudes of behaviour which give a clue to certain character traits.

This initial study takes place, not in the studio, but out in the world, among ordinary men and women going about their daily business. On the train, in a café, at the seaside—in fact wherever you can sit and watch people—you can select and perceive them without being observed. Take a notebook and write down everything you can about their characteristics, and finally think out the best way of making a photographic portrait of them. This may sound a waste of time, as the chances of your ever being able to photograph that particular person are extremely remote.

On the contrary, you will find that, after several months of conscientiously examining and writing about different faces, it will become progressively easier to do, and gradually you will find yourself getting a new insight into people—a new interest in the exciting variety of types, and a deeper realization that each person requires different treatment in the studio.

As long as we use people as pieces of still life, our portraits will be dull and uninspiring. People are not dull. They are full of many surprises, even a very plain face can be transformed into one of beauty by a happy expression! What a tremendous difference clothes, surroundings and atmosphere can make on each individual's character! Take you, yourself, for example. Are you exactly the same type of person always—every day—every hour and sometimes even every minute? Of course you aren't. We are all continually changing as our thoughts change, these changes being shown in our expressions and actions. Basically, our characteristic traits remain the same, and are revealed in various ways to the observant onlooker. The way we walk, dress, sit, speak, etc., can all categorize us as certain types. If portrait photographers would make greater use of the ever increasing number of techniques at their disposal to picture more of the exciting diversities in the character traits of the men and women in front of their camera, the phrase "stereotyped conventional portraiture" would cease to be so current.

Now let us look at a selection of people, noting all we can about them, and finally suggesting at least one way in which to photograph them if they ever chanced to appear before our camera.

We can only take quick glances towards our target in order to avoid embarrassment.

CASE I: MIDDLE-AGED LADY

Suppose, to begin with, there is a lady sitting opposite us in the train—a subject for a distinctive portrait.

Description

A middle-aged lady, wearing a striking "above the knee" length dress. Her fair (may be bleached) hair, swept back and up off the face is dressed in an immaculate style, and long earrings are dangling from pierced ears. The texture of the skin appears somewhat hard, matching the expression in the eyes. Her movements are quick and jerky. The natural tilt of the head seems to be slightly backward with the chin up and the eyes looking straight ahead or in a downward direction. As she has no one to talk to we cannot see the change of expression brought about by contact with another personality.

194

Facial characteristics

A long, thin face terminates in a square jaw. The forehead is high, the nose long and well shaped. The rather large ears are pointed at the top and the bottom, with the top of the ear well above the eyebrow line. The somewhat small, oval-shaped eyes are light hazel in colour, the cheeks slightly sunken, and the small, firm mouth has the top lip dipped in the centre and protruding slightly over the lower one. Dividing the face into thirds we find that A : B is the widest area, while B : C and C : D become progressively narrower (Fig. 9.1).

Suggested treatment

First let us consider the effects of the possible techniques.

Camera angle. A high viewpoint would be unsuitable in this case because of the hair style and the high forehead. Also the tendency of this angle to portray quiet, demure, characteristics would not fit this lady's personality. A level viewpoint could be used with a profile position of the face. A low viewpoint would emphasize the determined, forceful, positive characteristics of the square jaw. From a full face position, however, the low camera angle would exaggerate the shape of the jaw which would then overrule the character. Our choice of position for the face, therefore, must be a three-quarter view.

Our choice for the modelling light would be a spotlight in preference to a flood in order to give the crispness and vitality required. Its position for the three-quarter face being 45° to the rear. For a face in profile a strong rim lighting could be used. The eyes turned toward the camera results in a more personal portrait than would otherwise be the case. Even in a three-quarter face position the eyes can be turned towards the lens.

To sum up

This face would probably be seen in its best aspect from a three-quarter position, the camera being fairly low, and a spotlight used for modelling from a 25° or 45° angle. The brightness ratio would be 1 : 4 or even 1 : 6, and for effect lights, one on the hair close enough to give correct colour rendering only, and one used diagonally across the dress to render the texture and colour of the material. The eyes turning in the direction of the lens and a serious expression would admirably portray the slightly haughty, critical, determined, direct and positive characteristics.

A dark background would be most suitable.

This picture could be a starting point from which other suggestions would reveal themselves as the lady relaxed and conversed with you, the photographer.

195

CASE II: YOUNG LADY

Description

Now look across to the young lady on our right. At a guess she is in her thirties. An attractive woman, not slim, with an oval, well proportioned and well modelled face, framed by thick, short greying-brown hair. Her almond shaped eyes, hazel in colour, are very expressive. They twinkle when she smiles, have a natural dewy, kindly expression, and show a loving tenderness when she glances across at her husband. Her nose is fairly long with a bump in the bone structure. Her mouth is large, with well formed lips, and her flashing smile is really arresting.

The left side of her face is longer than the right, and she has a long, nicely rounded, neck. Her skin has a soft, peachy look, the make-up on her face has been carefully applied and her eyebrows well shaped.

Suitable techniques

Camera angle. A low camera angle would *not* be suitable in this case, partly because of the already long neck and large mouth, and partly because she is not a domineering, forceful type of person, nor does she need to be given any extra self-confidence or power.

The camera used from a position slightly higher than her eye level would be most appropriate, thus increasing the forehead space, and concentrating the attention on her expressive eyes.

Position. A full or three-quarter face position would be our choice. Do you notice that she has a natural tilt of the head to her left? This is important, and we must remember to sit her with the right side of her face nearest to the camera, so that, for a full face position, she can turn her head to the camera using her natural tilt—the other way would be unnatural and therefore slightly stiff.

Lighting technique

Modelling light. This should be a floodlight—at a reasonable distance, or diffused, in order to retain the softness of the skin texture. A brightness ratio of 1 : 4 or 1 : 6, to give the strength in the tonal quality which will help to portray the depth of character as well as the strong physique. The spot effect lights from behind the model can give the brightness and gaiety needed for a happy personality.

Background. Dark, so that the effect lights will show against it.

CASE III: YOUNG LADY

A third type of person, and this one very different from either of the other two. A young woman, age about 25, and on the plump side. Her short, straight, rather unruly hair, thin and straggly, frames a roundish face; spectacles are worn on a short pointed nose. The other features include fair eyebrows, a small mouth with the top thick lip protruding slightly over the lower thin one; a double chin and a short neck. (The division into thirds gives the space between the nose and chin as the largest). This lady has a cheerful expression, and is wearing no make-up. She appears to be a frank, open, happy personality.

Difficulties to overcome are short neck, double chin, glasses.

Points to emphasize are the happy candour of her expression.

Techniques

Camera angle. A too high viewpoint cannot be used because the top rim of the spectacles will throw the eyes into shadow. Otherwise we would choose a fairly high viewpoint to lengthen the nose and give increased width to the forehead. A level viewpoint would be unsuitable for head and shoulders because the already wide area between the nose and chin would appear distorted. The solution would be to get the camera further away—in other words take a three-quarter length portrait, using the camera from a height level with, or slightly below, the level of the model's eyes, or alternatively use a longer focal length lens. A low viewpoint could be used with discretion for a three-quarter face position.

Lighting. The modelling light should be a flood diffused or low powered, to be kind to the skin texture. The brightness ratio 1 : 4 would retain an impression of the frank, happy nature which has, as yet, none of the depth of real maturity. The spot effect lights can underline the gaiety. It would be best to use them across the clothes and on the background rather than on the hair, as the wispiness on the hair should not be emphasized.

Background. Dark—lit by the spotlight.

As a starting point we could have the model with her back towards the camera, leaning forward to bring her shoulders into a diagonal line. Her head could then turn towards the camera to the S.E.

Modelling light at 25° to the right of central (at E.).

The majority of arrangements would include the three-quarter length figure, and full face or three-quarter face position, with full use made of the diagonal line to keep the feeling of alertness. Does this lady not remind you of a bird, with quick jerky movements and bright beady eyes? Kind, friendly, dependable, vivacious, inquisitive and understanding are some of the adjectives I would use to describe this personality and yet physically one would not call her attractive.

CASE IV: TEENAGER

The girl sitting in the corner seat opposite to us now would make a good model. Quite young, around 20, of slight build, with long, medium-fair hair, a pear-shaped face and clear cut features. The face is well made-up—groomed eyebrows, pale complexion and no visible lipstick, which draws extra attention to her rather "overly-made-up" dark brown eyes with long black lashes. Her nose is of medium length, her mouth well shaped, and her dimpled chin long and pointed. Wrapping her black fur coat around her she leans back in the seat with her elbow on the arm rest, a cigarette between her fingers. Note how she bends her wrist back—she must be double jointed! Probably her general movements are supple and she would be able to pose quite naturally. Although her body is turned towards us, her head is leaning back and turned in the opposite direction in a rather affected, posed attitude. Large brass circular earrings dangle from a pair of small, well-shaped, ears mostly hidden by the long hair.

This girl obviously likes glamour. She is probably vain and moody; warm-hearted and gay at times, but could equally well be cold and aloof. She is not sophisticated in any real way, but is trying to emulate such a person.

To photograph her as she is sitting now would be quite characteristic; for one pose anyway.

There is no need to describe the necessary techniques because with this type of face and personality you are free to use any camera angle, or any power of light; even any background you choose, to suit the mood of the picture you wish to obtain. If the mood you choose is not strongly characteristic, it will be one that she acts at various times so you could not go far wrong. I think she would respond to glamour treatment rather than anything too serious.

CASE V: MIDDLE-AGED MAN

As a contrast to all that we have studied so far let us take someone more difficult —the middle-aged gentleman over there looking like a business executive.

Description
Of large impressive build, dressed in a well-tailored black suit adorned with a gold bangle, gold signet ring and gold wrist watch with matching metal strap.

A commanding figure, opulent, intelligent, self-controlled, determined, ambitious, somewhat vain and used to good food and comfortable living. He is used to giving orders and being obeyed but he is not a hard man—in fact the mouth shows generosity and an affectionate nature. The ears are large with fullness at the top. The blue eyes are centred behind large black rimmed spectacles. The Roman nose is of an impressive size, with deeply marked lines from the outer part of the nostril to the mouth. On his left this line ends below the corner of the mouth, but on his right it terminates about $\frac{1}{2}$ in. above the mouth. This would suggest that the sterner attributes of character are likely to be found in the left side of his face, while the benevolent sympathetic, kindly attributes might be found in the right.

In repose the mouth appears to turn down at the corners, but the lips are not thin, which infers that he is not a bad tempered individual. His complexion is pale, his skin smooth. What little hair he has is white and brushed back in an attempt to cover his head.

The shape of his rather large head is rectangular but rounded at the top. Dividing the face into thirds gives fairly equal spacing, but the jaw line is undefined.

Points to watch

1. Spectacles with heavy black rims can cause reflections in the eyes, and dark shadows from the rims.
2. The sagging jaw line can make the face and neck appear to be on the same plane unless the head is leaning forward, and turned to one side.
3. The black suit will need extra light.
4. His stature must not be dwarfed.

Suggestions for positions

As a business executive he could be seated at a desk, the desk being diagonal to the camera. The left side of his head should face the camera. His arms on the desk holding papers or pen, etc. His head must then turn towards the camera to an almost full face position, and his eyes directed to the lens. The camera will need to be fairly low to reach into the eyes, and retain the power of his personality, a spotlight from N.W. rim lighting the face, and as much of the black suit as it will reach. Another small spotlight must be used across the clothes but the beam must be small enough to avoid lighting any part of the face. In order to reduce the contrast between the pale complexion of the face and the black suit, any light from the front which reaches the face must be soft and of low power.

The light should be shielded from the top of the head otherwise detail will be lost in the thin white hair and the texture of the skin.

A man or woman of this stature is often more natural in a standing position.

Then comes the difficulty of the height of the lights. A way round the problem is to have the rim lighting from the back created by spotlights, and all the light in front to be reflected or bounced. Bouncing the light off white walls or white polystyrene boards, or by using the special lamps giving reflected light, will not only give reasonable lighting, but will allow the model freedom to alter his position without the lights having to be re-arranged. (This is quite an asset in the case of a very busy person with little time to spare for being photographed). Another small spotlight from the side can give extra light across the clothes.

It is not necessary to make the photograph full length just because the model is standing. A three-quarter length or even a head and shoulders portrait can be made with equal success.

Background

A black background would have to be well lit to prevent the picture appearing too dark generally. It would look rather well with a panelled wall background, or a door, or bookshelves, or part of a window. Otherwise a light grey background with all light kept off it except for one small light immediately behind the model to give the necessary relief. Shading the edges can be done during the enlarging.

CASE VI: ELDERLY GENTLEMAN

Take a look at that man over there dressed in the dark coat and hat.

What a lovely low key picture he would make. If he were to come to the studio to be photographed he would probably remove his coat and hat before you had a chance to see him. Make a note then to ask your models to bring their outdoor clothing with them into the studio, or you could miss a golden opportunity of a good picture.

Description

As he appears to be lost in thought, and oblivious to everything going on around him, we can look more closely at his features with no fear of being observed.

He has a squarish shaped face with almost equal divisions when divided into thirds, and a short neck. The features comprise the following:

Dark eyes set underneath dark bushy eyebrows and behind dark rimmed spectacles. Large ears, well shaped nose of medium length; thin firm lips, dipped in the centre; and square jaw with slight double chin. The skin is rough and swarthy—there is a deep crease between the eybrows and down each cheek.

Some characteristics

A man of character. I would say he has strong concentrative powers, strong likes and dislikes, he is a great talker and fond of the outdoors. He can be melancholy at times—has an ability for serious thought, is courageous, and interested most probably in mechanics.

Techniques to use

With his dark skin and dark clothes, he would, as I have already said, make an admirable low key study. A face, such as his, so full of character lines and expression makes a suitable subject for the low lighting, long exposure technique (see Chapter 14). This model looks as though he could sit still quite naturally for at least 20 sec., or longer if it were required of him.

If you are going to try the low powered lighting technique you will find it helps to have the model's arms resting on a table. This gives support to the head and shoulders and prevents movement. The modelling and effect lights can be used as required but all should be regulated for distance and brightness to allow for an exposure of at least 8 sec. You may have to close the lens aperture to f 11 or even f 16. The question I am sure you are waiting to ask is "Why not give a shorter exposure with wide lens aperture instead of stopping the lens down?" The answer you will find fully discussed and illustrated in Chapter 14. A similar, although technically different, quality of detail is revealed when a really long exposure is given for the interior of a building, although a shorter exposure might be adequate for recording easily visible objects.

Another point is the softness of all the edges of the lines in the face due to the fact that the subject is alive, breathing and probably invisibly trembling. The result is an alive looking person made of flesh and blood and not a piece of still life or stone sculpture.

It would be worth trying out for yourself. Take the same set-up twice: one with wide aperture and the shorter exposure, the other with the lens stopped down and the exposure increased.

To return to our model—the old man in the dark hat and coat. There are many techniques you can experiment with on him. The coarseness of his skin would register almost like cement with the spotlight from an oblique angle; or lighting with a flood in the 45° modelling position and a brightness ratio of 1 : 6.

A profile with rim lighting would be effective without his spectacles. You would not be at a loss for pictures if you were fortunate enough to have him in front of your camera, especially when he became animated in conversation.

CASE VII: YOUTHFUL MIDDLE-AGED LADY

The well-groomed young lady sitting opposite us now, has fortunately a friend beside her with whom she is conversing. This gives us a much better opportunity of watching her expressions as she speaks, smiles or listens.

Description

The short dark hair frames a well-modelled face set on a medium length neck. Dividing the face into thirds we find the middle third slightly narrower than the other two. The features are fairly regular, the complexion fresh and the slight double chin is enhanced by a well marked dimple. Behind spectacles, topped by narrow black rims, are a pair of confident, thoughtful hazel eyes. The right side of the face would appear to reveal the more character, but the left side seems thinner with a more definite, clear cut outline. Little make-up on the face is visible, and the lips are outlined with a quite pale lipstick.

The lady, whom I can well imagine being an efficient chairman or executive, is wearing a stone-coloured coat and pale green jumper.

Characteristics

As you will realize by now, in our summing up of personality traits, we are merely suggesting possible characteristics deducted from our perception of a person during a very few minutes. This can only be a guide to the type of portrait we judge to be suitable, and suggests a choice of technique to use for the first few exposures. Other facets of the character will unfold as we continue to search for them.

This is a very pleasant person, talented in some form of art—probably litera-ture. She has a methodical, analytical, and self-confident nature. She is interested in other people, is a very good listener, is sympathetic and courageous.

Technique

A conventional portrait with lighting to show good modelling would be my choice and probably, the most acceptable to her. A dark background would give the greatest contrast against the grey tone of her clothes. The strength of character could be depicted by use of the 1 : 6 brightness ratio and a rich quality print. A three-quarter face position with the right side of her face nearest to the camera would allow for defining the more clear cut left side against the dark background.

To visualize this more clearly by the diagram (page 30) we can place the model facing S.W. with the head turned towards S.E. and tilted very slightly upward. Focusing the eyes on a point directly in front of her will portray to the best advantage the keen interest she displays towards everything in which she is engaged.

Suitable lighting would consist of two floods, one for modelling placed at 25° to the right of central (roughly E.S.E.) with the second at S.S.E. to give a ratio of 1 : 6. A diffused spotlight for the hair and another spotlight to outline the shoulder against the dark background completes the set-up.

One of the important factors to remember in this case is that the clothes, although attractive in colour and well suited to the wearer, will be an all-over grey tone when rendered in monotone. Unless contrast is given by the lighting and the background the whole effect could be monotonous—face, clothes and background appearing in only slightly varying shades of grey.

CASE VIII: MIDDLE-AGED LADY

At first glance, this well-dressed, middle-aged lady, with the slightly sagging face, may not appeal to you as an exciting person to photograph; but let us look at her more closely.

Description

A short, dumpy figure with a short, lined neck, double chin and a sallow complexion. She has greying, wiry hair, a lined forehead, thick dark eyebrows, and small dark blue-grey eyes behind dark rimmed spectacles. Her well proportioned features are set in a squarish type face with a more pointed chin and a pointed tip to her nose. By the division into thirds she is a well-balanced personality. She is married, is wearing pearl earrings and is smoking a cigarette. Notice her practical hands—rather thick with short fingers. Deep nasal labial lines (lines from nose to mouth) extend below the mouth.

Characteristics

This is a pleasant personality, with strong likes and dislikes. Mentally alert, ambitious and determined—sometimes rather abrupt in manner, is capable of clear, logical thought and is used to talking.

Possible techniques

A three-quarter length figure would be the most suitable, giving more stature to a short person. As she is sitting at the moment, reading the newspaper, will do well for a start. By the chart, her body is facing S.S.E. and we will ask her to turn her head towards S.S.W. This will give a turn to the neck which helps to obviate the double chin and the shortness of the neck. Also, the left side of her face being the longer and thinner, will then be nearest to the camera. The camera angle being slightly below eye level will allow the eyes to be seen behind the spectacles.

Lighting

Modelling light, a flood diffused, 25° to the left of central; secondary, fill-in light also a flood diffused; or this second flood could be replaced by reflected light to help soften the deep lines in her face. A spotlight from N.W. level to add a touch of brilliance to the lighting, and a second small beamed spotlight over her left shoulder directed across the clothes only. Keep all stray light off the newspaper, or it will need printing down considerably during enlargement.

Background

This is another instance where a natural background of book shelves, or a corner of the room would add to the picture. It needs to be dark, intermingled with lighter tone, rather than solid black.

CASE IX: YOUNG MAN

We are indeed fortunate to find such a variety of types among a comparatively small number of people. The young man upon whom we will now focus our attention is representative of the modern generation and will make an exciting picture presented in a modern style.

Description

This youth, probably in his early twenties, is wearing a very striking white mottled three-quarter length fur coat. His wiry hair is thick and wavy, and is medium fair in colour. His regular shaped head terminating in a long chin, makes the lower third division of the face wider than the upper two. The bone structure of the face and features is well defined. The ears are small, and lie back close to the head. The well-shaped nose is short, and there is a wide space between the nose and the firm mouth, with its slightly protruding top lip. His eyes hold our attention—they are dark brown in colour, very expressive, and framed by long eyelashes.

Characteristics

What can we deduce from this analysis? He probably has a warm, affectionate, carefree nature and is ruled by his heart rather than his head. He enjoys life, is fond of change, but inclined to be lazy. Not naturally very intellectual, he can achieve his goal with perseverance. His conversation is often witty, he takes considerable pride in his appearance and is, most likely, very popular.

Techniques

We now have an opportunity of using a male model for some glamorous effects. His attractive features, coupled with his character traits and mannerisms, give us plenty of scope for some originality in posing, brilliance in lighting and crispness of definition which are some of the keynotes of modern portrait technique. It might be a good idea to start with the journalistic approach.

As our young model leaves the train, he dons his hat, picks up his immaculately rolled umbrella and steps out on to the platform, slamming the carriage door behind him. His coat still unbuttoned swings outwards from his slightly sloping shoulders as, hand in pocket, he walks jauntily down the platform. He turns back to look in our direction—does he sense we are watching him?

In that moment the picture is visualized. Full length, to be taken out of doors with, if possible, white buildings out of focus in the background. The figure, walking away from us, and then pausing and looking back over his shoulder. The point of the umbrella and the swing of the coat making diagonal lines in the composition. A crisp, glossy print will help the atmosphere.

In the studio, too, we can utilize the hat and coat for some of the pictures. As a starting point, for a head and shoulder or three-quarter length position, the backward glance will do well, and make an interesting comparison with the outdoor shot. To give the required crispness of definition, we will use the spotlights, both for modelling and for effect, with a brightness ratio of 1 : 6. A low camera angle, and the model's eyes glancing towards the lens, will portray a feeling of isolation, and happy superiority.

A more delicate high key effect can be produced by using floodlights instead of spots and, if necessary, placing diffusers over the lights. This will soften the shadows as well as give an overall softness of quality to the skin and to the texture of the fur coat. We will, of course, need a white background and the model must be asked to remove his hat which is dark in colour.

16 Children

A HIGHLY detailed analysis of child psychology is outside the scope of this book. I will, however, explain my methods of applying psychological techniques in my dealings with children in the studio; describe the lighting set up for daylight, tungsten, and flash and conclude by illustrating the photographic techniques with finished pictures of children in varying age groups.

AMATEUR SNAPSHOT v. PORTRAIT

If you are a parent and an amateur photographer you are probably interested in taking the casual snapshot of your child. There is a natural desire in any parent to keep a record of the quickly passing childhood days, and this inspires you to capture as many varied pictures as possible depicting the child's growth from year to year, or even month to month, from birth onwards. This intimate snapshot, which means so much to both parents in happy retrospect, is one which is important for the subject matter quite apart from the good or bad photographic technique.

On the other hand, a child's studio portrait must be a true character study, and show a natural expression whether smiling or serious. It must also be well composed, well lit, suitably exposed and processed and attractively presented.

The latter techniques present no problems to a student of portrait photography. The important skill to master is the ability to make a child completely happy and natural. This may not be difficult in the child's own home but in the studio where everything is strange to the child, it is another question. For this reason I suggest that some study should be made of child psychology, to help towards a greater understanding of the child's mind.

The essential question to ask yourself before embarking any further on the project of child portraiture is "Do I love children?" This is not just a sentimental feeling towards all the attractive babies and toddlers, but a sincere affection which embraces an understanding of the working of their minds. It means feeling with them, knowing when to ignore them and when to play with them. It means being able to make up stories, and to enter their world of make-believe. It means making sure they can trust you. A child never forgets a broken promise, so, when you say you will do anything you must be sure to do it—if you say you will give him anything you must do so. If you do not intend to, then refrain from saying anything about it in the first place. To understand children and to photograph them successfully, means having endless patience—patience to wait for that elusive smile, patience to deal with the child who thrusts a hand out for every toy the moment you show it, allowing you no time to make an exposure, patience with the lively youngster who will not remain in one position for more than a moment.

A child is as sensitive as an animal towards atmosphere, and will usually know instinctively whether an adult is a child lover or not. A child will react to expressions—if you want the child to smile and be happy you must show a cheerful happy countenance yourself. If you are tense, or impatient, you can be sure the child will behave in the worst possible manner.

If you do understand children, you have the key to success in child portraiture and you will very quickly discover your own ways of creating harmony and happiness in the studio.

SOME METHODS OF APPLYING PSYCHOLOGY

As I have said, the subject of child psychology is so vast, that even skimming its surface is outside the scope of this book. It is, therefore, something which we cannot study together in these pages, but our individual experiments will result in a better understanding of children, and this will become obvious in our relationship with them in the studio. This understanding becomes the silent communication of mutual trust, the silver thread which links the two minds, and is the inexplicable cord of harmony which must be kept intact throughout the whole photographic session.

The child is attracted by someone who obviously responds to his unspoken thoughts, his fears are dispelled and all barriers come down.

Each photographer must work out his own techniques, expanding his ideas as his experience widens. The recounting of some of my own methods of applying psychology in the treatment of children is, therefore, more in the nature of interest than instruction, although the techniques have been well tested over very many years, and have proved successful for me.

BOOKING THE APPOINTMENT

At the time of booking the appointment I make a note of the child's sex, name and age. I suggest the appointment is made at a time of day most suitable for the child, that is when he will not be tired or hungry. The mother is advised not to tell the child he is going to be photographed, but rather that he has been invited to come and see some of my toys, and perhaps he would like to bring one or two of his to show me. This prevents any fear of the unknown building up in the child's mind.

For a child of school age I suggest that a change of clothing should be brought to the studio. A different type of picture, showing the separate characteristics, can be made when the child is wearing sports clothes, school uniform or party dress. An insight into the younger child's favourite toys and the older one's hobbies is also useful when I am preparing the studio, selecting props, background, etc.

ON ARRIVAL

A child is greeted by name, and taken to the studio where his eye immediately alights on a large teddy bear sitting on the box, surrounded by either cars, or a doll's tea set or some other toy likely to appeal. If tungsten light is being used, one floodlight is already switched on making the room look bright and gay. For about ten minutes the child is allowed to get acclimatized while I discuss the required portrait with the mother. By this time the child is usually playing quite happily, and it is comparatively easy to encourage him to sit on the box and see what other surprises I have in store for him. Techniques obviously vary according to the age of the child. With some young children the sooner I start work with the camera the better, while others take longer to become natural in strange surroundings.

PARENTS IN THE STUDIO

Whether or not the parent should be allowed in the studio during the session is a problem which each photographer must sort out for himself. For me the solution lies in the answer to the question "how will it affect the child?" If the child is happy and likely to be less self-conscious in the studio with me alone, the parent can relax in an ante-room, where, if so desired, the proceedings can be overheard, but the child is unaware of being watched.

When photographing a baby or young toddler I find the presence of the mother in the studio a distinct advantage. One of her main tasks is to sit on the edge of the box or on a chair at the side, and be ready to grab the child in the event of a likely fall, or to replace her lively youngster in the required position. Parents can help too, in attracting the child's attention. This works well, provided it is done at the photographer's request and not in opposition to his needs! It is nothing short of chaotic for two or more people to try and attract the child's attention at the same time—the child merely becomes bewildered and the adults frustrated. It is also a fallacy that noises, such as rattles, bells, handclaps, etc. are indispensable. These have their uses, but there are also times when silence is the more impressive. In the silence even a faint sound, such as a clock striking in another room, or a small click, is enough to make the child look towards the sound.

For a young baby the most useful props are gaily coloured, especially red, moving toys, balloons, a red scarf to wave, a rattle, and a small squeaky toy (both to be used sparingly!) and soap bubbles, etc. A baby is either waving his arms around or keeping them straight down by his side, neither of which occupations is photogenic. To meet this situation I keep a supply of small, plastic, gaily coloured teddies. The baby can hold one without it being obtrusive in the photograph. I know it will almost immediately find its way to the baby's mouth, so the opportunities to click the shutter must not be missed. Of course, the plastic toys which the baby is likely to chew must be washed immediately prior to the sitting and kept in a plastic bag to comply with accepted standards of hygiene.

For toddlers there are endless ways of attracting their attention—the main thing is to do something which will not only induce the child to turn his head in the required direction, but will produce a suitable expression. It is all too easy to entertain a child and to be rewarded with an interested stare and the mouth wide open! Hardly the expression required for a portrait! Some of the props I have found most successful are the clay pipe and soap bubbles, puppets—a monkey puppet and Punch and Judy (these require the make-believe stories to accompany them), small dolls and teddies, which can be hidden down the reflex hood of the camera and can be made to come out when called, a dolls tea-set, aircraft circling round a central pivot and a musical box. These are a few suggestions, but any toy operated with one hand can be used—leaving the other hand

209

free to press the shutter release immediately the expression is right. Picture and story books, crayon books, stencils and cut-outs together with pencils, crayons and scissors, and a simple jig-saw puzzle are all kept in the studio to occupy the hands of the older child while sitting at the desk.

Some children are more interested in flowers, shells and even stones, than they are in toys. One small boy of four years old delighted in the feel of stones— the smoothness of a sea-worn pebble, another little three-year-old girl was more interested in flowers, and amused herself by plucking the petals from a marguerite and gave me a beautiful smile as the last remaining petal was pulled off.

Some children do not need entertaining in any way but are quite at home chatting about various things, their school days and holidays, their hobbies and recreations. With the intervals for changing clothes and backgrounds, and a refreshing drink half way through, the time passes quite happily. Nevertheless the photographer must be able to sense the child's feelings, and have a variety of things at hand to use if the need arises.

THE STUDIO SET-UP

Perhaps you would now like to come into the studio, before the child arrives to be photographed, and make a note of the general set-up (Fig. 16.1).

It is a fine summer afternoon. At one end of the studio there is a large window facing North. The walls and ceiling are white. The light is good, so there is every opportunity for taking the photograph by daylight. This is always more suitable for babies and children, because it is more natural, is soft on the skin tones, allows more freedom of movement, and is kinder to the child's eyes.

To prepare the studio takes very little time. Two sheets of white polystyrene 6 × 4 ft act as reflectors, and one 500 W spotlight gives the effect light.

The white box on which the child sits is placed at a slight angle with the wall towards the window, about 3 ft from the wall. AB and CD are the 6 × 4 ft sheets of white polystyrene, balanced against anything which will hold them upright. Between these two is the 500 W spot, high on its stand with the light directed downwards. If the reflected light from the ceiling is insufficient, a floodlight, in a wide reflector, could also stand between and behind the two sheets of polystyrene with the light pointing up towards the ceiling.

The distance between the window, the box and the polystyrene reflectors depends on the quality of the daylight and the exposure required.

The film to be used is one of 400 ASA.

An exposure of 1/30 sec. at f 8 or f 11 is usually fast enough to stop movement of the child and allows sufficient depth of field for reasonable focusing. The meter reading is taken against a white card held in the position in which the child will be sitting. (Meter adjusted for a 4× or 8× reading—see Chapter on Exposures.) The position of the box and reflectors is then adjusted to obtain the reading of 1/30 sec. ƒ 8 or ƒ 11. The camera lens and shutter can then be set ready for the daylight series of pictures.

To transform the studio from daylight to tungsten lighting takes only a few minutes during an interval if the light should suddenly deteriorate, as it is quite

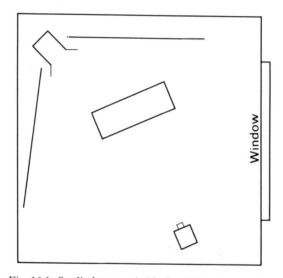

Fig. 16.1. Studio layout suitable for child photography

capable of doing in this country! The curtains are drawn across the window and the background paper, which is fixed above the window, is unrolled and the paper pulled down to floor level. The lights are then arranged as in Fig. 16.2.

A is a 250 W spotlight, B a 500 W spotlight, both diffused, directed down to light the hair or act as effect light on the back of the face and dress. C is a 500 W flood diffused, used as a modelling light, and which can be moved around to give the desired effect. D and E are 150 W floods directed on to a 6 × 4 ft sheet of white polystyrene placed at an angle, and well behind the camera. These act as the fill-in lights, but are stationary, which gives the photographer one thing less to think about during the session. F is another floodlight placed behind the child and directed up to the ceiling, to reflect light back on to the hair. If a high key picture is required, extra light will be needed for the background. The more

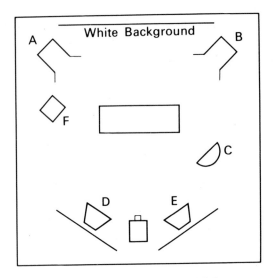

Fig. 16.2. Studio layout for artificial light set-up

back lighting is used, as opposed to frontal light, the more interesting the picture will be, but also the longer the exposure will have to be.

THE FLASH ALTERNATIVE

If we wish to take a picture by a single flash in place of the modelling light, the set up will be the same as for tungsten with the omission of the flood C.

The distance from the child at which the flash must be used, will depend on the flash factor supplied by the manufacturer, and will be coupled with the appropriate lens aperture.

The flash should be attached to the camera by an extension lead, enabling it to be placed on a separate stand, or held in the hand, at a height to give the required modelling to the child's face.

If two flash units are to be used, the second one, which can be either fixed on to the camera or on to a separate stand, will take the place of the fill-in light. The reflectors and the lights D and E will then no longer be required.

Electronic flash with three, or more, units connected to a central control will allow a variety of effects to be produced without any additional lighting. The built-in modelling lights are a great asset, enabling the correct balance of light to be visualized, but experiments must be made to standardize the most suitable positions.

A softer, shadowless result can be obtained by directing the flash towards the ceiling. The photograph is then taken by reflected light only which gives greater freedom to both photographer and child, but at the cost of any pictorial effects.

FINAL PREPARATION

Let us return to the daylight studio which we have been preparing for a child portrait session. Everything is in readiness; the background, lights and reflectors are positioned; the camera is loaded and the exposure calculated. It only remains to collect some toys together and place them on a small table behind a screen. Among the toys will be a pipe, and some soapy water. Bubble blowing is one of the most handy forms of entertainment for children of all ages, including babies.

It may be as well here to describe the box. It measures 4 × 2 ft and stands 18 in. high. It is made of white painted hardboard, the top and front panels being reinforced with wood. The top is covered with a soft white blanket to give greater comfort to the toddler. A mattress is slipped under the blanket and raised at one end by a firm cushion to enable a baby to lie flat and yet at a slight angle which is more photogenic than the completely horizontal position.

For a change from the box, there is a small red desk and stool to match, and three or four other stools of varying heights, one of them being long enough to seat two children side by side, yet low enough for their feet to rest on the floor.

Some of the techniques used can be more advantageously described by means of illustrations.

DAYLIGHT STUDIO

The lighting set-up as described in Fig. 16.1 is very versatile, reasonable results can be obtained whichever way the child faces, and whether the child is sitting or standing. The spotlight can be moved to give better effect lighting when circumstances allow, but with an active child, this is not always possible.

The first two illustrations show the spotlight used as the effect light, giving a touch of liveliness to the picture (Figs. 16.3 and 16.4).

Melanie is nearly two years old. She is sitting on the box facing the window with her head turned towards the camera. Her hands are busy opening and closing a small purse. The natural tilt to the head as it is turned is attractive, and there is a lively expression in the eyes. The daylight gives a soft texture rendering of the dress material, and good modelling to the face and arms.

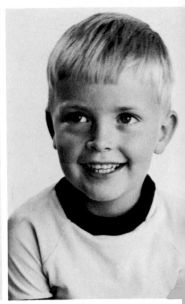

16.3 16.4 16.5

Fig. 16.3. Melanie given something to do
Fig. 16.4. Standing up
Fig. 16.5. Christopher nervous of the camera

In Fig. 16.4 Melanie is standing on the floor, still facing the window but, this time, looking up. In this arrangement more space is left above her head and in front of her eyes to give the required feeling of space. Note the arrangement of the lines: the lovely curved line of her arm flowing up and round her head and outlining the teddy with a series of short curved lines. The larger circle of her head overlaps the smaller circle of the teddy's head. Her hands, also, repeat the circular shape. There is intense interest shown in the child's eyes, as she watches her daddy "buzz" a toy plane.

DAYLIGHT IS A NATURAL LIGHT

Four-year-old Christopher is very nervous at the thought of having his photograph taken and says that he does not want to have it done. He is, however, quite happy to sit on a small pair of steps and take part in a bubble blowing competition, or watch a Punch and Judy show. The daylight studio appears little

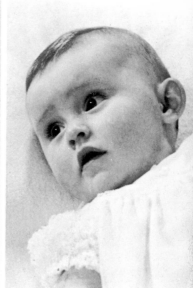

16.6 16.7 16.8

Fig. 16.6. David: all-over reflected light
Fig. 16.7. David: no fear of the camera
Fig. 16.8. Baby lying down

---

different from a normal room, there are no lights in front of him, and the window
beside him looks out on to a garden. This latter fact gives him a feeling of
freedom—there is a way of escape, whereas the studio lit by artificial light, with
a background covering the window area, can give a feeling of being shut in,
caught within the glare of bright lights, which, to a child, is unnatural and can
give rise to a feeling of apprehension, if not fear, until he has acclimatized
himself to it (Fig. 16.5).

In Figs. 16.6 and 16.7 David does not share his brother's fear of the camera.
He is a high-spirited youngster, incapable of staying in the same place for more
than a few moments. The daylight set-up allows for this, producing reasonable
lighting for the head turned in either direction, and the over-all reflected light
gives good quality in the clothes. Both children have very fair hair, which is well
rendered by the daylight, without any of the control needed when using tungsten.

When the daylight set-up is combined with a spotlight the naked spotlight is
usually too bright for a baby lying on the box. It can be softened by diffusing.

215

16.9 16.10 16.11

Fig. 16.9. Sitting position
Fig. 16.10. High key treatment
Fig. 16.11. Happy disposition

Katie can only just sit up on her own, but she will tire very quickly if allowed to do so for very long. The first few exposures will be made with her lying down, propped at an angle by a cushion underneath the blanket. In Fig. 16.8 the day-light is acting as an over-all diffused light, giving a softness to the skin tones, and lighting all the shadows in the white dress and blanket. This produces the high-key effect with the emphasis on the dark eyes. The eyes also hold the interest by their position on an opposing diagonal to the line of the body.

Katie is sitting up and turned round to face the window. The spotlight and reflectors have not been moved, but there is still sufficient soft modelling. The body leaning forward, with the arm forming a leading diagonal line, gives a feeling of movement, which is arrested by the turn of the head and the glance to the camera. The soft quality of the shadow tones, and the texture rendering in the dress, again makes a simple high-key picture with the attention on the baby's face and eyes (Fig. 16.9).

216

HIGH KEY EFFECT WITH TUNGSTEN LIGHTING

The following illustrations show the effect of the lighting set-up used in Fig. 2. The first two have the extra light on the background to make it softer in tone.

Pippa is a merry little girl with a decided twinkle in her eye, and a happy picture is the more characteristic of her delightful, mischievous, little self. The spotlight effect from behind gives a touch of brightness in keeping with the mood. A light background is suitable for a young child as it gives an idea of space and freedom. Reflected light on to the smocked pastel coloured dress gives soft detail. The body is facing in one direction while the head is turned to the opposite, which gives a feeling of life and movement. The hands are occupied— holding a small toy—which keeps them together and natural. Note that the back shoulder and arm are visible. Seeing the whole arm is much better than to see the hand and forearm protruding from the body without, apparently, any connexion (Fig. 16.10).

To sit the child sideways for a three-quarter view avoids any distortion of the hands and arms, and also allows for greater variety in the lines and background shapes.

Fig. 16.11 makes an attractive picture with Pippa trying her hand with the pipe. It shows her happy disposition and the merry expression in her eyes. However, it is more of a happy snapshot than a character portrait and is of only passing interest. This can be said, also, of Fig. 16.12. Any laughing picture is of an instantaneous expression and usually has only momentary appeal. But it may be useful to include in a series of "characteristic" pictures when the serious studies seem less natural.

Sometimes the opposite is the case, and the smiling expression will be in the minority in a series of pictures. All children differ one from the other, and all need individual treatment, both in the photographic techniques and in entertainment in the studio.

TUNGSTEN LIGHTING—GREY BACKGROUND

The following pictures, selected from a series, are of Katie, a serious-minded little girl, intelligent, and very fond of reading.

Katie also likes acting and posing in front of a camera! A natural picture has to be obtained when she is off her guard.

A grey background has been used to show the clothes to better advantage— especially the sun-bonnet with the light edge which forms an attractive shape.

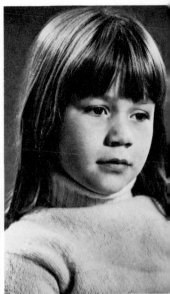

16.12 16.13 16.14

Fig. 16.12. An instantaneous expression
Fig. 16.13. Katie: a contemplative study
Fig. 16.14. A happy disposition

Also the effect lights from behind are stronger against a slightly darker background.

Katie is imaginative, and Fig. 16.13 is a contemplative study, obtained during a pause while she is thinking what to write next. The spotlight behind acts as the main light, giving modelling to the near side cheek by the small triangle of light. The elbow has been trimmed off to give greater concentration to the face and hand. When two lines, such as the diagonal lines of the arm, are obviously going to meet, it is unnecessary to show the point at which they do meet. Trimming should not occur at either the elbow joint or the wrist, but anywhere in between which will maintain a feeling of implied continuity.

Fig. 16.14 concentrates attention on her thoughtful, yet happy expression, and shows to advantage the well-modelled, sensitive lips. The backward slope of the body denotes a relaxed position, and is prevented from being too static by the slight tilt of the head and the slant of the eyes.

218

In Fig. 16.15 the face is framed by the sun-bonnet, the lines of which are interesting, the shape repeating the shape of the face. The light edge and the dark interior, in close proximity to the light side of the face, form a lively interplay of light and dark across the picture. Trimming off the unnecessary back of the bonnet focuses attention on the face, particularly the eyes.

HIGH KEY VIGNETTE

The word "vignette" savours of the old-fashioned portrait, as it was a popular style in the last, and early part of this, century. But for certain subjects its simplicity and charm is unsurpassed by any other technique, and during the last few years many parents have requested a portrait of their child finished in this way. The portrait must be taken against a white background, and the enlargement of the head only is printed through a circular hole cut in a piece of cardboard. The hole is cut slightly larger than would appear necessary and the card must be kept on the move during the exposure. The head must be positioned correctly on the paper as it will be isolated on the white background, and if too central, or too high or low, it will look unsatisfactory.

Vignetting is a technique more suitable for a soft focus portrait than one of critical definition. The gradual fading out of the tones implies a delicacy which needs to be maintained throughout.

Fig. 16.16 shows a charming baby girl with a very appealing expression in her dark eyes. The effect of vignetting is the gradual fading of the tones in all directions from the eyes outwards. Or you could put it the other way round and say that there is a gradual strengthening of the tones towards the eyes, leading the viewer to the focal point of the picture. A studio camera with a 12 in. portrait lens used on a $\frac{1}{4}$ plate film is responsible for the soft definition. The exposure, with tungsten lighting is $\frac{1}{10}$ sec. f 8. The soft quality of the lines and shadows gives a roundness to the features, a natural texture to the skin, and liquidity to the eyes.

ELECTRONIC FLASH

One of the great advantages of electronic flash lighting for certain types of portrait and the photography of young children is the knowledge that all movement will be arrested by the very short exposure time.

In Fig. 16.17, baby Ian is enjoying a "rocking session", backwards and

219

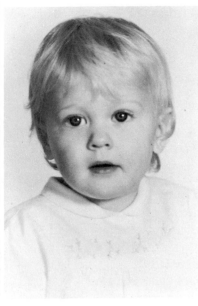

16.15 16.16 16.17

Fig. 16.15. Framed with a bonnet
Fig. 16.16. Vignetting: gradually fading tones towards edges
Fig. 16.17. Flash is especially useful for the mobile very young

forwards. Releasing the shutter the moment he touches his toes results in a happy picture showing the hands and feet in clear detail. The use of flash allows the photographer more scope to take pictures of children in action, especially useful for the young ballet dancer when the freedom of movement can produce more graceful curves. The use of a smaller aperture than is possible with tungsten lighting gives greater depth of field, and consequently over-all sharpness.

Two flash heads are used; one above and to one side of the camera, the other on the camera. The surrounding daylight gives overall reflected light and softens the shadows. The baby is sitting sideways, enabling the arms and legs to be in the same plane as the face, and so avoiding any distortion.

INCLUDING HANDS—TUNGSTEN LIGHT

Unlike adults, children are not self-conscious about their hands. Children use their hands continually and naturally. Their hands are pliable and well modelled, and provided they are positioned suitably, they will always photograph well and add a further touch of character to the picture.

Although a child cannot be actually posed for a photograph he can be placed in a position where he is likely to adopt an attitude similar to one which the photographer has in mind. The child seated on a stool, with the appropriate size of table or desk in front of him, will, almost certainly at some time, put his elbows on the table and cup his face in his hands; or use the hands in some way which can be termed photogenic.

Susie is quite unaware of what she is doing. She is watching a soap bubble being blown, which gives the natural tilt to the head, and the interested expression. The exposure must be made quickly because the hands will probably not remain in the same position for many moments. Her head is resting on her left hand. The third finger of her right hand is pressing into her face—the other fingers are barely touching the cheek—natural, pliable, photogenic (Fig. 16.18).

Charlotte is concentrating so hard on some problem of her own, concerned with her hands; I think she is putting an elastic band round the fingers of her right hand. The intense interest has brought the hands up close to the face which makes a good arrangement of line and shapes. This opportunity must also be seized quickly—or the expression, which makes the picture, will be lost (Fig. 16.19).

Deborah is a skating enthusiast and her movements are mostly poised and graceful. She is a quiet, thoughtful child, and when seated at a table, sideways on to the camera, she adopts this beautiful position quite naturally. The back lighting, the modelling in her arms, and the lovely shape of her well-groomed head, all add to the charm of the picture, but the expression on her face and the thought behind her eyes are the factors which provide a lasting attraction (Fig. 16.20).

Jonathan clasps his hands quite spontaneously as his attention is attracted by a gaily coloured parrot swinging on a bar. The back lighting gives modelling to the face and hands, while at the same time it lights the dark jumper, across the chest and on the sleeve. The fair hair is lit sufficiently by the frontal fill light.

Note the upward diagonal line of the forearm, implying movement. The horizontal position would be more static and not in harmony with the eager alertness of the expression on his face (Fig. 16.21).

Simon is seated at the desk with a sheet of drawing paper. His hands are naturally placed, as he curves the paper backwards. This is just a spontaneous movement, but it suits the over-all arrangement. The back lighting gives a depth, as well as a lightness, to the picture and renders the white shirt and fair hair with good tonal gradation (Fig. 16.22).

The pliability of a child's hand is shown in the low angle shot of Jonathan.

16.18 16.19 16.20

Fig. 16.18. Watching a subject out of the picture
Fig. 16.19. Concentration
Fig. 16.20. Graceful movement

Taken in the daylight studio, he is sitting on the small pair of steps, and is just about to reach out for a soap bubble which is floating towards him. One second later and the whole arrangement would have been useless. This emphasizes the need for the photographer to be always on the alert to catch opportunities as they arise. The lighting arrangements must also allow for this freedom.

It is interesting to note the difference in the shape of the head between the low camera angle of Fig. 16.23 and the higher one of Fig. 16.24. The latter shows a triangular shaped head coupled with a shy, reserved sensitive nature, while the former depicts a squarer shaped head and a more positive, courageous, adventurous character.

Note, also, how the daylight from the window takes care of the detail in the shirts—both the white and the navy.

There are few children who use their hands for expression more than Jane. An attractive little girl, of few words or sounds, but a variety of expressions and

222

16.21 16.22 16.23

Fig. 16.21. Watching a parrot out of picture
Fig. 16.22. Spontaneous movement of the hands suits the over-all arrangement
Fig. 16.23. Jonathan: pliability of a child's hand

mannerisms. Her hands and wrists are very pliable, and her arms are continually poised ready for action. She is graceful in her movements and her limbs are well proportioned. The lighting arrangement is similar to that shown in Fig. 16.2 (Figs. 16.25, 16.26 and 16.27).

For a profile position (16.25) it is almost essential to have an assistant to amuse the youngster, while the photographer awaits the opportunity to release the shutter. In 16.26 Jane is occupied with the tea-set but looks round on hearing her name called, while in 16.27 a soap bubble is floating past her.

A composition of curved and diagonal lines is always useful in portraying a lively character or a happy disposition. The body facing one direction, with the head turned and looking up places the eyes on a diagonal line, and implies movement. The sunny effect of the back lighting adds to the charm of the natural smile (Fig. 16.28).

Joanna refused to be photographed without her pet cat. While she is holding

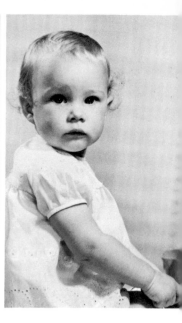

16.24 16.25 16.26
16.27

Fig. 16.24. Higher camera angle
reshapes the head
Fig. 16.25, 16.26. Jane uses her
hands with great expression
Fig. 16.27. Jane reaches for a
soap bubble

16.28 16.29

Fig. 16.28. Susie: diagonally placed eyes implies movement
Fig. 16.29. Joanna is only unselfconscious if allowed to hold her pet cat

---

puss she is quite unselfconscious. Joanna is kneeling on the floor and leaning forward to keep her head on the same plane as that of the cat. The arms fall quite naturally into a pleasing position—fortunately the line of the right arm is visible behind the cat's body. The upright and curved lines of the archway in the background stabilize the diagonal composition (Fig. 16.29).

The box is on its side with one end towards the camera. In a moment of relaxation Christopher lies full length along it and cups his face in his hands. This is so completely natural that the opportunity cannot be missed. The modelling light is quickly positioned and an exposure made. All models must be allowed to relax at intervals, but the photographer must always be vigilant for possible characteristic attitudes and expressions which, once missed, might not be seen again during the session (Fig. 16.30).

Occasionally a quick series can be taken with one shot rapidly following the other. A game of "peep-bo" was responsible for 16.31 and 16.32. In 16.33 Fiona

16.30 16.31 16.32

Fig. 16.30. Christopher lies full length on a box on end, towards the camera
Fig. 16.31, 16.32. Fiona. Series of movements taken in rapid succession

is holding the bulb attached to a rubber tube which activates a small toy donkey. An attractive dress and pretty hair style add greatly to the charm of a full length picture. The flexibility of the arms and legs suggest vitality, and one can well imagine Fiona becoming a proficient dancer.

If a child wears spectacles, it is wise to include them in some of the pictures. They rarely present any problem as the lenses are not, usually, very thick. If the primary light is used in the normal position for good modelling, and the secondary light is bounced off a white surface, there should be no trouble with the light being reflected in the spectacle lenses. On the rare occasions when this reflection cannot be eliminated by a movement of the light, or a slight downward tilt of the head, it is advisable to have the light spots on the part of the spectacle lens which is over the face, not over the eyes themselves. The spots can then be taken out in the finished print without affecting the expression in the eyes (Fig. 16.34).

Fig. 16.33. 16.34 16.35

Fig. 16.33. Fiona: The third position
Fig. 16.34. Torben: the problem of spectacles
Fig. 16.35. The school cap photograph

When a young boy is wearing his school uniform, either a blazer or a suit, he will be delighted to have a picture of himself in his school cap, especially if it is a new acquisition (Fig. 16.35).

Groups of children are never easy to photograph. So often the expression of one is the better in one position, and the other in another. In this picture, fortunately, the children are both natural. They are interested in what they are being shown and are oblivious to the photographer. The delightful roundness in the modelling of their faces is obtained with the use of a 12 in. portrait lens on a $\frac{1}{4}$ plate studio camera. This also shows the eyes to advantage. There is, of course, little depth of field, so the two heads must be on the same plane, and the focus must be accurate (Fig. 16.36).

In arranging two children for a head and shoulder portrait, it usually works if you have the smaller child in front, and the bodies overlapping rather than side by side. This gives a better outline, and a more unified composition. The

227

16.36
16.37

Fig. 16.36. Adam and Sarah: the
difficulty of grouping children
overcome by interesting them
Fig. 16.37. Andrew and James:
the smaller child placed in front
with shoulders overlapping

228

back lighting centres the interest on the two faces, which show up well against the darker background (Fig. 16.37).

Fig. 16.38 is a group arranged as a natural conversational study. The child is intently listening to her parents. The composition is such that all the heads are on a different level, obtained by using separate chairs rather than the box, and they have varying spaces between them. The back lighting on the father's face and the off-central position of his head, make him the focal point of the picture, while the direction of his glance leads the interest towards his wife. An informal arrangement for a group is often the most satisfactory, as it is only possible for the photographer to clearly see the expression on one face at a time, and the likelihood of everyone looking pleasant is far greater when the positions are natural, and when there is no necessity to look at the camera.

CHILDREN AT HOME

There are times when you will want to photograph children in their own surroundings, that is, in their own home. The main difficulties to be overcome are usually, 1. the lack of space; 2. unsuitable backgrounds; 3. the unknown light source, all of which can be overcome by a little ingenuity.

AVAILABLE LIGHT

In Fig. 16.39 the mother and baby are taken in a small lounge by the bay window. The baby is lying on the floor on a white blanket, stretched across the bay, and the mother kneels beside him. At the moment before the shutter is released, the mother gently "scoops" the baby's head and shoulders a few inches from the floor and leans her head against his. (Turn the picture sideways and you will see the position).

The only light used is the available daylight—the only reflector is the white blanket on the floor. The camera is hand held. There is an interesting arrangement of line—the heads represent overlapping circles—one dominating the other. It is fortunate that the baby is not looking towards the camera as well as the mother.

Fig. 16.40 shows a new born baby, only six days old, taken in a very small bedroom, close to the window. The window is covered with net curtaining which spreads the light over a wider area. The mother is sitting on the edge of the bed, holding the baby in her arms. The camera is hand held from above. The photographer is standing on a chair. It is just lucky that the little hands are together,

16.38
16.39

Fig. 16.38. Group can be arranged
as a conversation piece
Fig. 16.39. Mother and child by
the light of a small window

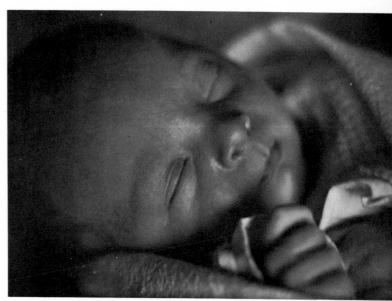

16.40 16.41

Fig. 16.40. Six days old, by curtained window light
Fig. 16.41. With close ups lack of depth means focusing on the nearside eye

the thumb placed on the chin, and that the eyes open for the exposure. Patience is required, probably more than any other attribute, when photographing tiny babies. No props or toys of any sort are of any use at all at this age, it is just a question of how long you can wait for what you want, and being ready to seize the opportunity when it comes.

Fig. 16.41 is not an enlarged head, but the picture is the full format of the negative. The baby is the same six day old boy as in Fig. 16.40 and the picture is taken under the same conditions of lighting, etc. With the close-up lens on the camera and full aperture there is very little depth of field. However, the focus being sharp on the nearside eye concentrates attention where it is required and the rest, being slightly out of focus, gives a "dreamy" appearance.

FLASH

In Fig. 16.42 this one-year-old boy was taken sitting on his father's knee in their lounge at home. The chair is placed in the centre of the room to allow as much

231

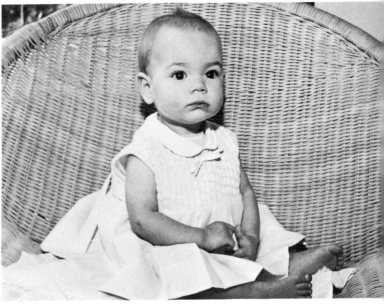

16.42 16.43
16.44

Fig. 16.42. Christopher: by a
mixture of flash and daylight
Fig. 16.43. Subject contained in
the background
Fig. 16.44. Plain background and
a useful prop

232

space as possible between it and the wall behind. The picture is taken with available daylight and a single flash held above and to one side of the camera. The flash is nearer to the child than the camera, producing the attractive dark outline round the far cheek.

BACKGROUNDS

The close-up head and shoulder pictures so far illustrated present few difficulties regarding backgrounds, but when a full length figure is required a suitable background becomes a necessity.

In Fig. 16.43 there is a one-year-old baby girl, photographed at home in the lounge. A round-backed wicker chair is selected for the seat and background combined. The advantage in this is two-fold: first, the child is secured in one position for a few moments anyway! Secondly, the chair's curved back and slightly well-shaped seat give a degree of safety for the child. The disadvantage is the proximity of the child to the background with the consequent lack of depth in the picture. The discomfort of wicker work for a baby is overcome by the use of a pillow. The chair is placed near the window to get the maximum daylight, and a single flash used above and slightly to one side of the camera.

Fig. 16.44 is the same little girl photographed two years later, this time with her baby sister. The plain light coloured wall forms a suitable background, and, all the furniture being cleared from the corner of the room, the children's rocking horse is positioned as far away from the wall as space will allow. This well-loved toy has several uses: 1. it keeps the children safe and in one place; 2. they are familiar with it and therefore inclined to be more natural; and 3. it adds to, rather than detracts from, the picture content. The children are facing the window, and a single flash is used above the camera.

The background shapes are interesting and the line flows easily from one figure to the other. The horse's head is not too insistent, there being less tonal contrast between it and the background than there is between the children and the background.

The unknown elements in at home portraiture are not always a disadvantage to the photographer—the rocking horse is a pleasant surprise!

Many parents are under the impression that children are happier when photographed in their own home. I do not altogether agree with this, as, after the initial shyness has worn off, a child enjoys a visit to the studio. The exciting lights, and the many varied toys with which to play, make a happy time for any youngster, as long as the photographer is fond of children.

233

17 Enlarging Techniques

WE MUST now study ways of reproducing the selected character traits on photographic paper, using any of the enlarging techniques which seem to be appropriate. Here the darkroom work becomes exciting and original. Only the photographer who has taken the picture can really know the type of personality he is trying to portray. The subtle differences in contrast, in depth of tone, in surface texture and in colour, all play a part in defining character.

SELECTING THE NEGATIVE

Perhaps the selection of the negative is more important than any other stage. It is always a temptation to glance through a strip of film and select one that looks the best. This practice may be satisfactory in landscape, or still-life photography, but is of little use in portraiture.

The almost imperceptible differences of expression—impossible to see on the negative, only become visible in the print. The wisest procedure is to:

1. Make contact prints of the whole film. These can be made in one strip, if preferred, as the correct exposure for each separate film is not so important at this stage.

2. From the strip of contact prints select the few most successful for enlarging.

3. Study the selected prints, and with the help of a mask made from two L-shaped pieces of card, decide on the tilt and the shape most suitable for the mood of the picture. Outline the area to be printed with pen or pencil.

If you find it easier, you could make an enlarged print of the whole of the selected frame, and mark the correct trim on that. The larger print makes it easier to decide which printing controls are necessary. By drawing on the print itself or by sketching on the back of the print, determine the areas to be controlled, either by shading-in or holding back. This is the time to decide on the aim of the finished print, and to make a note of the appropriate techniques to be used.

THE ENLARGER

What concerns us most about the enlarger is the type of illumination, and the effect this has on the quality of the print.

Broadly speaking there are three types of enlarger illuminants: Condenser, Diffused, Cold cathode. Of the three the condenser is the most brilliant, and therefore gives the utmost contrast from the negative. The other two being much softer in quality, would require a more contrasty negative in order to produce a similar print (on the same grade of paper) to that made with the condenser. The exposed film then must be processed to provide a contrast suitable for the type of enlarger illuminant to be used.

For all these exercises we have at our disposal a condenser type as well as a cold cathode. We are, therefore, able to make use of the enlarger as another tool for defining character. The greater brilliance and clarity of the condenser will convey the feeling of vigour, and vitality, as opposed to the quieter, more gentle rendering of the cold cathode. All character lines will be more clearly defined on a print made by the condenser illuminant. Therefore if much retouching has had to be done on the negative in use, the work will be less likely to show on the print if the cold cathode or diffuser type of illuminant is used.

While on the subject of enlargers it is appropriate to mention here a few routines which help maintain good print quality.

1. Keep the enlarger covered at all times when not in use.
2. Clean the two glass plates in the negative carrier with an anti-static cloth, and the lens with a lens tissue or brush, before commencing work.
3. Make a mask to fit the negative area to be enlarged, to prevent any unwanted light reaching the printing paper.
4. Shield the chromium columns of the enlarger with black paper or card to prevent light being reflected from them on to the printing paper.
5. Check for any stray light issuing from the enlarger lamphouse, or from any other source in the darkroom.
6. Make various sizes of oval, square and circular shapes from strong black paper, and fix these to pieces of thin wire about 12 in. long, with pieces of black

adhesive tape covering the incision holes in the paper. Small pieces of modelling clay on the end of thin wire are also useful. These are to be used for control in printing.

7.   Make large pieces of black card with a hole of varying shape and size cut in each, just off-centre. If preferred, two cards only need be used—one card being placed over the other to vary the size of the hole.

FOCUSING

Several aids are available to help ensure accurate focus. One such is the Scoponet, which focuses on the grain structure of the film. This is most useful when the negative is slightly soft focus or when the cold cathode enlarger, particularly, is being used and the negative is too dense to see through clearly. In such cases, and where there is no Scoponet, or similar device to hand, the simplest way to adjust the final focus is to replace the negative in the carrier with an old one which has been scratched with a pin. Focus on the spot where the two scratches cross. Care must be taken in withdrawing or replacing the negative carrier not to disturb the focus. To this end it is also advisable to set the lens aperture ready for use before focusing, and to focus on a piece of paper of the same thickness as that intended for the final print.

PAPER

We now come to the point where we must make the choice of the most suitable printing paper. To begin with we will discuss some of the types of paper available, and then examine each one as a technique for emphasizing a particular facet of character.

In the beginning it is better to choose a certain make of paper, and use it strictly according to the manufacturer's instructions until its peculiarities are well understood, rather than to switch from one make to another. It takes time and much practice to know how to get the best out of each type of paper, and it is unfair to judge without sufficient practical knowledge.

The two main types of printing paper for use in enlarging are bromide and chlorobromide.

Bromide
A paper of high sensitivity with little latitude in exposure time, giving pure black image tones, and delicate rendering of detail. The rich quality of the blacks

depends on the print being developed to finality. As exposure and development times are interrelated, the exposure should be such that the print is fully developed between $2\frac{1}{2}$ and 4 min. according to the developer and temperature combination. The rule is—minimum exposure for maximum development. A fully developed bromide print will tone to a rich sepia by use of the sulphide toning process.

A bromide paper can endure various controls during development, such as the use of warm developer on stubborn highlights, without the risk of colour change. The water-bath development—30 sec. immersion in plain water between brief developing times—can also be used if a softer result is needed.

Bromide paper is, characteristically, clean and crisp, owing to the clarity of the well-separated tones throughout the whole scale (see step-wedge, p.243).

A portrait print using the top end of the scale only (e.g. high key), will give an impression of lightness and delicacy, but the cool colour of the greys will tend to make it appear somewhat cold and detached.

The use of the full range of tones, from maximum black to maximum white will go with an exact, formal, or scientific turn of mind, while the lower end of the scale (e.g. low key) may suggest more vigour and vitality, but the pure black tones lack the warmth usually associated with human beings.

Bromide paper is eminently suitable for the presenting of a portrait in only the two "tones" of black and white. Here the purity of the tones is essential and the success lies in the correct exposure and development to obtain the maximum quality at both ends of the scale.

The two-tone portrait lacks intimacy but may be recognizably characteristic in costume, position, or mannerisms.

Chlorobromide

Chlorobromide is a paper of less sensitivity than bromide, but with greater latitude in exposure time. The general rule is for adequate exposure and minimum development. The development time is usually between one and two minutes, to obtain the normal warm black image colour. Prolonged development will make the tone progressively blacker, and will eventually, destroy the warm quality of the chlorobromide which is one of its chief characteristics. This paper is unsuitable for sepia toning by the sodium sulphide process, but varying colours from warm black to brown can be obtained by lengthening the exposure time and altering the constituents of the developer. Developer formulae will be given later in the chapter.

All warm tone prints look lighter under the yellow safelight than they really are, so development must be stopped just before the desired depth. The prints, especially those done on the matt surface paper, appear darker when dry than they do in the wet state. Allowance must be made for this. A chlorobromide print will also lose quality in the highlights if the print is left in the fixing solution for too long.

A part of the beauty of a chlorobromide paper lies in the rich, warm quality of the shadow areas, of the print. A glance at the step-wedge shows that there are more separated tones in the lower end of the scale, which makes the paper suitable for low key pictures having broad areas of dark tone. Chlorobromide is especially suitable for portraiture because of the characteristic warmth of tone. This gives a naturalness to the skin texture, and to the personality as a whole. Any picture with large areas of light tone will have vitality and daintiness, but will lack the crisp cleanliness of a similar picture printed on bromide paper. The choice should be made according to the interpretation we wish to put on its subject.

PAPER SURFACES

There are three main paper surfaces, produced by most manufacturers, which are of use to us as part of a technique: glossy, lustre and matt.

Glossy
The glossy surface reproduces the longest range of tones, especially when it is glazed. Because of the deep blacks it reproduces shadow detail better than any other surface. These deep blacks contrasting against pure whites give great impact to any print. A glossy print is always used (not always being glazed) for reproduction purposes. The glossy surface will emphasize grain, also scratches, retouching marks, and any blemishes. It is not easy to carry out hand work finish on a glossy print.

Lustre
As its name implies this paper has a slightly rough lustre surface. It is not a smooth surface such as a glossy or semi-matt, but it has a sheen, which gives it a good reflective quality. A lustre surface tends to hide the image graininess in the print, and absorb some of the marks and blemishes. It is reasonably easy to do hand work on a lustre surface print.

238

Matt

A matt surface does not have a long contrast range. It is more inclined to absorb light than to reflect it. For this reason a wet matt print will show well-separated black tones, but on drying, some of the darker tones tend to merge into one another. A matt print is easily finished.

Unless a print is especially required for reproduction the paper surface should be chosen according to the character of the person, or the particular mood we are trying to portray. If we consider a glossy surface to have not only impact but a clean, vibrant, strong, arrogant and even flamboyant nature, we shall begin to understand how we can use a paper surface as a technique for portraying character. In like manner a lustre paper is a good average; it does not appear to be so forceful as the glossy, but is more communicative than the matt. It has a cheerful simplicity, but no very great depth. For the latter property we turn to the matt surface especially when used for a low key. There is a serenity, a mystery, an unassuming power suggested by this surface and the harmony is maintained throughout its tones. We shall be applying this technique in a practical way at a later stage.

PAPER GRADE

Paper manufacturers have tried to ensure a good quality print from each negative contrast by supplying paper in at least three different contrast grades—soft, normal and hard, and some have stretched the scale further still to "very soft" and "very hard". It would seem that the choice concerning the paper grade for a particular negative should be a simple matter. But this is not so.

It is true that a negative which appears thin and flat when held against white paper requires a hard paper to produce as much contrast as possible from it and that a strong, contrasty looking negative needs a soft paper to shorten the tonal scale. But in this calculation we have omitted the essential factor—the subject matter itself.

A current mode among many photographers is to produce portraits in, almost, the two tones of black and white. These may be critically sharp, very blurred or with exaggerated grain. Many of the pictures are produced in this style for a purpose. The particular technique is chosen as a means of expression (which is what this chapter is all about!), but some are similarly produced merely for impact, and in this case, the photographer has projected his own image rather than that of his subject.

239

The purpose for which a picture is being produced must be considered through every phase of processing.

If the resulting picture is for reproduction, then the grade of paper chosen should be one which will pair with the negative to give the type of print required by the particular newspaper or periodical.

We are concerned, at the moment, with the expression of personality, character, or mood, as the subject of our picture. Therefore our choice of paper grade must be one which will convey this to the best advantage.

Let us consider the apparent qualities inherent in the two opposing grades of paper, hard and soft, when used in conjunction with a normal negative.

Hard paper

A hard paper, paired with a normal negative, will emphasize the sterner qualities within the subject. It may suggest a dynamic, forceful personality, or a person with strong, powerful physique. It can also indicate a cold, aloof, temperament.

Pairing a hard paper with a negative already strong in contrast will emphasize these characteristics to an even greater degree, possibly to the point when they can no longer be termed true, and the picture then becomes one that has impact only, as it has lost all trace of its communicative power.

It is occasionally possible that the use of a hard paper with a normal negative will transform a plain, unintellectual, perhaps colourless personality into one that is far more alert and exciting.

Soft paper

The soft grade of paper, when paired with a normal negative, will have the opposite effect. Its use will put greater emphasis on the more gentle, quiet, thoughtful, benevolent characteristics.

We come to the conclusion, then, that both hard and soft grades of paper can be used, even with the same normal negative, to depict a differing mood or opposing character trait which, to some degree, is within every human being.

Tonal quality of print

As well as the character, or the particular mood, of our subject, we have to think of the tonal quality of the print we wish to produce. If the effect is to be in a delicate high key, a subject with a very short tonal range and with all the tones in the upper part of the scale, the print must be made on a soft grade of paper— a paper which is incapable of producing very deep blacks. The more ethereal we want the picture to be, the softer must be the tonal quality.

A print that is required to have the full tonal range—from paper base high-lights to rich deep black shadows with as many intermediate tones as possible, must be printed on a normal paper—a paper which is capable of producing a full range of tones.

At the other end of the scale we have the low key print, in which the subject contains large areas of dark tone. Our choice for this will be the hard grade of paper, because the greatest number of separated tones are at the lower end of the scale, finishing with a deep black.

STEP-WEDGE COMPARISONS

In order to show the distribution of tones more clearly, we will compare a step-wedge made from a piece of the normal grade of bromide paper, and one from each of the other grades—hard and soft. When making the step-wedge we must ensure correct development, which, in the case of bromide paper, is until development is complete.

To avoid a common error, it is important to note that a bromide paper must have sufficient time in a developing solution before it will produce a good black tone, regardless of the length of exposure. It may be useful to prove for ourselves the correct time required to develop the particular paper we intend to use, so we will make our own tests.

We must cut six strips from a sheet of bromide paper and number them 1–6. These must be exposed to light for a few seconds and then developed separately in developer kept at a constant 68°F. No. 1 must be developed for $1\frac{1}{2}$ min., No. 2 for 2 min., No. 3 for $2\frac{1}{2}$ min. and so on. As all the strips have had a similar exposure it will be simple to ascertain the time at which the maximum black is obtained. This will be the *minimum* time for which this particular bromide paper must be developed at 68°F.

Now we can return to the development of the step-wedge, and, by developing to finality, we will find the maximum tone values of white and black of which the paper is capable. A piece of chlorobromide paper should be developed according to the makers instructions—usually between 2 and 3 min., the exposure being made adequate for such development.

Normal bromide

The step-wedge made from the normal grade of bromide paper shows an equal distribution of tones throughout. This paper, if used with an average negative, will produce a print having a full range of tones from black to white (Fig. 17.1).

241

Hard bromide

The hard grade of bromide paper has a shorter tonal scale than the normal. The intermediate tones are missing, making the step between each tone much steeper. The majority of separated tones are made up from dark greys. For this reason a hard paper is usually the more suitable for a low key picture having large areas of dark tone (Fig. 17.1a).

Soft bromide

The soft grade of bromide paper has a longer tonal scale than the normal— easily visible from the step-wedge. The steps are shallow, giving more inter- mediate tones—the majority of which are at the light end. This means that the soft paper will be the more suitable for all prints of a subject that is predominantly light in tone, such as high-key subject (Fig. 17.1b).

If we make a step-wedge from each packet of paper that we have in stock, and fix it to the *outside* of the packet, it will be a great help when we need to choose the right paper to suit a particular negative and to express a certain personality. From this step-wedge we shall be able to see, at a glance, the paper grade, the surface, the tonal distribution and the colour of the paper base.

COLOUR OF PAPER BASE

Most enlarging papers are obtainable with the emulsion coated on to a white or ivory base, and there are still a few which have a cream base.

The choice of colour is really one of personal preference, but there is a ten- dency towards the use of cream or ivory for male portraits having a dark back- ground, and white for any portrait that has large areas of light tone. This is because the cream, or ivory, enhances the warm beauty of the skin tones, and gives a deep richness to the dark shadows, but will tend to make all large areas of light tone appear slightly degraded. For this reason, portraits having light backgrounds will appear to have greater clarity of tone when printed on a white based paper.

In the following experiments we will concentrate on the normal grade, white based bromide and chlorobromide papers, obtaining a variety of image tones by controlled processing.

TEST STRIPS

Having selected the most suitable paper we must now make some tests to deter- mine the correct exposure. We will make these first on the bromide paper and then on the chlorobromide.

17.1
17.1a
17.1b 17.2

Fig. 17.1. Step-wedge made from normal bromide paper
Fig. 17.1a. Step-wedge made from hard bromide paper
Fig. 17.1b. Step-wedge made from soft bromide paper
Fig. 17.2. F. W. Tyler, Esq. Normal glossy bromide 2 sec. exposure

243

Bromide paper

We need a strip of paper, not necessarily very wide, but long enough to cross a portion of the background, the face—including one eye, and the clothes. This should take in a sample of the lightest and darkest tones. As a bromide is a rapid enlarging paper, the exposures are likely to be comparatively brief. The first strip we will expose for 2, 4, 8, 16, 32 sec. and develop it for $2\frac{1}{2}$ min. at 68°F.

From this strip we can judge the approximate exposure time. Taking this to be 8 sec., we will make five further tests each on a separate strip of paper at 6, 7, 8, 9, 10 sec. We will mark the time on the back and placing each one on the enlarger baseboard, successively, in exactly the same place. After exposing the strips we develop them all together for the $2\frac{1}{2}$ min. at 68°F. We can now make a truer estimate of the exposure and determine the amount of control which may be required.

The final print will be developed at the same temperature, 68°F, but must remain in the solution until development is complete. This may be at the end of the $2\frac{1}{2}$ min., but development can be continued, if necessary, for 3 or 4 min., to reach the maximum black.

The golden rule for bromide paper can be said to be "minimum exposure and maximum development".

Chlorobromide

Our next print will be on chlorobromide paper, our aim being the warm-black image tone. We shall make the test strips in a similar way to those on the bromide paper, with the exception of the exposure time. This will be comparatively longer, as the chlorobromide is somewhat slower in emulsion speed.

We shall find a difference in the developing technique. The makers will supply the data for this, giving the developing time as approximately $1\frac{1}{2}$–$2\frac{1}{2}$ min., at 68°F. This $2\frac{1}{2}$ min. must be considered the *maximum* developing time if we are to produce a warm-black image tone. The longer the development time, the blacker the image tone will be. Our exposures, then, must be sufficient to allow for the correct depth of tone to be obtained in *less* than the maximum development time.

For chlorobromides, the rule should be "adequate exposure and minimum development".

WORKING TEMPERATURE

We have mentioned 68°F as being the temperature at which solutions should remain constant. This is an average safe temperature.

Hydroquinone, the chemical responsible for making good black tones in a print, will not work at all in a temperature below 55°F.

For a bromide print the recommended working temperature is 68°–70°F maximum.

For chlorobromide there is more latitude in the selected temperature, but it must remain constant throughout the process. A temperature of between 70°F and 75°F will ensure a warm image tone, but the method makes it difficult to transfer the print from developer to stop bath at precisely the correct moment, and even 1 or 2 sec. error, either way, can be enough to spoil the print. It is safer to keep the solutions at 68°F and to control the warmth of the image tone by giving increased exposure time and by developing for $1\frac{1}{2}$ min.

STOP BATH

It is not essential to use a stop bath for a bromide print to "arrest development", though it is useful for conserving the fixing bath, especially with "rapid" fixers. A chlorobromide, however, depends on the stop bath to terminate the development.

FIXING

It is not advisable to keep a print in the fixer for more than 10 or 12 min. After this time the highlights may begin to bleach out.

CONTROLS IN ENLARGING

Quite a number of controls can be used during the enlarging process to emphasize or minimize certain characteristics. For areas that are too light or too dark in tone, a piece of card, with or without a hole cut in it, can be placed in the enlarger beam and kept on the move all the time. The corners and edges of the print also can be darkened by control and so direct attention to the face.

To darken an area where there is unwanted detail, it is more satisfactory to fog. To do this make the main exposure first, attending to the control of small areas, such as shielding the hair, or printing up the hands, etc., then proceed in the following manner: Stop the lens down to the smallest but one aperture, turn out the enlarger light, remove the negative from the carrier (replace the carrier to prevent any leakage of light, and remove the orange cap). Having a piece of card held ready over the face area and keeping it continually on the move, switch

245

on the light for a predetermined exposure. The test strip to find the fog level of the paper and the time required to darken it to the required tone, should be made at the same time as the normal tests.

This darkening of extraneous highlights gives a sense of harmony to the picture as a whole, as well as concentrating attention on the essential element.

There are times when we would like to add a distinctive touch to the picture in honour of the renowned personality we are portraying—or, perhaps, as a more pictorial way of describing particular achievements, occupations or hobbies, or even to emphasize a certain quality.

SCREENS

One way to emphasize a certain quality in the subject is to place a diffusing screen between the lens and the printing paper, during the whole, or part, of the exposure time.

A piece of nylon stocking, or similar material, placed over the lens for a portion of the exposure will have the effect of softening the image outlines, but does nothing towards the characterization of the subject.

A fine mesh screen placed half-way between the lens and the paper for the duration of the exposure will soften the contrast of a print by adding tone to the highlights. In so doing, it adds tone to the whole print, dark areas as well as light, by removing the subtle intermediary tones from the dark areas. This technique, then, is useful for reducing the contrast in an average tonal subject, or for one that is predominantly light in tone, but is unsatisfactory for a print with broad areas of dark tone.

A screen of tissue paper, Windolite, finely woven material, or anything of a similar nature, can be placed in contact with the paper to give various results.

The beauty of a picture treated in this way depends on the material used for the screen. Too coarse a texture, if placed in contact with the paper, will supplant the portrait by its own image. A piece of fine white material will give a very different result from a similar piece of black. It is worth experimenting with different screens in order to discover the one most suitable for the particular character you are trying to express.

A few illustrations will suffice to demonstrate the technique.

Fig. 17.2 is the late Frank W. Tyler, F.S.A. The letters after his name— Fellow of the Society of Antiquaries—give a clue to his life's interests. He was also a genealogist. A great proportion of his time was taken up with studying and investigating the past.

He was a quiet, retiring, kindly, trustworthy personality, exuding a vital interest in his work, yet apparently having a deep inner serenity which enabled him to relax at will.

What techniques shall we employ to give as true a picture as possible of this man as a genealogist of the calibre described? The choice of the low key effect to express the depth of intelligence, thought and serenity, has been made when taking the picture also the inclusion of books to suggest the background of a study. It is left to us now to choose the style of printing. A hard grade paper, which would be the choice for large areas of dark tone, would indicate a clever, perhaps brilliant man in his field of work—which he was—but an unapproachable person—which he certainly was not. An ordinary print on soft paper would not show sufficient vitality. The use of a screen will add a distinctive touch to the picture and will also soften the tones.

A piece of tissue paper is placed in contact with the printing paper emulsion for the duration of the exposure. (Normal glossy bromide, exposure 2 sec.) (Fig. 17.3).

The grainy effect is quite pleasing if we wish to emphasize his work. His dealings with old parchments, is suggested by the whole portrait having a textured surface. The dark tones have merged together, simplifying them to the point of monotony. However, these could be controlled, and, in a large print, this could be acceptable as a distinctive portrait.

A screen of white chiffon gives a very similar result. Possibly the most disappointing feature of these two screens, is the loss of communication through the eyes. It is the mouth which captures our attention in preference to the eyes, and it should be vice versa, especially when the eyes are so expressive.

Still using the same type of paper we will make a print with a piece of *black* chiffon in contact with it, and give an exposure of 4 sec.—being double that of the other two. The result is very different, as you can see at a glance. Instead of the dark tones being merged together they are beautifully separated. The rendering of the eyes is exceptionally good and the power of communication, strong. The lengthening of the tonal scale throughout enhances the deep serenity which is so marked in his character, and the textured surface illustrates the distinctive quality of the man and his profession (Fig. 17.4).

These experiments have been made on bromide paper for ease of reproduction, but, pictorially, a warm-toned chlorobromide would suit the subject admirably.

A black chiffon screen, on a *hard* grade of paper would give a greater degree of contrast (grade for grade chlorobromide is of slightly greater contrast than bromide) which could help to express the vitality which is needed.

Fig. 17.3. Tissue paper; normal glossy bromide 2 sec. exposure

248

Fig. 17.4. Black chiffon screen; normal glossy bromide, exposure 4 sec.

249

Our chosen printing technique, therefore, for this particular subject is the following:

The print will be made on a piece of hard, glossy, chlorobromide paper, diffused with a black chiffon screen throughout the exposure. The exposure will be double that required for an undiffused print. The print is processed in a special developer to give a warm-black image tone.

One more example may be given of the method for choosing the suitable printing technique for a particular personality.

This portrait (Fig. 17.5) is of a tall, slim, brown haired, fair complexioned young woman, wearing a brown-green jacket and coloured scarf. She is a natural, warm-hearted person, and friendly in a rather shy and reserved way. She is temperamental—being subject to moods of exhilaration and depression. As might be expected, she is artistic, and has the artist's craving for perfection in everything. Her hobbies include painting and dressmaking.

From what we now know about her, how shall we choose the most suitable printing techniques?

Let us take each trait in turn and consider the way in which to represent it on photographic paper.

1. Appearance—fair complexion, brown hair and brownish toned jacket.

For the best representation of her physical appearance we would choose (a) a bromide print, fully developed and sepia toned, (b) a warm-tone chlorobromide print.

The natural, friendly, but shy personality can be shown by:

(a) soft or normal bromide paper with lustre surface,
(b) warm-black chlorobromide, lustre or matt surface,
(c) either paper diffused with black chiffon.

The gay temperament can be expressed by a white glossy paper either bromide or chlorobromide. The mood of depression can safely be ignored. The artistic qualities are well represented by the use of a screen.

Attention to detail, which is the hallmark of a perfectionist, will be expressed most vividly by a white glossy bromide—clean and crisp.

We can summarize the technique to reproduce as many of the characteristics as possible in one print as follows:

The print will be made on white normal, glossy bromide, or white chlorobromide developed to a warm-black image tone. The bromide print can be toned a rich sepia, with the sulphide-toning process, or with one of several toners available in a variety of colours. A screen of black chiffon will be used in contact with the paper during the exposure (Fig. 17.6).

Compare the rendering of hair, clothes and particularly eyes in Fig. 17.6 with that in Fig. 17.5. The use of the screen gives the print a distinctive charm, in keeping with the personality, and the natural friendly nature is expressed through the beautiful rendering of the eyes.

These few experiments will suggest to you other ways of exposing a print to produce a picture with a difference. It is well to remember, though, that "a print with a difference" may be pictorial, but if it is not characteristic of the subject, it is not strictly a portrait in the sense in which this discussion is being held.

CONTROLS IN PRINT DEVELOPMENT

Let us now see if there are any ways in which we can control the print production, as it passes through the processing stage.

Bromide paper

There is little that we can do during the development time for bromide paper, apart from assisting underexposed highlights to develop a little further by touching them with warm water or more concentrated developer. As we have already seen, bromide paper required full and sufficient development to produce its best quality. No amount of control at the development stage will produce a print superior in quality to one that has been exposed correctly in every tone to allow development of each one to finality. We come back again to the realization that a good bromide print requires minimum *sufficient* exposure and maximum *sufficient* development.

There are times, however, when the result we are aiming for does not require any black tones, in fact the picture is to represent a mood, depicted in shades of white and grey. In this case we have a means of control that we can use for prints, although at one time it was more generally used for negative development. This control is known as *water bath development*.

For this control, a dish of plain water, at the same temperature as the developer, is placed alongside the developing dish. The print is immersed in the developer for 30 sec., and then transferred to the water bath where it should remain, motionless, face down for a further 60 sec. This is repeated until the required depth of tone has been reached. The process allows for the highlight areas to continue developing after the shadows have exhausted the supply of developer, thereby producing a print with greatly reduced contrast.

251

17.6 17.5

Fig. 17.5. Maureen: normal glossy bromide 2 sec. exposure
Fig. 17.6 Normal glossy bromide; black chiffon screen. 4½ sec. exposure

252

A soft working developer can produce an extra soft result; alternatively a contrast developer will give a hard quality to the print. Apart from that any controls when using bromide paper must be made during the exposure.

Chlorobromide

In a chlorobromide the image colour can be varied during the development process from black to warm-black, brown-black, or even brown, but, in most cases, extra exposure will be needed.

Three ways of doing this are as follows:

1. By diluting the developer with water. The amount of dilution must be found by experiment, but if it is more than 2 : 1, a few drops of potassium bromide (10 per cent solution) should be added, together with a drop of Johnsons 142. Extra exposure for the print will be needed, and the development can be continued until the required tone is reached.

This developer will soften the contrast in a print.

2. Extra potassium bromide can be added to the normal strength developer, again the amount must be found by experiment. The exposure of the print should be increased, but the development time should not be prolonged.

3. A special low energy developer can be used. The image tone can be varied by straight development using D.163 for black tones, D.156 for warm-black and D.166 for brown-black.

AFTER TREATMENT OF PRINTS

Points to remember when developing prints are:

1. *Warm* tone prints appear lighter under the yellow safelight than they really are.
2. Allowance must be made for any print to darken slightly during the drying process. This is especially important for a matt surface print, which reflects more light when wet than it does when dry.

A slightly over-dark print might benefit from a quick run through a reducing solution. For this purpose a 10 per cent solution of potassium ferricyanide, and (in a separate large bottle) a 10 per cent solution of plain hypo should always be kept in the darkroom ready for use.

For over-all lightening a print, immerse the whole print in a dish containing some of the 10 per cent hypo solution, with one or two drops of the 10 per cent

253

"ferri" (the mixed solution should be a pale lemon colour). Rock the print for a few minutes, and then transfer to the washing tank for half an hour. A print that has been through a stop bath before fixing will take a longer time before the "ferri" begins to work.

This process can be repeated if the print is still a little dark when dry, but fresh solution must be used, as the mixture lasts only a very short time.

A stronger solution of "ferri" can be used to lighten small areas of light tone, but care must be taken that the image is not completely removed, which can happen all too quickly. It is rarely satisfactory to try to lighten areas of dark tone by the same method. The unevenness of tone becomes visible in the dried print, and the black is devoid of quality.

For small prints the quick run through a weak solution of "ferri" is usually sufficient. As the "ferri" works on the highlights first, the print should look brighter after treatment but the blacks should retain their quality.

REDUCING A LARGE PRINT

Large prints often benefit from localized reducing—even very minute spots can be lightened with care and patience.

Let us "reduce" a 20 × 16 in. print in which there are some highlights without sufficient tone separation, some stray hairs over the forehead, a few blemishes on the skin, and the grey dress lacks variety in tone.

We must first soak the print for 10–15 min. to soften the emulsion, then blot off all the surplus water with a clean towel. The print is laid on a flat surface such as the underneath of a 20 × 16 in. dish or a large enamelled tray (a butcher's tray, or any white enamelled metal sheet is admirable), and placed on the table at which we intend to work.

We have a large dish of water beside us (or a sink with running water), a little pot with a fairly strong solution of the "ferri" mixture, some cotton wool and a spotting brush. We will cover the print with a smooth towel (except for the portion on which we are going to work). In one hand we must hold a piece of cotton wool which has been wrung out in plain water, and in the other hand the spotting brush, or small piece of cotton wool rolled round a matchstick. The spotting brush must, of course, be used for the major part of the work, the hairs and blemishes are too fine for the cotton wool.

Having dipped the brush in the "ferri", we just touch the blemish, with the same movement used for ordinary retouching, and immediately wipe with the wet cotton wool in the other hand. This process is continued in quick succession,

254

touch—wipe—until the required amount of work has been completed. At intervals we can immerse the whole print in water and then blot with the towel and continue. Keeping the print blotted prevents any solution from running down it, which could be disastrous. When the necessary reduction has been completed, the print must be washed in running water for half an hour. This process does take some time but is often well worth while.

Another print reducer which can be used is made, very simply, by adding some tincture of iodine to a tray of ordinary water. The dry print is placed in this solution and removed when the highlights take on a slightly blue tinge. A short soak in *plain* hypo will remove the blue tone. The print should then be washed and dried as usual. Localized spots can be removed with the iodine in the same way as has been described with the "ferri", with the one difference— a piece of cotton wool wrung out in plain hypo must be used in place of the piece dampened with water.

INTENSIFYING PRINTS

A print that is a little too light when dry can be improved by intensification, provided it has had sufficient exposure. In other words, if the print is under-exposed, nothing can be done with it, but if it is fully exposed and under-developed it can be improved.

One method which gives slight intensification is to bleach the print in the bleaching formula used for sulphide toning, followed with a wash in running water for at least half an hour, and then to re-develop in an ordinary M.Q. print developer. (Not a warm-tone developer).

For greater intensification the chromium intensifier can be used. This intensifier is used for negatives and the formula can be found in any photographic book dealing with the subject. A word of warning, though, when using chromium for prints. Make certain that the washing time between the bleaching and re-developing is adequate, otherwise print staining may occur at some future date. The chromium gives a warm-black tone to the print, which is quite attractive.

Some photographs appear more characteristic if the prints are toned with sulphide or selenium, especially so if the model is auburn or brunette, and wearing a brown colour. It is possible to get three different colour tones from the use of sulphide—brown-black, warm-brown, or cold-brown. The brown-black is particularly useful if the model has very dark brown hair and is wearing pastel shades. The selenium tones to a beautiful purple-reddish-brown.

255

SULPHIDE TONING

This is most suitable for bromide prints which must have been fully developed and washed completely free from hypo.

Stock bleaching solution

Potassium bromide	50 g	($\frac{1}{2}$ oz)
Potassium ferricyanide	100 g	(1 oz)
Water to make	1000 ml	(10 oz)

For use take 1 part of the stock solution to 9 parts of water.

This solution will keep indefinitely if put in a dark bottle away from the light, and can be used over and over again until exhausted.

1. Soak the well washed and dried bromide print for a few minutes to soften the gelatine and then bleach in the above solution until the image is pale yellow.

2. Rinse the bleached print in water for 1 min. (longer washing will impair the tone).

3. Put the print in the sulphide solution where it will immediately darken to a sepia tone. When all action is finished transfer to washing tank.

4. Wash for half an hour.

Stock sulphide solution

Sodium sulphide (pure)	200 g	(4 oz)
Water, to make	1000 ml	(20 oz)

For use take 3 parts of stock solution to 20 parts of water.

Discard the used solution immediately.

If a colder brown tone is preferred, the prepared print should be placed in the sulphide bath first for a few minutes. After a brief wash it is then bleached and toned in the manner already described.

Occasionally a print where the deeper shadows are more black than brown will give more distinction. For this it is only necessary to remove the print from the bleaching bath before the dark tones have bleached out.

18 Understanding Colour

No STUDY of portrait techniques would be complete without the inclusion of colour. Many amateur photographers concentrate on colour transparencies, and seldom expose a black and white film. If you are among this number, and your subject is portraiture, you will quickly realize that this chapter cannot be divorced in context from the rest of the book, but that it is a study of an extra technique— essential if we are to understand the detailed search for character and personality in portraiture.

You will soon realize that we are attempting to use colour creatively—as a technical tool—and not only scientifically, when correct colour rendering would be the main incentive. To illustrate my meaning, let us imagine that we have a charming, attractively dressed, model in front of our camera. We follow the film manufacturer's instructions regarding the light sources, the brightness ratios and the exposure, and, finally, send the film away for processing.

The resulting transparency proves the exposure to be correct, and all the colours to be faithfully reproduced. In this instance we have recorded our subject quite accurately in colour but have made no attempt to use colour creatively.

In this chapter we are going to explore colour, and try to discover ways of exploiting it to interpret personality, mood and atmosphere, with even greater clarity than is possible in black and white. We shall consider the psychological aspect of colour, the relation of one colour to another, and the mixture of colours, as applied to light. We shall discuss the lighting and exposure techniques where they differ from those already described in previous chapters. Finally I shall suggest a few controls which may be a starting point for future experiments.

PSYCHOLOGICAL ASPECT

In everyday life we are surrounded by colour. We like, or dislike, certain colours. We use colour to express our emotions. We choose colours for house decoration and dress materials according to our temperament, and the effect that colour has on our personality. We have become so involved in colour that all too often, we accept it without understanding much about it, or, sometimes, without really seeing it.

COLOUR CHARACTERISTICS

Let us refresh our minds by investigating the five main colours, red, blue, green, yellow, purple, separately, considering some of the qualities which are associated with each.

Red

Red is the most powerful, active, exciting, assertive colour of all. Red has "impact", hence its use, so often, as a focal point in a picture. Red is universally used as a signal for danger, because of the sharp brilliance of its colour when contrasted against any other colour.

Red can be horrific through its association with blood, and dramatic though its connection with fire. In these illustrations red is hard, domineering, intensely active, and indicative of anger, rebellion, danger and extreme heat.

The positive characteristics of red are excitement, gaiety and joy. We think of red decorations, of holly berries and robins associated with Christmas festivities. The bright cheerfulness of red makes it attractive to children, even to babies.

The red ray is strong and powerful. It may sometimes help to lift depression in a strong type of person, but its violence is too overpowering for anyone who is nervous or weak.

Blue

Blue is quite the opposite in character to red. It has a calming, cooling influence, and is less assertive.

Blue is a positive colour, and belongs more to the spiritual side of life.

We talk of "a heavenly *blue*". Church furnishings are often in blue, probably adapted from the painters who robed the Virgin Mary in blue and white.

Blue denotes freedom and expresses a joy of life. We think of the lark soaring in a bright *blue* sky, or the pleasures of swimming in the deep *blue* Mediterranean Sea.

258

Blue is the colour of honour and of royalty. We talk of being "true blue" and "blue-blooded".

Negatively blue denotes depression and extreme cold. We speak of "feeling blue" and of being "blue" with cold. We also describe an extremely cold atmosphere as "ice blue".

Coloured light rays are used in the art of healing, and the blue ray is said to have great antiseptic power, to be electric, and to have a calming effect on the patient. It can also relieve pain to a certain extent.

From the foregoing we learn that blue emphasises the spiritual, and is a colour of poise, serenity and joyous freedom. It calms the mind of a worried, excitable or fearful person, but it can also make one feel physically cold, and mentally aloof.

Green

A positive thought about green is its luxuriousness—the "green" of the Emerald Isle, and the trees turning "green" with fresh leaves in spring, thus we associate green with renewed life and energy. It is not vibrant like red. It steals upon our consciousness rather than bursting in on us as red is inclined to do.

Green is neutral; it is neither hot nor cold; it is harmonious, and a peaceful, soft colour. Green will advance when related to yellow, and recede when related to blue.

Green is the colour of nature, and, to keep healthy, everyone needs the green of the trees and fields. Were it not for parks and commons the town dwellers would be starved of green, and would periodically have to visit the country to be re-vitalized by the green light ray. Negatively, green stands for withdrawal. A person is said to "turn green" before fainting, to "look green" with fear, or with sickness. Green is also used as a descriptive term for an inexperienced person who can be imposed on too readily. Jealousy has been referred to as "the green-eyed monster", and "I was green with envy" is a phrase which is often heard.

Yellow

Yellow is a joyous, uplifting, golden colour. It is associated in our minds with sunshine, with spring flowers, and fluffy chicks—the colour of Easter and new life.

The yellow light ray is known as the "Ray of Wisdom"—the reason, perhaps, why a golden crown represents kingship, and a golden halo adorns the saint's head in religious pictures.

259

Although yellow is predominantly positive and uplifting by nature, it does have its negative side. Yellow is suggestive of cowardice and disease. We talk of "a yellow streak", and of "yellow jaundice". A plant is sickly when the leaves turn yellow.

Yellow, when it is related to red, becomes more active, and suggests autumn, and falling leaves, with eventual decay.

Purple

Purple is associated in our minds with royalty, and with all kinds of pomp and ceremony. It conjures up pictures of rich velvet, or satin, fabrics in folds of deeply saturated colour, or the flowing robes of honour as worn by royalty. Purple has a solemn dignity. Being composed of blue and red it acts as a balance between the two. It can be said to be active in a slow, majestic way, and passive in its dignified solemnity.

Purple has also been used to symbolize the erotic.

The paler shades of purple have a softer dignity, and a sense of noble serenity.

Negatively purple is associated with death, and funerals, but even so, it maintains its royal dignity.

COLOUR RELATIONSHIPS

A valuable aid to any student of colour is the Munsell colour wheel, which shows the five principal colours, fully saturated, and all the intermediate hues in steps of decreasing saturation. The contrasting and harmonizing of individual colours can be ascertained at a glance.

Fig. 18.1 is a greatly simplified form of the Munsell wheel, but it will serve as a visual aid to our study.

The three complementary colours red, green and blue, being shaded, are easily distinguishable. Equilateral triangles connecting three colours, show immediately the colours which will harmonize with one another. An endless variety could be made but illustrating them all would make for confusion.

Fig. 18.2 shows what is meant by the term "complementary colour". (When dealing with coloured light, as opposed to pigments or dyes, the colours red, green and blue in equal proportions add up to white. We shall refer to this again when we are using filters over the lights for colour control).

Using the above wheel for reference, let us look again at each of our five principal colours now in its relationship to other colours.

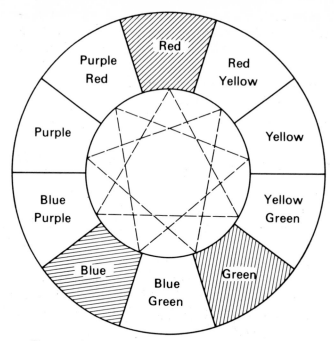

Fig. 18.1. A colour wheel for staging colour relationships

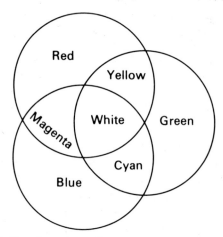

Fig. 18.2. Complementary colours
Red + Green = Yellow
Red + Blue = Magenta
Green + Blue = Cyan
Red + Blue + Green = White

261

Red. Red is one of the complementary colours. Its opposite or contrasting colour on the wheel is blue-green. Red is a warm, advancing colour, while blue-green is cold and receding. Red is related to purple-red on the one side and red-yellow (orange) on the other. The temperature is cooled by the purple-red, and its excitement modified by the red-yellow. Vivid colours of these two relatives will clash and give a loud, noisy, effect. Desaturating one of them will give a more peaceful effect and make a pleasing arrangement.

Red, blue and yellow-green are connected by the equilateral triangle, which means that red will compose well with either or both, particularly if one, or two, out of the three are desaturated.

Red, desaturated to shades of pink, has all its characteristics modified, and it becomes more self-effacing and delicate.

Red has the greatest impact of any colour: it is also the warmest colour, and adds warmth to any other colour mixed with it. In strong colour it can be garish and hard.

Blue. Blue is the coldest, most receding colour and will cool down any other colour which is mixed with it. The opposite colour to blue, and the one, therefore, to contrast most strongly with it is red-yellow.

Blue is related to blue-purple on the one side and blue-green on the other, both cold colours because of the blue content, but obviously slightly warmer than the blue alone.

As we have already seen, blue composes well with red and yellow-green if one or more are desaturated. The more desaturated blue becomes, the more ethereal and the more icy cold its appearance.

Green. Green, as we have mentioned before, is neutral. It neither advances nor recedes, it is neither warm nor cold. In order to make green advance and be warmer it must be mixed with its relative, yellow-green; to enable it to recede and become cooler it must be mixed with its other relative, blue-green.

The equilateral triangle links green with blue-purple and red-yellow.

The colour to contrast most strongly with green is purple-red.

Green harmonizes with all colours and has a calming effect.

Yellow. Yellow is an advancing, warm colour, and the mixing of any colour with yellow will create a feeling of warmth.

Yellow contrasts most strongly with blue-purple.

Yellow is related to red-yellow (orange) on the one side and yellow-green on the other, both of which are warm colours but the red-yellow is the more active.

Yellow will harmonize with blue-green and purple-red. Desaturated blue-green enhances a passive yellow subject, while desaturated purple-red creates a more active atmosphere.

Yellow is formed when green light is added to red light.

Purple. Purple is more active, warm and advancing than blue, but less active than red.

Purple contrasts most strongly with yellow-green.

Purple is related to the active purple-red on the warm side and the more passive blue-purple on the cold side, although the blue content of purple will make it always cold in comparison with red, yellow and green.

Purple will harmonize with red-yellow and green. Equal areas of purple-red and blue-purple will clash and give a noisy, discordant effect.

To sum up our findings, so far, regarding the colours illustrated on the wheel, we can tabulate as follows:

1. Each colour contrasts most strongly with the one immediately opposite it. Saturated colours of both in one composition will give maximum brilliance and maximum impact.

2. Equal areas of strong contrasting colours, or of strong unrelated colours, will clash. Desaturating one or more of them will make a pleasing arrangement.

3. Each colour is related to the one on either side of it.

4. Colours at the three ends of an equilateral triangle within the wheel will compose well together.

5. Warm colours from red to green on the right of the wheel—are advancing colours.

6. Cold colours—from purple-red to blue-green on the left of the wheel—are receding colours.

7. All colour characteristics are modified by mixing with other colours or by desaturating.

LIGHTING AND COLOUR

We studied methods of lighting for various types of face, and for the characterization of personality in the earlier chapters.

In the main these techniques still apply, but the fact that we are now using a colour film instead of a black and white means that we have two additional factors to consider:

263

1. The balance between the type of colour film in use and the colour temperature of the light.

2. The effect of light on the various colours in the picture.

1. *Colour film*

If you habitually use colour films you will know that *reversal* films are obtainable in two main types: those balanced for use with daylight and those balanced for use with artificial light.

The artificial light film is sub-divided into: Type A for photoflood lamps (3400°Kelvin), and Type B for tungsten lamps (3200°K).

Using a daylight film in conjunction with artificial light will result in an overall red-yellow cast, as the colour temperature of daylight is very much higher (i.e. bluer) than that of any artificial light, with the exception of blue flashbulbs and electronic flash. These two light sources are used with daylight film (which will give correct colours in the "blue" light of day), but any other light needs a correction filter to obviate the yellow cast.

On occasions we may wish to mix daylight with artificial light in the studio, e.g. when photographing the subject near a window. Now the choice is ours. A daylight film will give a general feeling of warmth to the picture, while the Type A or B film will produce a much colder, bluish effect.

It is advisable to have all the lamps in use of the same colour temperature.

The experiments that we undertake together will be made on Type B reversal film in conjunction with tungsten lighting.

2. *Effect of light on colour*

A parallel beam of light from a high-powered spotlight gives, as we already know, a sharply defined, bright, contrasty light, with clear cut dark shadows. The effect of this on strong colours will be to make them appear brilliant but rather harsh, and darker or more intense than we might expect. The light colours will lose some of their tone by being too bright, and the overall contrast of the colours will be increased. The crisp clarity of the light is unfeeling, and, while the mood of the picture may be gay, it will lack emotion.

The cone-shaped beam of light from a flood emits a much softer light, giving more transparent shadows. All colours appear more natural, less harsh, and have more emotional feeling. The intensity of the light can be controlled by the distance of the lamp from the subject—the nearer the light the more brilliant will be the colours and vice versa.

The softer the light source the more restful and emotional will be the mood conveyed. A diffusing screen, made of butter muslin or translucent paper stretched over a frame, and placed between the light and the subject will soften the brilliance of the light without dulling it, which latter effect results when a diffuser is placed directly over the light.

A soft over-all illumination can be obtained by bouncing the light off reflectors. These are made of aluminium foil (dull side) or pure white paper, stretched over a 3 × 2 ft piece of hardboard. Some reflectors made of bright coloured paper are useful for certain effects—when an over-all colour cast is required.

A colour film cannot cope with extreme contrasts, therefore the lighting ratio must be such that the overall contrast range is low. An average subject can be lit with a brightness ratio of 1 : 2 or 1 : 3, but if the colours of the subject are of *very low* contrast—either all dark or all light, the brightness ratio can be increased to as much as 1 : 6 if necessary. This allows for variety in lighting, it makes back lighting possible and gives scope for characterization and imagination. The lighting then, must always be considered in relation to the subject colour contrast, and to the exposure, and the whole related to the character and mood of the subject.

BACKGROUNDS

Backgrounds play an important part in any portrait, but perhaps more so in colour than in black and white. An unlit background appears dead, and the subject is made to look static. Coloured background paper can be used but it is difficult to have a sufficient variety of colours to suit every picture, or to control the light and shade on it. A more comprehensive and satisfactory way is to have three rolls of background paper—one each of black, white and grey, together with a variety of pieces of coloured gelatine for use over the background lights.

Black background

Any colour, seen against black, will appear more saturated and luxurious, and in a transparency, more brilliant and luminous. It is most effective for low key subjects, and subjects containing only one strong colour.

Any light that is required on the background is produced by light passed through a selected piece of colour gel.

White background

White, being a mixture of all colours, appears, when used as a background, in a transparency, to reduce the intensity of each separate colour. It also attracts attention to itself, by its brightness, which again, weakens the picture. A glow of coloured light can be produced by the coloured gelatine, which will enhance instead of weaken the colours of the subject. If a mixture of colours is required on the background, a separate light for each colour must be used. This will add one colour to the other on the white background paper. In a colour print white is seen to be "white" as opposed to "bright", and therefore will not weaken the colours as it does in a transparency. Instead it makes them appear more saturated and isolated, more clear cut and emotionless.

Grey background

Grey is a neutral colour and will quieten or tone down any colour that is mixed with it. Grey paper, then, is very useful as a background, because it does not draw attention to itself. Light of the required colour can be directed on it where necessary, in the same manner as described above. By this means the interest is centred on the subject, and the softly echoing light on the background lends harmony to the theme of the picture.

As a precaution, all other lights are switched off while the background light is being positioned. This ensures against the risk of unwanted coloured light straying across the model's face.

EXPOSING FOR COLOUR

In some respects the exposure calculations for a colour film are simpler than those for black and white. Correct exposure is essential, the film has very little latitude—a contrast range of only 4–1—and variations in exposure time are reduced to a minimum. The control comes mainly in the arrangement of the colours and in keeping them within the contrast range of the film.

If a subject is comprised of light and dark colours we know that all the colours cannot be recorded correctly at the same time. If we expose for the light colours the dark ones will be underexposed. If we expose for the dark colours the light ones will be overexposed and possibly bleached right out. If we were using a black and white film we could compromise, or expose for the highlights and add more light to the shadows. This is not possible with colour—we must reduce the colour contrast in the subject. Keeping the contrast really low will give more latitude in the exposure time, thus allowing for variations in depth of tone to suit individual requirements. For certain subjects we may wish the colours to be rendered darker in tone than the normal "correct" exposure produces them. Reducing the lens aperture by $\frac{1}{2}$–1 stop achieves this. Alternatively, opening the lens aperture by $\frac{1}{2}$ stop will desaturate the colours more than average. The suggestion of only $\frac{1}{2}$ stop in this direction is because the lighter colours so quickly lose their delicacy of tone and take on a "washed-out" appearance. If the colour contrast cannot be sufficiently reduced it is better to calculate the exposure for the light colours and let the dark look after themselves. At times it may be possible to substitute black for the dark colours. This would give a much brighter effect, as underexposed colour looks clogged-up, and it is impossible to underexpose black in a colour transparency. At the other end of the scale, of course, it may be possible to substitute white for the palest colour, as it is likewise impossible to overexpose white. This latter control may be less practical, because the white will take on a colour cast from any stronger colour in close proximity to it.

Exposure calculation can be executed in the same manner as described previously for black and white. The only difference is that for colour the white card reading is used and multiplied by a factor of 5 (or, alternatively, the film speed ÷ 5 which will mean only one adjustment for the whole film). This gives the correct average colour tone, and the controls for darker or lighter results can be used as described above.

Control by exposure

It may be that our subject is made up of all highly saturated colours to create a vibrant, happy mood. In this case calculating the exposure against a white card ×5, and then the reducing of the lens aperture by $\frac{1}{2}$–1 stop, will ensure the full brilliance of the colours.

These same bright colours can be used to produce a quieter, more ordinary effect by calculating the exposure as before and opening the lens aperture by $\frac{1}{2}$–1 stop, thus slightly desaturating the colours.

If the subject consists of pastel shades only, the calculated exposure must be given without any further adjustment, as the delicate shades will not allow for any variation, unless the aim is to make the tones darker, when the lens aperture can be reduced by $\frac{1}{2}$–1 stop.

Whether the colours are highly saturated, or desaturated, there is scope for control in the exposure, provided the *contrast* is kept *low*. The greater the increase in contrast the less latitude there is in exposure. Exposure, then, can be useful as a means of putting that little extra feeling into the mood of the picture.

Control by lighting

We can also control the contrast range of the picture, to a certain extent, by careful thought about the lighting. For a high key portrait, as we have seen before, we do not want any dark shadows on the face. To avoid these the secondary light or reflector is brought close enough to give a brightness ratio of 1 : 2. If, on the other hand, we have composed our picture with only dark colours, we do not want a very light face to upset the harmony. We can maintain both the low contrast and harmony by using diffused back lighting for the main light, combined with the minimum amount of secondary light, preferably from a reflector.

CONTROL BY COMPOSITION OF COLOUR

If our picture is to be a sincere attempt at conveying a definite message graphically, we must arrange the colours with as much care as we lavish on the differing tones in a black and white photograph. The fundamental requirements are similar to those for any other art form—i.e. a knowledge of the techniques which will satisfactorily reproduce a preconceived idea in the mind of the artists.

We can aim at simplicity or chaos, harmony or discord, surface or depth, brilliance or dullness, hardness or softness, strength or delicacy, etc. The themes are endless, but so are the mixtures of colours from which we can choose the most suitable to convey our meaning.

Let us have a quick look at some of the ideas that have been suggested, and consider how we may express them in terms of colour.

Simplicity

Simplicity can be created by monochrome, that is by using one colour on its own, in varying shades, composed, if desired, with black and/or white. Alternatively, a certain colour, composed with one or two of its related colours, can be the main theme, and a very small area of contrasting colour used for emphasis. Lighting, whether by spotlight, or flood, diffused or reflected, should be simple but effective.

Chaos

All strong colours in close proximity, in various jagged shapes and opposing sizes, help to achieve a feeling of chaos. Colours are separated, one from the other, rather than blended. Lighting is strong, directional and precise, as even chaos must be ordered to appear chaotic! A wide lens aperture is used to allow differential focusing. A confused background containing a few blobs of opposing colour, especially red, appears very discordant when out of focus.

Harmony

Harmony, as opposed to discord, is produced when, either one colour is used alone in varying shades, or when several related colours are intermingled. The colours are blended together rather than separated. Any repetition of coloured shapes should appear progressively lighter in shade as they decrease in size. Colours between the blue-green, and yellow-red, on the colour wheel, merge together naturally and, in their darker tones, are soft and restful. The colder colours, on the opposite side of the wheel, will also blend harmoniously if the colours are muted to soften their somewhat harsh characteristics.

Soft lighting and differential focusing allow the colours to blend more easily, but care must be taken to ensure that the background contains no distracting colour.

Discord

The use of equal areas of highly saturated unrelated colours, in close proximity, will produce discord. Harsh lighting and sharp focus will intensify the feeling.

Surface and depth

These can be taken together because either is obtained by a careful balancing of the warm, advancing colours with the cold, receding ones. The fact that the most advancing colour is red and the most receding one is blue, suggests that the greatest possible feeling of depth will arise by placing a highly saturated red subject against a desaturated blue background, while a highly saturated blue subject against a desaturated red background will tend to be static.

Depth is easily obtained by placing any highly-saturated colour against a colder, more desaturated one. When, however, the subject is a highly saturated blue—which is the coldest colour—depth can be achieved by making a background of progressively desaturated shades of blue or black.

Brilliance

All colours show their greatest brilliance when highly saturated, sharply focused, and lit by undiffused directional light. The brilliance is intensified when seen against a black background in a transparency, but it is a white background which gives impact to the brilliant colours in a print.

Red, by nature, is the most brilliant colour, closely followed by its relatives red-purple and red-yellow.

Dullness

Colours are only dull if they are muted with grey, or are dark in shade and unrelieved by any lighter shade of the same, or contrasting, colour.

Any dark shade of colour gives a subdued effect, but particularly the ones

269

related to blue—blue-green and blue-purple—the opposite colours to those which give the greatest brilliance. Diffused flood lighting, or reflected light on dark colours, helps to create a cheerless mood. Dullness should not be confused with "softness".

Hardness

Most colours are said to be "hard" when they have a bright, metallic appearance, but red is the colour we associate more often with a hard temperament. A large area of highly saturated colour, in critically sharp focus, spotlit and contrasted against a large area of equally strong contrasting colour, such as blue, will make the red appear hard and emotionless.

The warm red-yellows, yellows and greens should not be used as hardness is contrary to their nature.

Softness

All too often colours are used in their strong shades, and sharply focused to intensify their brilliance. By so doing the emotional and mysterious mood is overlooked: the beauty of "softness" is particularly suitable in pictures of young women and children.

Any chosen colours can be used, either desaturated or in dark shades, according to the desired mood of the picture. In both cases the colours should be related to one another, and should blend together harmoniously. Diffused or reflected light will heighten the effect, and so, too, will a slighly soft definition.

Strength

The darker shades of colour will give a feeling of strength and power, particularly if they are composed with black. Small areas of light colour are needed for contrast, and for these it is better to substitute white for colour to allow for the correct exposure of the dark tones. Pictures composed of only one strong colour with black and white, are very effective, and certainly powerful in their simplicity.

The closing of the lens aperture by a $\frac{1}{2}$ stop will strengthen the colours to a certain extent, and increase the definition.

Delicacy

To characterize a dainty, sensitive nature desaturated colours are preferable. Compositions can be made of the triangular combinations (on the colour wheel), of contrasting or harmonizing colours, but all the shades of colour used are of a similar desaturated quality. A picture may be soft or hard, simple or chaotic,

270

have surface or depth, be brilliant or dull, etc., meanwhile maintaining its delicate nature. The feeling is conveyed by the colours themselves as well as their arrangement. If you can imagine compositions of colours such as (a) pink, grey and white, (b) mauve-pink, pale green and white, (c) yellow, brown and white, (d) mauve, orange and white, (e) blue, mauve-pink and white, etc., you will agree that each one conjures up in your mind a picture of delicacy. You will also realize that each composition contains white. In a similar way that black adds strength to a composition of highly saturated colours, so white adds delicacy to one of paler colours.

As we have said the themes are endless, but these suggestions may be a starting point for your own adventures in the control of colour.

To gain a deeper knowledge of colour, it is a good plan to train yourself to *see* colour, wherever and whenever you can. One source of study is the advertisement on the hoarding, or in the magazine; another is the illustration in a book—photographic or otherwise. If you will (a) analyse the colour combinations in each case, (b) assess your emotions regarding them, (c) try to discover the underlying reason for the selection and arrangement of the colours, and (d) imagine your attempt at conveying a similar message by a different composition. You will learn to understand the use of colour far more quickly than by merely reading about it. Train yourself, also, to become aware of the colours worn by individual people, the colours in which their homes are decorated and furnished and endeavour to connect these colours, and shades of colour, with some of the known or imagined, visible characteristics of the owner.

We, as individuals, must assess our own response to colour and not rely on what others say. The response to colour is as individual as personality.

271

19 Retouching, Finishing and Presentation

We now come to the final stages in the production of our portrait, which are: retouching the negative, finishing the print, and mounting the print.

NEGATIVE RETOUCHING

First a word about retouching itself. It is an art to be used and not abused. Retouching can both enhance and destroy character. Careful retouching can lift an ordinary, commonplace portrait to one of distinction, but over-retouching, or bad retouching, is worse than none at all.

Male portraits seldom require any retouching, unless a small amount is needed to minimize an overly dark shadow—due to a lighting error—or to moderate the lines under the eyes due to tiredness and those in the forehead which are the outcome of strain or worry. These must be only softened—not entirely removed. The remainder of the facial lines and wrinkles visible in the negative, will be absorbed in the tones of the print, and the removing of them only results in the destruction of character.

Portraits of all young women need slight retouching. Skin blemishes are removed, as they are a temporary disfigurement and are often more conspicuous in a photograph than in life. The complexion, too, can be smoothed to its natural softness.

It is the portrait of the middle-aged lady which needs the most skilful retouching. The amount of work to be done varies according to the personality of the sitter. Each one will need to have the lines in the neck and face softened, the complexion lightly smoothed, and all blemishes removed. But the lady who spends much time in glamorizing her appearance, and disguising her age, will require more work to be done on the negative (where the size of negative makes that possible), if the resulting photograph is to be a true likeness.

Retouching, in this case, does not falsify the character as one might suppose, but aims at perfecting her make-up. The "beautifying" is all part of her character.

Broadly speaking retouching means the working on a negative with a brush or pencil except in the case of small negatives which can hardly be retouched. The actual stroke, or stipple, used is as individual to the person who does it as handwriting. In the main it should be a free flowing movement in a series of "squiggles"—similar to a figure 8—which will blend in with the surrounding tone, and not straight lines or dots which would create a false texture. A retoucher works according to the requirements of the negative—sometimes a broad open stipple, sometimes a much finer one. Lightness of touch is of great importance otherwise each stroke will be visible on the print.

There is little point in further discussing retouching as an art. The main thing we want to know is how to perform the art ourselves, and how to train ourselves to see on a negative what needs to be done and what is better left undone. As in all other arts, there is no quick way to success which eliminates practice. But practicing the right way can save a great deal of time. It is also an advantage to know something about the tools in use and how to handle and care for them. Together, then, we will discuss first the equipment, then retouch a selected negative, and finally compare the unretouched print with the retouched.

EQUIPMENT FOR NEGATIVE RETOUCHING

Fortunately there is no great monetary outlay in purchasing the necessary tools for retouching and finishing, and only very minor replacements are ever required —such as medium, pencil leads, and brushes.

It is, therefore, worth buying the best quality at the outset and taking care to keep everything in good working order. The first essential is some kind of desk at which to work. If you are likely to spend many hours at a time in retouching you are advised to consider your comfort, and get one that is large enough to sit at in an upright position. Very small desks are only suitable for occasional work.

A portable desk (Fig. 19.1) can often be purchased second-hand, or is reason-

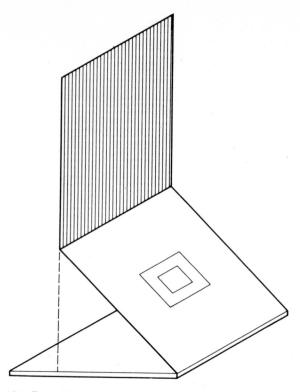

Fig. 19.1. Retouching desk which is portable and simple to construct

ably easy to make at home. The three main pieces of wood are hinged to fold flat when not in use.

The base should be covered with a reflective surface—plain white paper is quite suitable. Unless the room is in darkness when you are working, it is a good plan to hang a dark cloth over the hood and down each side to prevent the distraction of stray light. A light is shone directly on to the white base and reflected back through the negative being retouched. If possible, the panel holding the negative should be made to revolve. This makes it much easier to turn the negative in all directions while working on it.

Retouching medium

This is rubbed on to the negative to form a "tooth" for the pencil work. It can be used on either the back or front of the film. It should be non-sticky, and there should be no visible evidence of its application. Johnsons of Hendon supply a

274

good one. If a medium becomes sticky after a time, it can be thinned with turpentine. Any error in retouching can be removed by a second application of medium, and turps will remove the medium as well as the retouching.

Pencils

Special retouching pencils are supplied by any photographic dealer, and the long leads provided with them range from Nos. 1–6. The two most generally used are Nos. 3 and 4—No. 3 being the softer. Before the lead is used it must be sharpened to a fine point.

Glasspaper block

This is obtainable from a dealer in artists' materials and is used for sharpening the pencil leads. Insert a lead in the holder leaving about $1\frac{1}{2}$ in. free, and screw firmly in position. Hold the glass block between the thumb and forefinger of the left hand and the pencil loosely in the right, in such a way that the whole of the exposed portion of the lead is in contact with the block. Move the lead in a circular motion over the block, at the same time twisting the pencil round and round between your fingers and thumb. Now you will see why it must be held *loosely*! In this way you will get a fine point graduated from the holder to the tip. The graphite left on the block is useful for putting on with a stump to lighten large shadow areas.

Always return the lead within the holder when not in use, as a fine point is easily broken.

Knife

A knife, suitable for retouching either negatives or prints, is obtainable from suppliers of surgical goods. The quality of the work done depends a great deal on the shape of the knife, and the way in which it is used, and its condition.

Fig. 19.2. Retouching knife. Shaped for the correct angle to the film surface

Fig. 19.2 illustrates one useful type of surgical knife. It can be sharpened at the tip for the removal of small spots and lines, as well as further down the blade for paring the film. It is well to remember that the knife is made of steel and reacts to temperatures. It is always sharpest in cold, frosty weather! Knifing a negative requires a great deal of practice. It should be done before any medium is put on the film. The emulsion must never be "scratched" away, but pared gently layer by layer. To do this successfully the knife, like the pencil, must be held very lightly between the thumb and forefinger, and in a sloping position. If it is held upright and gripped too firmly it will be impossible to do anything else but "dig" right through the film surface.

The knife must be kept sharp always, and for sharpening it a piece of fine carborundum stone is required. Again, the touch must be very light as the delicate edge is very quickly blunted. An unwanted negative is useful to keep handy for testing the blade.

Martins dye, black

Some retouchers use a black dye in preference to a pencil. It blends in well with the tones of the negative and can be used on either the back or film side without the application of medium. It must be used very dilute, and the matching of the denser areas must not be attempted in one stroke. Remember it is a dye and, as such, cannot easily be removed. The dye should not be used direct from the bottle, but a few drops should be placed on a palette and diluted with a drop or two of water, or, better still, wetting agent.

Spots and scratches on a negative are filled in more easily with dye than with paint. Dye should not be used on prints, as the colour is liable to change during the course of time, resulting in a pinkish stain. This stain, if it should occur on a negative, is harmless.

To apply the dye a spotting brush is needed.

Brushes. Fine sable hair brushes should be used. These are obtainable from any art, or photographic dealer, in various sizes. Nos. 00 and 0 are needed for fine work and a No. 2 for a broader wash. It is essential to protect the brushes when not in use, to prevent any damage to the fine points.

Water colours. Black paint can be used instead of the dye for spotting a negative but good quality water colours in lamp black and ivory black are needed in any case for print finishing. It is inadvisable to use paint instead of a pencil for retouching, except in a particular circumstance, when it should be used on the back of the film. Paint does not blend in with the negative tones like the dye, and is therefore more likely to show as light marks on the print.

Magnifying glass. A light, easily held, magnifying glass is a great aid to the retoucher, particularly if the negative is small in size.

Having assembled our equipment we can now retouch our selected negative.

Fig. 19.3, from untouched negative. A contact print from the whole negative

276

is made and the required area for the final print is clearly marked. We must study this print and determine the improvements to be made within the selected area.

WORKING ON THE NEGATIVE—STEP BY STEP

1. Assemble the desk, adjust the light to give bright, reflected illumination, and clean the glass in the negative carrier.
2. Study the negative and compare it with the contact print.
3. Knifing must be done first, before any medium is applied. The knifing to be done in this case is merely the small piece of hair which has caught the light, and will be too big an area to fill in easily on an enlarged print. Being a dark background it is simple to knife away on the negative.
4. Application of the medium is done as follows: lay the film on a clean flat surface, emulsion uppermost. Cover a small piece of cotton wool with a soft, fluffless rag (an old handkerchief is ideal) to form a pad. Put a drop or two of medium on the pad, and rub lightly over the whole negative, using a circular motion. Wipe over, very lightly, with a pad of dry rag. Wiping may not be necessary if the medium is put on finely—the surface should be clean and there should be no visible signs of any medium having been applied.
5. Sharpen the pencil to a really fine point. Then, with the length of lead about $1\frac{1}{2}$ in. out from the holder, position the pencil between the thumb and forefinger at a sloping angle. It should be held so loosely, that if anyone were to pass behind you he could remove the pencil from your fingers without any effort. Gripping too firmly will result in breaking the point off the pencil as soon as you start work on the negative. A loosely held pencil means a light touch and less finishing on the print.
6. Begin work by removing the definite skin blemishes—the larger ones will need a few "squiggles" the smaller ones just a touch. The precise way of spotting, whether with brush or pencil, is to barely touch the film surface with the pencil point, and draw the pencil back towards you. Two or three light touches are better than one decided lunge, which may result in a broken pencil point or fanning out the tips of the bristles.
7. All highlight areas should be worked on first, taking care to maintain the shape, as this preserves the modelling. Begin with the *forehead* where the highlights are usually to be found above each eyebrow and near the hair line. Always work across the forehead, never up and down. Never do any work at the edges of the face or the effect of roundness will be destroyed. The horizontal lines across the forehead can be well softened.

Fig. 19.3. Print from unretouched $2\frac{1}{4} \times 3\frac{1}{4}$ negative

Fig. 19.4. A print from the retouched negative. The unwanted portion has been trimmed away

8.   Highlights on the *cheek bones* come next. Work across these, following the bone formation of the face, but do not lose their shape.

9.   There is a highlight down the *nose* which stops short of the tip. If you feel your own nose you can feel where the bone ends. This gap between the highlight on the bone and the little highlight on the tip should always be visible.

10.   The highlight on the *chin* should be worked across, again keeping its shape.

11.   The half tones are now worked on where necessary, revolving the negative in order to follow the lines of the bone structure.

12.   The nasal labial lines—that run from the nostrils to the corners of the mouth—can be softened by working on them from the outside inwards. It might be likened to the filling in of a trench in such a way that the trench is narrowed, its depth slightly reduced but its shape maintained.

13.   The deep shadows under the eyes are softened in a similar manner. These should never be entirely removed or the eyes will appear to be unnaturally close to the surface.

14.   The lines round the *neck* can be softened and the skin texture lightly smoothed. Care must be taken to prevent the neck losing its natural roundness while you repair the ravages of time! The shadow from the jaw should never be removed, and any blemishes which are visible within the shadow can be ignored, as they will not show on the print.

At this point it is as well to turn the negative and view it through the reverse side. It is much easier to ascertain the amount of work still needing to be done when viewing the negative through the back. Knowing when to stop work is very important, and as a general rule, the aim should always be to do the *minimum necessary.*

15.   The *arms* and *hands* need some attention. The skin texture can be smoothed, and the veins on the hand softened to make them less obtrusive.

16.   The *hair* may have pockets of deep shadow. These can be lightened by rubbing a light graphite on to them. The graphite, left on the block after pencil sharpening, can be applied by a special stump (obtainable from any dealer in artists' materials) or a small tuft of cotton wool.

It is now time to make another contact print from the retouched negative for comparison with the original.

You will notice that her left eyelid is still drooping. It needs to be raised, as the droop is only caused by a weakness in the eye which is affected by light. As a general rule it is better to leave any work connected with the eye until the print stage. It is all too easy to make one false stroke on the negative and destroy the expression—the intangible, indescribable, hidden something—which accounts for the eyes having been described as "the windows of the soul".

Observe that the highlight shapes on the forehead, cheek bones and chin have been maintained. The skin texture has been smoothed, and the veins on the hand softened. The features are unaltered and no character lines have been entirely removed. An enlarged print from this negative will need very little finishing.

It is almost impossible to retouch a negative which is smaller than $2\frac{1}{4}$ in.^{2}. Instead all the work must be done on the print. If much is needed, and several duplicate prints are required, either an enlarged negative can be made and retouched, or an enlarged print can be "finished" and a copy negative made from it.

PRINT FINISHING

This term covers any work which is done on the surface of the print.

It consists of removing any spots and blemishes, either black or white, increasing the brightness of highlights, and generally smoothing the skin texture where necessary.

Two methods can be employed: finishing with the knife, brush and pencil, or reducing with chemicals (see Chapter 17) first, and then finishing with brush and pencil.

The requisite tools for the first method are:

1. A large piece of hardboard on which to work.
2. Retouching knife and stone for sharpening.
3. Sable hair spotting brushes Nos. 00, 0 and 2.
4. Tubes of artists water colours—or airbrush colours, in lamp black and ivory black, and a palette.
5. Indian ink.
6. Gum arabic or retouching medium.
7. Retouching pencil and glasspaper block.
8. Wax polish.

Seat yourself at a table with the piece of hardboard resting against the table edge and sloping towards you. An adjustable table lamp, positioned at the top of the board, will give good, even light.

Place the print, which must be perfectly dry, on the board and cover the lower half with a piece of clean, white paper. This serves two purposes: first, to keep the print clean, and second, to use for testing the colour of the paint to match the required print tone.

Knifing

The knife is sharpened at the point for the removal of black spots, and a little further down the blade for the larger blemishes. It is again held lightly between the thumb and forefinger, in a sloping position for general knifing, but slightly more upright when the point is being used.

To begin work on the black spots, use the tip of the blade, and just "pick" the surface of the spot until it disappears. Care must always be taken to ensure that only the emulsion itself is touched with the knife and never the paper base. Passing to the general dark blemishes, the wider part of the blade is used and the surface is "pared" away layer by layer until the tone matches its surroundings.

Knife work on a print has one great disadvantage—it is difficult to cover up traces of the operation on the paper surface. Hence it is much wiser to remove the spots and blemishes by negative retouching.

Spotting

Put a little water colour on the palette, using the lamp black for a black tone, or the ivory-black for a brown-black, and spread it with a few drops of wetting agent or water. Leave to dry.

Moisten the brush on the tip of your tongue, gently twirling it at the same time to keep the fine point. Now twirl the brush on the palette on the edge of the dried paint. Very little paint is needed. Test the colour on the plain paper and select a spot within the matching tone. The action of spotting is to touch and draw back, not to push forward. If the brush is held in the upright position and the point pressed straight down on to the spot, the paint will circle the outside of the spot and the brush hairs will fan outwards. The brush must be held lightly in a sloping position and the paint left on the spot as the brush is drawn backwards.

The habit of moistening the brush on the tongue is derived from necessity. There is no other medium which enables the paint to adhere to the print as easily as does the slight moisture of the tongue. If you prefer to try something else use a pad of cotton wool soaked in wetting agent, or water. If the paint is made too wet it will not stick to the emulsion.

Should the spot not be removed at the first attempt leave it to dry before trying again. On the light tones very, very little paint is needed, in fact the re-moistening of the brush is usually sufficient without re-charging with paint.

Glossy prints which are intended for glazing are spotted with Indian ink instead of paint. This is waterproof, and enables the print to be wetted before glazing without affecting the finishing.

Glossy prints which are to be left unglazed can be finished with paint mixed with either a drop of gum arabic or of retouching medium.

Matt prints can be finished with a brush and paint as usual or with the retouching pencil and a soft lead. If pencil is used the print should be held in the steam from a boiling kettle for a few minutes to "set" the graphite.

Wax polish

All print surfaces, with the exception of matt and glazed glossy, can be lightly polished with a pure white wax polish used sparingly. This has a dual purpose— it both prevents the finishing marks from being seen and from being wiped off in the course of time. Use the polish after mounting.

PRESENTATION

The techniques practised throughout this book, have a primary consideration in common: to produce a "living" portrait, whether the truth is revealed through a mood, an idea, or something more personal. So far we have been involved only with ourselves and our model, but now we have reached the stage when we must introduce a third person—the viewer.

We aim at his acceptance of our portrait as a reality, whether or not his response is favourable. If a picture is unsuitably mounted, the viewer immediately becomes aware that he is on the outside—that he is only looking at a photograph on a mount. To involve the viewer completely we must use presentation techniques imaginatively. Today we are free to do this, as the restrictions regarding standard sized mounts for use in exhibitions have very largely been removed. Mounts may be of any colour, size or shape, according to the photographer's creative vision.

Colour of mount

Mounts of a definite colour are sometimes most effectively used for colour photographs, when their role is to enhance the theme of the picture. But for monochrome a coloured mount will, all too often, attract attention to itself and so defeat its object. Whereas a black mount for a predominantly dark in tone subject, a grey for a half tone, and a white for high key, will all give greater impact to the picture content than to the mount.

Size of mount

The size of the mount depends on the mood of the picture. An idea, or emotion, which needs space to convey its meaning needs a large mount with the picture suitably—not necessarily conventionally—placed.

The greatest impact which can be given to some subjects, is to flush mount the picture to its particular shape.

Shape

The shape of the picture is all important. We thought about this before making the enlarged print, when with the help of two L-shaped pieces of card we selected the picture content. The over-all shape may be upright, horizontal or square. The essential factor is whether or not the shape suits the subject. If we have used a particular shape with the sole object of presenting something different, the result may or may not be successful. But in either case we shall have failed to use the technique creatively.

Mounting

The best and cleanest method is dry mounting. The requirements are:

1. Ruler.
2. Adhesive dry-mounting tissue.
3. Fixing iron.
4. Trimmer, or knife and steel rule.
5. Dry mounting press, or household iron.

Method

The first essential is to ensure that the print and the mount are absolutely dry, then proceed as follows:

1. Straighten the print. Place the print face down on a soft but firm surface. Hold one corner between the thumb and forefinger of the left hand. Hold a ruler in the right hand and place it lightly but firmly diagonally across the back of the print. Holding the ruler still, draw the print out from under the ruler. This will turn one corner outwards from the centre. Repeat the process for all four corners. The print will then curve slightly backwards. *Note*: Do not straighten a print immediately after heat drying or the surface will crack.

2. Apply the tissue. Take a piece of adhesive dry mounting tissue the same size or a little larger than the print and lay it over the back of the print. With a heated fixing iron, tack the tissue to the print from the centre outwards to form

a diagonal cross, leaving the corners free. This prevents any ruckles occurring in the tissue when it swells with heat. Substitutes for a fixing iron are a soldering iron, or any piece of *smooth* metal which can be heated. The handle of an old spoon will suffice. The correct temperature must be found by trial and error. No harm can result from a tool which is insufficiently hot—the tissue will just not stick, but too great a heat will not only burn the tissue, but make a shiny mark on the print surface. If you can just touch your hand with the heated tool it is about the right temperature. Experiment with an old print first and you will quickly discover the right heat.

3. Trim the print and tissue together. If you do not have a trimmer or a guillotine, you can use a steel ruler and a *sharp* knife.

4. Position the print on the mount, carefully measuring the distances. Hold the centre of the print down firmly with the fingers of the left hand, leaving your thumb free to raise one of the corners. With the heated fixing iron in your right hand tack the tissue to the mount. Repeat the process with the other three corners.

The final stage should be accomplished by using a dry-mounting press, which gives firm, even, pressure and uniform heat over the entire surface.

There is no equally good substitute for this machine, but a makeshift tool, which is used by many amateur photographers, is the household iron. This is very good for small prints, but is not so satisfactory with big enlargements.

However, to obtain the best results with a household iron, proceed as follows:

1. Heat the iron to its lowest control—below "silk"—to start with. The temperature can always be raised slightly if necessary, but more trouble is caused by over-heating the iron than by having it too cool.

2. Place a large piece of hardboard on a table and have ready a piece of plain white paper, greaseproof paper or fluffless blotting paper, which is larger than the photograph and mount.

3. Rub the heated iron over the hardboard and the paper to dry out the damp which may have been absorbed from the atmosphere.

4. Place the photograph to be mounted, on to the hardboard and cover with the piece of paper.

5. Press the iron squarely on to the centre of the print.

6. Raise the iron, remove the paper to ensure that it is not sticking to the print surface. It will only do this if there is any dampness present or if the iron is too hot. Replace the paper.

7. Press the iron again on the centre of the print. Hold it there with firm

pressure for a minute or two and then slowly and firmly work outwards towards the corners and edges. Finally press the edges all round. This means that half the iron will be over the mount.

8. Pick up the mounted photograph and bend the mount slightly inwards. Look along the surface of the print and if a bubble is seen, re-apply the heat.

9. Test again as before, and if no bubbles are seen, bend the mount slightly backwards at each of the four corners. If the print leaves the mount in any place, re-apply the heat.

Note: If the iron is not hot enough, the tissue will stick to the print but not the mount. If the iron is too hot the tissue will stick to the mount and not the print. Too much heat usually results in the destruction of the adhesive power in the tissue, and the whole operation has to be repeated with a fresh piece. It pays to have patience and use a cooler iron, even if it means keeping the pressure on the print for a longer time.

10. Put the photograph under an even weight for a time. If the print is to be flush mounted, and the tissue is more or less the same size as the print, there is no need to trim until after the mounting has been completed.

If the print to be mounted is a glazed glossy, at stage 4 you should cover the print with the chromium sheet from your glazing machine. Without the protection of this sheet the heat will destroy the glaze.

TITLING AND SIGNING

If your picture needs a title, take care to write it neatly. The same applies to your signature. These finishing touches are all part of the presentation, and untidy lettering can detract from the message of the picture.

CONCLUSION

IN THE foregoing chapters we have discussed the many techniques that are a part of camera portraiture, including the lighting and arrangement of the subject, the exposure and development of the negative, and the production and presentation of the print. We have analysed certain types of people: the shape of head and facial features, the characteristic lines and wrinkles, the general mannerisms, etc., and attempted to use psychology to comprehend their behaviour. We have explored the ever-changing emotion of light and colour, and have sought to make ourselves more aware of it in everyday life.

The aim of the book has been to provide a basic training, from which foundation the photographer can further his own creative imagination, whether or not he has accepted the challenge of portraiture.

But we have concentrated mainly on the interpretation of character and personality in the conventional approach. The underlying principles are the same for most other types of portraiture whether the application is for fashion, advertising, glamour, journalism, or any other. The field of portraiture is wide, the approach is unique. Each photographer must develop his own way of presenting his message, and must select the techniques suited to the purpose.

A wide variety of approach can be seen among the pages showing examples of the finished portrait. Some pictures there are my own but many have been drawn from other countries. Some of these will attract, others, perhaps, repel, but most will stir the imagination and form a powerful stimulant for your own individual work.

Index

289

290